ARMY OF LIARS

ARMY OF LIARS

How Digital Media and Artificial Intelligence Are Corrupting Truth and Endangering Humanity

ANDREW V. EDWARDS

ROWMAN & LITTLEFIELD
Lanham • Boulder • New York • London

Published by Rowman & Littlefield
An imprint of The Rowman & Littlefield Publishing Group, Inc.
4501 Forbes Boulevard, Suite 200, Lanham, Maryland 20706
www.rowman.com

86-90 Paul Street, London EC2A 4NE

British Library Cataloguing in Publication Information Available

Library of Congress Cataloging-in-Publication Data

Names: Edwards, Andrew V., 1956- author.

Title: Army of liars : how digital media and artificial intelligence are
   corrupting truth and endangering humanity / Andrew Edwards.
Description: Lanham : Rowman & Littlefield, [2024] | Includes
   bibliographical references and index.
Identifiers: LCCN 2024005878 (print) | LCCN 2024005879 (ebook) | ISBN
   9781538194157 (cloth) | ISBN 9781538194164 (ebook)
Subjects: LCSH: Information society. | Digital media. | Artificial intelligence.
   | Misinformation. | Technology—Social aspects.
Classification: LCC HM851 .E345 2024 (print) | LCC HM851 (ebook) |
   DDC 303.48/33—dc23/eng/20240430
LC record available at https://lccn.loc.gov/2024005878
LC ebook record available at https://lccn.loc.gov/2024005879

♾️™ The paper used in this publication meets the minimum requirements of
American National Standard for Information Sciences—Permanence of Paper
for Printed Library Materials, ANSI/NISO Z39.48-1992.

This book is dedicated to my wife, Luchy, who has been there for me always. I also thank Rand Schulman, who strongly encouraged the idea of this book. Finally I would like to thank Randall Martin, who interviewed me on the radio and helped me understand that this subject matter was as important as I had suspected.

CONTENTS

AUTHOR'S NOTE

This book may be considered an attempt to capture a moment in time.

Technology continues to move at a terrific pace, and each week we see new developments that often seem to render old arguments obsolete and that present us with new challenges we had not dared imagine. While attempting to keep the book up to date, I am also aware that technology is moving so fast that some things may have changed between the writing and the publication of the book. So too with a rapidly evolving political spectrum where indictments and insurrections are as common as press conferences used to be.

Where possible, I am keeping my focus on the bigger picture and away from month-to-month challenges, but our time horizons have become very short indeed. What you are reading represents my best attempt at delivering a meaningful experience in a fast-changing world.

FOREWORD

Rand Schulman

Andrew and I have been in conversation about the internet for over twenty years, from different perspectives—Andrew as a content creator, in the broadest sense (images and words), and I as a technology innovator, executive, and disruptor. However, we both hold a fundamental position that seems to converge and be synergistic—truth is contextual and will prevail, and *"information wants to be free,"* as Stewart Brand says. It may need a little help getting there without causing collateral damage. This book explores our themes and observations over the years.

My background is in persuasion and mass communication, pre-internet. During college I studied the great communicators—McLuhan, Innes, and Ogilvy. Armed with an English degree, I copywrote direct mail content for business reply cards (BRCs)—those unwanted little slips of paper you find in your favorite print magazines. At the agency I learned about segmentation, targeting, testing, and optimizing toward conversions, or defined objectives. I loved utilizing quantitative metrics to optimize qualitative words/images to create greater conversion rates. Left and right brain stuff.

Back then, the measure of interest was a return of the BRC. We'd test copy in different demographics: "Buy today and get one free" or "Buy today and get half off." It was very crude, yet we created a basic engagement model for conversions. And then we started adding in different measures, demographic, psychographic, and econometric data until we could form a very accurate picture of our target and convert them to our objective.

Fast forward a decade or so, to the mid-1990s, and we started applying these known "old-world" marketing practices to the new digital paradigm. I have been a founder, executive, and board director at some of the first digital analytics companies, Keylime acquired by Yahoo!, IBM, and Adobe, all enabling the internet as we recognize it today.

It doesn't matter whether you're selling hats, airline tickets, or content, "Big Data" and the rise of the web as a channel gave us a start. However, our big breakthrough was the creation of the cookie, or page beacon, invisible pixels inserted on a web page that allows the site to gather information about the visitor, in either a personal (if allowed by the visitor) or in a nonidentifiable way. We slipped these cookies onto your computer when you were visiting the page. When aggregated across the internet, this anonymous visitor behavior enabled us to precisely target our offers to those visitors who would convert: either they would stay longer or buy more.

The search engine and these analytics companies enabled the internet with a new emphasis on *conversions*, rather than just informational "brochure-ware." This new focus drove real business models and was the reason for the Yahoo! interest in Keylime, and the Google interest in Urchin (which eventually became Google Analytics). While hat sellers could sell more hats, media companies could optimize what readers read and saw, creating greater visitor engagement and allowing media to sell ads and subscriptions to advertisers and even data to those who shared the same appetite for the reader profile information. The old world became the new world at warp speed.

While my companies built those platforms and capabilities, Andrew built companies that put those technologies to work with Fortune 500 firms like Coca Cola, Michelin, and Century21 Real Estate. We have been professionally collaborating since those early days, and along the way we cofounded the Digital Analytic Association, which empowered thousands of practitioners in the science of digital analytics. Yet, I think it's fair to say, we both recognized we were creating a potential dystopian environment that, in the wrong hands, might benefit from public naivety.

Today, any person, or state, can utilize our tools to optimize conversions, and the relativity of truth can be manipulated and conflated as "fact"—or alternate truth. Perhaps, and cynically, this may be an example of "Social Darwinism" at work? A "dumbing-down" of civilization.

Was the election stolen? Are there Jewish space lasers? Not for me to judge. Perhaps this should be governed by the deep state, and firewalls built? Maybe not. However, there are solutions on the horizon that give us options. Perhaps we can have an objective third party, like a FICO score, rating and footnoting what is fact or when fact becomes truth or not? Perhaps that is part of a nanny state; and if so, is it an infringement of one's right of free expression? But one can't legally scream fire in a crowded theater without repercussions.

John F. Kennedy said, *"The educated citizen knows how much more there is to know. He knows that knowledge is power, more so today than ever before. He knows that only an educated and informed people will be a free people, that the ignorance of one voter in a democracy impairs the security of all."*

Clearly, we need to be informed, but I am optimistic, as some answers are beginning to surface. Guard rails like the General Data Production Regulation are being created. Watermarks are now being applied to Generative AI-based content and large language models (LLMs), and objective scoring is being used by applications like *Ground News* to spotlight the content creator, publisher dynamics, and ownership bias, displaying the source and the context of a news report. While the wisdom of the crowed gets hijacked by tactics like "flooding the zone" with disinformation and outright misinformation, new technology is helping combat the rapid rise in these "alternate facts."

I can't say we didn't see it coming.

Based on several decades as a digital pioneer, Andrew shares his wisdom and explores the digital frontier, looking for truth and fact and for those who are lying—or whatever it's called these days.

PREFACE

In 2015 I wrote a book called *Digital Is Destroying Everything: What the Tech Giants Won't Tell You about How Robots, Big Data and Algorithms Are Radically Remaking Your Future*. It was well reviewed, but unfortunately not very widely read.

Three things I will say up front:

First: it predicted a crazy number of things that came to pass sooner than later (if I do say so myself).

Second: my timing was off—nobody wanted to hear it.

Third, and most important: digital is *still* destroying everything, and it's much farther along than you thought. In fact, I will argue that digital technology, chiefly in the form of digital media, has almost destroyed the topology of truth, and in doing so, has also gone a long way toward undermining the democracy upon which we have long depended for a way of government.

Evidently some of the most important names in digital technology are more unnerved than one might have expected. In an industry known for a "boil the ocean" optimism, it is instructive to see tech CEOs signing on to open letters about the dangers of artificial intelligence, essentially asking the world to pause AI development until we can better understand it. This letter,[1] signed by the likes of Bill Gates and Geoffrey Hinton, the man they call "the father of artificial intelligence," is by all appearances not more than a placeholder so the tech giants can later say they told us so—but of course none of them have any intention of slowing anything down. Hinton recently quit his post at Google so he could speak openly about the dangers. But the rest, perhaps predictably, will run headlong into the most advanced technologies, perhaps hoping that what they find there is an aid to humanity and not the engine of its destruction. Unfortunately, it appears their collective hopes are flagging, and if the tech bros are uncharacteristically worried, we ought to be paying attention to that.

In May 2023, Sam Altman, CEO of AI poster child OpenAI (maker of ChatGPT) testified before Congress to say, "When this technology goes wrong, it can go very wrong. . . . We want to work with the government to prevent that from happening."

For anyone who has observed the Muskian[2] insouciance that characterizes typical tech bro bravado, the above comment must come across as sobering indeed.

I'm writing today with a plan that amounts to nothing less than saving humanity from digital destruction. This destruction in 2023 takes the form of an army of liars, digitally assembled, digitally manipulated, and bent on taking the United States back to a pre-Enlightenment, proto-Christian state where only well-financed, white Christian males have anything that resembles a combination of rights such as those outlined in the United States Constitution. This digitally enabled army of liars attempts to obtain their inglorious end by the persistent poisoning of the American political dialectic. They aim to transform it from a so-called marketplace of ideas into a gateway to fabulism that includes accusations of child rape and cannibalism and every type of blood libel that might have been outlined by the Nazis' own "Elders of Zion." In fact it was none other than Steve Bannon, a chief advisor to Trump, who in 2018 proclaimed that his goal was to "flood the [public information] zone with shit,"[3] presumably so that nobody believes anything anymore.

The impact of digital technologies goes well beyond digital media.

Today, *everything in the world* runs through digital domains in one way or another. We already may have ceded human sovereignty to the artificially intelligent Borg, but maybe, just maybe, it isn't too late to save some smidgen of humanity from the clutches of the destructive algorithms that power social media disinformation. And perhaps the same type of insights I offered in 2015—many of which were considered too early and too dire—will help save us now.

You're very likely thinking, "*Who is this guy, and why should I listen to him?*"

I can understand that reservation. So here's something to think about: My background in digital marketing goes back to the early 1990s, when I built some of the very first websites. Technology was such that at one point I was tasked to develop an interface that would not be larger than nine kilobytes in size. For reference, SEO Optimizer in 2023 says that the average web page "load" is two megabytes. That makes my 1994 interface 0.005 times the size of a current web page. Bandwidth was poor in those days! And we had no clue that there'd be anything like "social media."

Later, in 2004, I helped found the Digital Analytics Association. This organization continues today, and digital analytics remains the science behind audience measurement.

Audience measurement is one of the most important tools in digital advertising today. In fact, it is the most important aspect of what I will call "digital propaganda." This is because digital advertisers and publishers today can carefully target audiences and craft messages in real time in a manner that can often prove entirely convincing to that targeted audience. I intend to make the case that digitally powered propaganda is taking the United States apart almost exactly as an external enemy might wish to do.

Further, I will make the case that this digitally savvy external enemy may turn out to be the same one that we defeated in the Cold War, and that Russia saw the Cold War only as one phase in a forever-war for global domination. Americans may have moved on from the Cold War, but Russia, apparently, never forgot and certainly never forgave. They continue their onslaught today; no longer communist, they are instead openly fascist. And their brand of fascism has found more than a mere foothold inside the American electorate. This foothold was not achieved by accident. As I intend to show, the attainment of this foothold relies heavily on the type of digitally manipulated disinformation that has managed to brainwash millions of Americans into believing that men who wear dresses are the equivalent of Jack the Ripper.

Perhaps most importantly, I intend to make the case that the lion's share of our troubles with disinformation tie back not so much to the Steve Bannons of the world, but to the technology giants themselves. For Facebook (Meta), Google (YouTube), Twitter (X) and other social media platforms can *only* exist in a world where they are shielded from liability for what the general public posts to their promotion platforms. That shield is accomplished by a 1996 law known as Section 230 of the Communications Decency Act. Section 230 sets up the social media enterprise with a combination of rights and protections not afforded to any other type of publisher. In essence (and as was recently upheld by the Supreme Court in a liability case called *Gonzalez vs. Google*), Section 230 says that no social media company can be held responsible for what anyone posts to it. The same law also grants them the right to remove anything from their properties that they don't want there.

My position on this is clear: Section 230 is a dangerous anomaly. My intention is to demonstrate that this outdated law is at the root of our challenges with disinformation and that we would be much better off as a society without it.

For many years I consulted with companies of every size about how to understand the traffic coming across their websites and their apps. These companies were attempting to assemble audiences and deliver successful messaging to those audiences. Often, they spent heavily on these efforts. They were, in general, trying to sell more widgets. None of the groups I worked with were in the business of stoking hate for profit with targeted disinformation. In this corporate environment, it was my job to explain digital technologies to senior marketers, as well as the social trends that proceeded from these technologies.

On the strength of that reputation, I was given a chance to publish a book about digital culture. That book was called *Digital Is Destroying Everything*. I am pretty certain my publisher, in the early stages of the project, was not expecting a dystopian take on the subject when they asked me to write a book. The reason I think so is that they ended up not publishing it. Not because it wasn't good enough! No, in fact my editor loved the manuscript and made almost no changes. But even as the book had been typeset, even after the cover had been designed and the galleys were at the printing press, a senior executive at this publisher thought it was too negative, especially because some of my points conflicted with some of their own business plans as regarded digital business models. *Digital Is Destroying Everything* ended up in print via another, smaller publisher.

I include this tale because it reveals how controversial that book was then. It may help to explain why this book may also prove controversial, especially as regards my assertions about Section 230.

Here are some of what that book predicted in 2015:

- the disappearance of the local newspaper and nearly all journalism generally
- the destruction of retail as we knew it
- the disappearance of rational discourse, and its dreadful impacts on the democratic process
- a major crisis in higher education
- the ceding of decision making to algorithms in every aspect of life

. . . and more.

And yet, as noted above, practically no one was tuned in to this kind of message back then. It was a time of boundless digital optimism. Barack Obama was president—his second term! Some folks (not me) said we were "post-racial." Many more said digital technology offered us a boundless future with no downsides. We really were going to be able to stream any movie, song, or human utterance anytime, anywhere, and for almost no money. Everyone had a blog. Digital had swept away those lousy gatekeepers, and everyone could publish their own personal cri de coeur by clicking a button. We would have a perfect utopia of digital expression where all of humanity's most cherished dreams would be laid out for all to partake, and moreover, it would be free, free, free!

These predictions aged like milk, as they say.

Instead of a digital utopia, we are at the precipice of digital destruction.

This destruction is upon us chiefly as a result of audience targeting; real-time content recommendation; nefarious, tech-aware state actors; radical religionists who have made a tentative peace with the one sliver of science that benefits them; and the power of persistent hate-mongering. These liars all have made common cause, with an eye toward the destruction of the type of liberal democracy we have become accustomed to in the West, in order to replace it with a narrow form of Bible-fueled fascism that wants to crush diversity and put all power into the hands of a small cabal of preachers and mob-boss politicians.

Of course the digital threat is not *only* due to the overt (and covert!) actions of bad actors and the way they hide behind laws that protect digital platforms (a.k.a. Section 230). We are also confronted with new technologies, generally referred to as artificial intelligence, large language models, and especially "generative" AI, that are maturing before our eyes and that threaten to run a race for sovereignty against all humanity in ways we could never before have imagined.

Artificial intelligence has been manifested most notably in the form of apparently "intelligent" chatbots that can answer questions and even write original content, depending on what a human prompts the tool to do. The most well-known example is OpenAI's ChatGPT, but this is only a small parcel upon the artificial intelligence landscape. AI already is embedded in more business models than the public is even aware of, and while AI is not necessarily a bad thing and can be a boon to humankind, there is, as mentioned above, a general call for some kind of hiatus, or at least a review of circumstance so that we don't let our machines outsmart us before we can even understand what they are up to. My intention is to lead that discussion in a way that is both insightful and illuminating.

To be sure, digital media manipulation and artificial intelligence also work together. For there is no way for Facebook, for instance, to recommend stories about making oat milk smoothies *in real time* to a person who has evinced an interest in tofu, without the intervention of artificial intelligence and the algorithms that drive AI.

My goal is to expose the underlying dynamics of these digitally driven phenomena in a way that helps people understand why their untrammeled expansion is an existential threat. Throughout, I will try to point the way toward truth and the light-of-day as best as I understand it.

Humanity's story is one of brinkmanship. We seem always to be one or two steps away from the precipice, but somehow, having recognized a threat, have organized ourselves to defeat the threat and see another dawn. May we also succeed in this task now, in this place, in our time.

1

~

CAN TRUTH SURVIVE A
DIGITAL ONSLAUGHT?

Today we are compelled to do battle against a digitally empowered army of liars who have managed to corrupt the terrain of truth itself. They have achieved this by deploying audience-targeting, message-manipulation, and nonaccountability in a combination that has proven successful in creating entire political movements based on daring, shameless lies and the proliferation thereof. Together these three factors have created a sluice-way for a flood of purposeful disinformation that threatens to swamp civilization in no less a complete fashion than when the Little Conemaugh River burst its dam and washed away the town of Johnstown, Pennsylvania, in May 1889.

Never before in US history have we seen a confluence of technologies and untruths manifest in a way that threatens the very existence of rational discourse, and of liberal democracy in general. It is no coincidence that the rise of disinformation almost exactly matches the rise of social media itself. It would be hard to argue that misinformation and disinformation, these days, comes from any source *other* than digital media. It comes to us chiefly in the form of platform-driven social media at sites like Facebook, X (formerly Twitter), and YouTube (which is owned by Google).

Digital has substantially altered (if not destroyed) any number of things we had every reason to believe were permanent: print media, retail, music, apartment rental, real estate, and many other industries have been completely remade by digital technologies. Digital has, since COVID, even transformed our very working habits—many of us no longer commute but work from home because of the extraordinary power and adaptability of digital technologies. But of all these sectors, the media landscape, perhaps, is what's been transformed most completely.

THROUGH THE LOOKING GLASS

It is as if humanity has passed from a reliance on fact into a new world bound only by false narrative, manufactured outrage, and relentless manipulation—much as Alice stepped from her Victorian parlor through a mirror and into a world where everything was backwards, where caterpillars were haughty, and where chess queens ordered heads chopped off for even the most insubstantial infractions. That was a world of fantasy, but suggests important parallels to ours.

Where Alice encountered the hookah-smoking caterpillar, we encounter Rudy Giuliani, bleeding black from his temples, parroting election-fraud insanities, under oath and in front of Congress—election fraud lies that he sourced from dubious, unverified digital sources of only the most questionable provenance. Where Alice spent time at the court of the execution-minded Queen of Hearts, we are continually in the court of the likes of Marjorie Taylor Greene, a one-woman wrecking crew who retweets obvious lies she sourced on the internet (Jewish Space Lasers) while daring you to call her out. According to Red Queen Marge, all liberals are deserving of death, and she gleefully calls for their heads on pikes).[1] It would be funny, in a very dark, twisted sort of comedy, and perhaps once we are past her type of threat, we can laugh again. Finally, where Alice met the walrus and the carpenter, we instead have the likes of Lindsey Graham and Donald Trump. This pair of charlatans can be found weeping for the souls of their oyster-like bed of followers, upon whose financial flesh they feast even as they can hardly wipe their tears fast enough to take the next bite.[2]

Whether or not you agree that we are in a world that seems ruled by the irrational, much like the one in which poor Alice was trapped, it remains that at least three critical factors set this age of digital liars apart from the past:

- Our world is characterized by digital technology that enables a limitless number of liars to post unlimited amounts of lies before a targeted, global audience of vulnerable media consumers.
- The persistence of these lies guarantees their enshrinement in recommendation engines and artificial intelligence applications in ways that guarantee the propagation of untruth.

- Finally, and in a manner I will describe in a later chapter, we are also now, as a civilization, suffering from a form of information overload, and especially suffering from exposure to masses of uncomfortable, contradictory information that heretofore only the most specialized educations might have prepared us for in the fields of cosmology, physics, aerial phenomena, and the very nature of reality itself. This may seem altogether un-digital in nature, but I will discuss how digital technologies, especially as related to search and archiving, have provided easy access to esoteric knowledge that, until recently, was, for better or worse, not widely disseminated.

Together, these factors create an atmosphere of doubt, enmity, and irrational imaginings that threaten to overwhelm all good sense; and to throw civilization back into the primordial muck from which truth helped us climb out.

It is critical to human survival that we understand exactly how this has been permitted to happen, what it means presently, and what must be done to save us all from a world bounded by rumor and darkness. One major contributor to our social media disinformation dilemma, and perhaps the most important and most difficult to fix, is a 1996 law called Section 230 of the Communications Decency Act. This law effectively sets up the business model whereby a Facebook or a Twitter can amplify hateful messages without exposure to any legal liability. I will discuss this in more depth later.

In addition, we must recognize a profound irony in that much of the lying found in digital media comes from those who would deny science. I am talking chiefly about religionists here and afar, many of whom evince a belief that their chosen deity can, for instance, cure disease through prayer and that science is a hypocritical farce that contributes nothing to the human project. Except, of course, the technology upon which their digital jeremiad relies entirely!

One of my favorite examples is where climate-change deniers, faulting all scientists as proponents of an impossible agenda designed to cover the earth with solar panels, will at the same time rely 100 percent on advanced computer science to deliver their climate-denying rhetoric.[3]

I don't notice how they are claiming that *computers* are examples of science-failure—merely that all geophysicists are delusional clowns.

We saw the beginnings of digital untruths even before the arrival of Donald Trump's presidential candidacy. But we were neophytes then, and perhaps can be forgiven for having been blindsided by the sudden onslaught of brazen, organized lying, fueled in part by social media. And Trump may have been the first politician to successfully manipulate digital media for political gain.

Whether Trump was a digital pioneer or not, we can thank Donald Trump's former campaign advisor, Kellyanne Conway, for coining the phrase "Alternative Facts." She did this when she described press secretary Sean Spicer's foundational untruth about the size of Trump's Inaugural crowd.[4] Soon lost in a Sargasso Sea of other lies even more outlandish, this was an early, official lie that was promulgated on the very night of the Trump inauguration. In an ill-fitting suit and appearing exactly as amateur as he truly was, Sean Spicer told the world, "This was the largest audience to ever witness an inauguration, period, both in person and around the globe." However, any casual comparison between, for instance the Trump crowd versus the Obama crowd showed, to anyone in possession of even a halfway-functioning set of faculties, that the Obama crowd was several times larger and that, in fact, the Trump crowd was smaller than you might have expected. Trump obviously knew this and could not face the fact.

The Presidency of Lies began very quickly, and it began with the crowd size. According to a January 17, 2017, *USAToday* article, on NBC's *Meet the Press*, host Chuck Todd asked White House counselor Kellyanne Conway, "Why did the president ask the White House press secretary to come out in front of the podium for the first time and utter a falsehood?" Conway responded: "Don't be so overly dramatic about it, Chuck. . . . You're saying it's a falsehood. And. . . Sean Spicer, our press secretary, *gave alternative facts* to that."

The article goes on to say that while there may be alternative data sets or alternative explanations or estimates, there absolutely is never any such thing as an "alternative fact." This is because a fact is an established thing in the world. It can be independently verified as having taken place or to be demonstrably true over a long enough time to make its reaffirmation as close to certain as anything can be. A perfect example would be the comparison of photographs showing the two crowd sizes: one for Trump, one for Obama. The photography shows very clearly that the Obama crowd was much larger, and that the Trump crowd was not remarkably large by any means.

But liars don't care about fact-checkers, nor have they any regard for people who would rather hear truth than lies. And it turns out Kellyanne gave these liars a concept they could deploy over and over even though it is dishonest, illogical, and self-serving. "Alternative Facts" became core to the GOP playbook and has been part of it ever since.

This novel concept openly rejects arguments based on demonstrable facts by simply denying the existence of the underlying facts, while brazenly substituting them with lies deemed suitable by the liar in question. That this concept has succeeded beyond anyone's wildest prediction tells us we have not yet climbed from the primordial muck, but have only succeeded in peeking out above the lowest levels of mud, perhaps to see the sky briefly before being plunged back into darkness. We are hauled down into a dungeon built of targeted disinformation by cynical digital manipulators who crave power and despise the human project in general.

This combination of powerful, digital media and orchestrated untruth has pushed millions of Americans to believe dangerous fabulisms that call for the murder of liberals, the extinction of homosexuals, a final solution for Jews, and the apotheosis of a cruel, hypocritical form of Christianity that pulls us back to a pre-Enlightenment era of witch-burnings, pogroms, and blind faith in an unworthy priesthood.

It may come as a surprise to the logical thinker that we already have, and have had for a long time, large institutions devoted to the promotion of alternative facts. Many refer to them as "churches." Let me say that I am not anti-religion, and that I find the introduction of a concept I will call "Christian mercy" one of the most important moral events in history. However, and most unfortunately, very few churches spend any time at all talking about mercy. Instead they talk about how if you don't believe in their god, that you will burn in hellfire. Or that if you don't accept that the Earth was created only a few thousand years ago and that dinosaurs were contiguous with humans, and that the theory of evolution is an insult, that you also deserve to be stripped of your rights and denied a full and happy life. We don't know enough to say whether Jesus is an alternative fact, but the Christian Evangelists' "young earth," and the lack of evolution thereat, are certainly alternative facts. Worse, they are alternative facts *even though science never claims to have established any facts about the nature of reality.*

A true scientist, like intelligent people generally, will point to evidence about the geology of the earth, and the obviousness of its age, and to natural selection, and the predictability of that process, but they will not deign to call them "facts" because we all know they are nothing more than very well proven theories. And yet the religionist will mischaracterize these findings as if they are unfounded dogma, and then call them "facts" only to set them up as a straw man for their "alternative facts."

In the twenty-first century, only the devout Christian will assert that it is a "fact" that the earth is only four thousand years old; and a "fact" that their creator built us out of mud only a short time ago. And just the way the Trump Organization will boldly state a lie and then double down on it and triple down on it, there are Christians that persist in their own pretenses and their own world of alternative facts as well. Which goes a long way toward explaining why evangelicals have formed such a large part of the Trump constituency.

Beyond the Christians, there are others who indulge freely in alternative facts.

Of particular note are what are called "Q-adjacent" beliefs that find a ready audience on platforms like X and Facebook. According to the Anti-Defamation League, "Q Anon is a decentralized, far-right political movement rooted in a baseless conspiracy theory that the world is controlled by the 'Deep State,' a cabal of Satan-worshiping pedophiles, and that former President Donald Trump is the only person who can defeat it."[5]

The corpus of Q-adjacent beliefs is too voluminous to catalog here, except to say it is a continuing source of disinformation on a grand scale. In fact, the Q-paradigm seems almost perversely focused on topping the last idiocy with something even more outrageous. Hence, we went from doubting a birth certificate, to doubting election results, to doubting that Western medicine can be effective (e.g., COVID anti-vaxxers), to doubting that liberals are not cannibals.

Alternative facts have metastasized and gone viral over the years, and for some, they have proven very profitable. And if you are a shareholder at Meta or Google (X went private), then you are among those who have profited! X and Facebook and Google all not only permit, but also *promote* these theories upon their platforms; and both enjoy total immunity from any consequence of their selling advertising adjacent to these damaging, hateful theories.

The big platforms enjoy this immunity because of the above-mentioned Article 230 of the Communications Decency Act. This law carves out a special niche for digital platforms that allows them to make billions of dollars *promoting* hate and division without owning even one iota of responsibility. I am sure the act was never designed to have brought about this result. But the platforms do amplify hateful messages and are at the same time extraordinarily profitable. I will have much to say about this peculiar law in a later chapter. For now, suffice to say it is a unique type of carve-out that grants digital platforms the right to immunity from anything they amplify upon their platform, as well as the right to delete any content they choose not to amplify. If this sounds like a very profitable and at the same time a very inequitable business model, perhaps it's because it is. There is little doubt that, if social media is the tree upon which hateful content flowers, then there can be less doubt that the roots of that tree are nourished by the law known as Section 230 of the Communications Decency Act of 1996.

Alternative facts notwithstanding, I aim in this book to take up the cause of truth itself. I do not claim to be in possession of any game-changing amount of general facts, nor do I claim to know any ultimate truths about life or anything else. My premise is that digital media, fueled by a unique ability to source questionable authority from a toxic stew of hateful assertions, *plus* the parallel ability to target the most gullible with unsupported disinformation, has created a new and unique world of false ideas that has come to dominate our national discourse. I aim to expose the technological underpinnings of the assault on truth, as well as the way universal access to information has succeeded only in eroding trust in all forms of expertise. My hope is to build a constituency that will demand better media accountability, and perhaps enable others to identify, fight, and defeat the army of liars that is attempting to destroy civilization as we know it.

2

DIGITAL UNDERPINNINGS

Computers, at least until very recently with the advent of ChatGPT, have not been much in the way of advancing ideas, or even activities, on their own. No, the problem has always been *people*. Or, as an old comic book character named Pogo once observed: "We have met the enemy, and he is us."

To put it perhaps more academically, the problem is not the technology, but how the technology has been used. We have been on this ride before and should not be surprised that the dynamics are not so very different even if the details diverge. Two major technologies offer important parallels—and neither one of them represents exactly a success story in how we have dealt with them.

The first is that carriage-load of technological wonders including steel, combustion, rubber, and electronics that we call "automobiles." It was only 125 years ago when cars were not much more than odd-job buggies with spoke wheels and a rudder for steering. They exploded in popularity and absolutely changed the American way of life; and soon after, the rest of the world's as well. By what stretch of the imagination can we say that we have controlled this technology? Indeed, we have not. We have made a provisional peace with cars, with laws regarding licensing, taxes that fund the building of roads, and yet more laws that attempt to make these ground-missiles rather safer than they would be otherwise.

Has anyone thought to blame the cars? Of course not. Nor could the automobile be avoided, because someone was bound to be inventing it—and indeed, much as with other technologies, different teams in different parts of the world were working to perfect the automobile at the same time in very similar ways. Henry Ford in Michigan, Karl Benz in Germany, and others were all developing automobile technology at the same time. Their eventual offerings were remarkably similar to one another, even as they had been working independently.

But perhaps the most relevant question for us would be to wonder what kind of world we would have today, if we had no laws to govern roads, or rules of the road, or automobile safety, or any regulations about lead in your gasoline and smoky pollutants in the air. We know air quality is bad enough *with* air quality regulations (and I don't hear much pushback about it from the right!), but that only underscores how much worse things would be *without* environmental regulations.

The second illustration would be about the advent of the nuclear bomb, and as a by-product, nuclear power to generate electricity. For almost the entire first half of the twentieth century, physicists wrestled with the notion of atomic structure and how it might be put to use. The science was almost impossibly arcane, and even today represents puzzles that seem to defy logic. But it was all just an exercise written in chalk on university blackboards, until the threat of war came knocking at the door of academia. Once it became apparent that atoms could possibly release enormous amounts of energy, it was then assumed that someone, somewhere would work on it until they had the makings of an explosion exponentially larger than the explosion yielded by any bomb that had ever been built. A single atom, when split, would, according to the calculations of the best minds in the world, cause an explosion large enough to destroy a city. And that would be just the start.

The United States in the 1930s and 1940s ran a hidden, massive program to develop a nuclear bomb. Tens of thousands worked in secret. Entire semi-covert cities were erected: one in Oak Ridge, Tennessee, to process a form of isotope, and another one in the New Mexico desert at Alamogordo, where they tinkered with uranium and plutonium until they had enough to make a big noise in the desert. By 1945, they had made a big enough test-noise to deploy it in an attempt (successful) to defeat the Empire of Japan and end the Second World War. In August 1945, one bomb was dropped on Hiroshima and then another one on Nagasaki, both medium-sized cities in Japan. Each bomb resulted in a giant fireball, and the immediate death of hundreds of thousands of men, women, and children.

There was a debate then about whether nuclear technology could have been avoided. The consensus was that it could not have been avoided. Just like with the automobile, there were teams working on it in Germany as well as the United States, and the notion of a nuclear Hitler was not to be countenanced.

In addition the point must be made that the advent of nuclear power did not necessarily result in a bomb. Nuclear power was never the culprit, because instead of the bomb, we might have focused on free electricity for all. Nor was the internal combustion engine to blame in and of itself. No, it was how humans used these technologies that caused what trouble there was.

The same can be said for digital technologies and artificial intelligence especially. As we will discuss, AI has the potential to be enormously helpful or enormously destructive. Moreover, digital technology, like nuclear power, was *always unavoidable*. And like our history with nuclear, we are having difficulty managing it, even as we learn more and more about it every day.

My position is not anti-digital. That would be like going anti-water because we didn't build a seawall. There is much to admire in digital. Perhaps my personal favorite digital technology, even with its whiff of big-brother, is the EZ-PASS system on the toll roads that are so prevalent in the Northeast. Some of us may recall a thing called a "toll booth" and our impatience while inching up to the toll with a quarter, or a dollar, or five dollars for a person asphyxiating in the middle of traffic. These tolls could result in very long delays, sometimes as much as an hour in the big cities. These days you don't even slow down. Above, a camera winks at you as it registers your EZ-PASS going by at sixty miles per hour.

Let them track my movements! Just don't slow me down.

Digital is always throwing off these benefits to humankind, almost as if they were incidental to the larger project. The real question is: What is the larger project? Can we expect to survive the destruction of truth by digital media? Are computers, and artificial intelligence especially, poised to take over decision-making powers in human society? Finally, are humans still important?

I don't know the answers to any of these questions. But I have some ideas that may be helpful.

FROM MUDDY TRACE TO SUPERHIGHWAY

Many of our most serious problems with digital technologies can be traced back to the innocence and the boundless optimism of an earlier day. This would be very much like how humanity has been forced to deal with innovations in its recent past, as suggested above. The pattern is familiar: first, a brand new, epochal technology that is rapidly adopted. Then, a proliferation of that technology that succeeds beyond anyone's initial plans—but with major, not to say ruinous downsides. Followed by a period of resistance to any sort of regulation; finally by a universal admission that the technology would prove worthless without our putting it in harness for the good of all.

I mentioned above a late nineteenth-century innovation called "the automobile."

In the early twentieth century, automobiles began their meteoric rise to transportation supremacy. At first there were claims that cars simply were not suitable for the public, and that they were in fact exceedingly dangerous. One lawmaker wanted each "horseless carriage" to be preceded by a man on horseback, waving a flag. The parallel with digital technologies would have been that brief period when internet purists clutched pearls to hear that someone had dared advertise, for instance, via email. The public did not object to email ads in 1995, and they didn't care what naysayers said about cars in 1905, either.

Once the car became popular, the attitudinal poles shifted. Now cars were everywhere, and you could not stop them. Nor could you propose any moderation in their development. The notions that they might pollute too much, or be dangerous death traps, or that traffic might need management—all of these were at one point derided as unworkable, meddling, and timid in the face of brave innovation. For decades, every car manufacturer fought the notion that cars might be unsafe. They said that seat belts were unnecessary, that safety glass was an unworthy refinement, and that emission controls were nefarious in and of themselves. This is the phase we are at today with digital: no meaningful regulations. We are driving fast on hairpin curves with no guardrails, but the digital optimists see no rough patch.

Today, who wants to drive an automobile without seat belts or anti-lock brakes? Or on busy roads without traffic lights? It took decades before the public began to support regulations on automobiles. But now it is taken for granted that these regulations make the technology only that much more effective.

It ought to be much the same with digital.

It is important to note that until very recently, almost no one in the mainstream media—or elsewhere!—wanted to point a finger at the Lords of Digital. Even Yours Truly, in 2014 when I was writing my first book, I held out hope that we might avoid some of the worst possible effects.

Today, I'm pretty sure that was too optimistic.

Perhaps today's attentive reader is more likely to agree with me that digital may, indeed, be in the business of "destroying everything" than they might have been in 2015. That year saw no shortage of pie-eyed digital optimists. We already talked about how some were too early calling the United States "post-racial," only for racism to come roaring back. Digital optimism in 2024 seems equally unfounded.

There is no shortage of other examples of unwarranted optimism from the pre-Trump era. For instance, the Online News Association in 2015 said that the next year "would be a time of growth and optimism."[1] Do you imagine they knew, at the time, that by 2023, nearly every independent news source in the United States—thousands of local newspapers and most national magazines—would be as dead as an old tin lizzie? How many of those paid journalists have since become unpaid gig workers with a Substack account and a job at the coffee bar?

At about the same time, *Bloomberg* was reporting that the *New York Times* was "optimistic about their role in the social media world."[2] Today the *New York Times* has no role at all in social media. Nor does any other news organization, except to the extent that they may have an "X" account.

Eric Schmidt is a former CEO of Google. In 2015 he was (and perhaps still is) essentially a digital optimist. In his 2013 book *The New Digital Age*, he said, "The most significant impact of the spread of communication technologies will be the way they help reallocate the concentration of power away from states and institutions and transfer it to individuals."

His claims in 2015 would never have been characterized as overly optimistic. That his unbridled optimism may have been self-serving is another matter. He wanted to propose that we would all be much more powerful, having been granted access to the Google machine. And it turned out to be true—just think about all that information right at your fingertips! And yet no one had really foreseen back then that so much of that information would turn out to be false, misleading, hateful, ruinous, and, by the way, written and disseminated often enough by bots and hackers working to foment discord. What was vaunted as the flowering of the human spirit came out more like turning over a big flat rock and finding out that the life scurrying about under the rock is what you're going to have for dinner.

Mr. Schmidt may have imagined a world of shared ideas and shared goals. He may or may not have imagined how awful, and how phony many of those ideas would be. Nor did he foresee that we might end up with one million cynical manipulators, lying in concert so as to bring patent insanities into mainstream discourse. Each one of the cynical manipulators would qualify as a member of Schmidt's newly empowered "individuals." But much as murder wasps are not ladybugs, nor are all individuals the same, nor ought the murder wasp be expected to deploy their newfound power for anything but the most nefarious purposes. And yet the big tech outfits, Google among them, have seen fit to empower the murder wasps along with the ladybugs, as their cash register rings in deafening fashion. Meanwhile, the murder wasps continually attack the ladybugs by skillfully deploying (for instance) Google's vertically integrated communications platforms.

But this minor problem would never get in the way of profit at Google. Schmidt, and many more like him, saw great advances in their collective wealth via the business model enabled by the law we know as Section 230. Remember that, according to the definitions of 230, Google (or YouTube) are just providing a platform! The hate-spew is only an accident, a minor by-product of the affair. They don't have anything to do with those lies that are promoted all day and all night on YouTube. They will say that they have no control over it, and that they frankly have no connection to it, even as their logo remains at the top of the screen at all times. Clearly, they are running well ahead of the lawmakers, who have absolutely failed to understand the dynamics of digital media.

Remarkably, the big platforms also refuse to distinguish between the dollars that come from legitimate advertising, and the dollars that come from promoting ISIS videos.[3] Oh, they will *try* to get rid of such evil up to a point, and as long as it isn't inconvenient, and also *entirely at their own discretion.*

Finally, as they will vacantly claim, they really can't be expected to get rid of all of it!

They can, however, keep all the money.

There have been other major changes since the publication of my book in 2015. Back then, Amazon was only just starting to turn a profit. And Jeff Bezos had only just rescued the *Washington Post* from bankruptcy. To his credit, he has done little to make that newspaper less valuable.

Today, Jeff is fighting off unions. And sending rockets into space.

And so is another billionaire, named Elon.

Elon Musk, a South African diamond-mine scion with an electric car company and a launching pad, in fact now owns X, which is the de facto global town square, for better or worse (mostly worse). A self-proclaimed "free-speech absolutist," many contend he is actually a right-wing fascist. Probably it would be tiresome to cite the numerous examples of Elon disparaging the "woke" agenda, and seeming to side with Putin about Ukraine, and then how he appeared at the 2023 Super Bowl in the company of Rupert Murdoch who owns Fox News. Later, after the October attack on an Israeli music festival, it would be noted with puzzlement that for some reason it was X that seemed to promote the *most* disinformation, by comparison with other platforms. There is little uniquely digital in the self-absorbed mania of a multibillionaire who pals around with fascists, and if this were all he had done, any discussion of his antics would have little place here. But the damage caused by the platform he now owns is continuing, regardless whether Musk thinks ill or well of X in general.

But the most significant thing that has changed since the publication of *Digital Is Destroying Everything* is the way that X and other social media platforms have powerfully impacted political discourse in the country and around the world. I did, if I may say so, predict that we might see seasons of online nastiness, but it did not occur to me we would have so much of it nor that we would see it so soon. Nor did I expect social media to play a pivotal role in the election of a Neo-fascist American president from the borough of Queens.

Back in 2015, Donald Trump was a television reality show host of a particularly tacky sort.

Today, Donald Trump is an oft-indicted has-been with his own useless Twitter-wannabe and a tentative reservation at a government hostelry. But in the interim, Donald Trump successfully weaponized Twitter as an engine of hate and division; and even if he never holds office again, the damage has been done.

In many ways, social media and Trump were made for each other.

He is shallow, self-aggrandizing, a serial liar, a brutal fool who makes simple-minded assumptions, and perhaps most important, he is both persistent and vulgar. Hence there is no filter to keep his innermost id from spilling out right onto the screen, time and time again. This, of course, could also characterize the type of outrage that drives engagement on social media.

We mentioned how it seems at times as if we have turned over a big flat rock, and that social media is what is scurrying to hide from the light. Trump shoved the rock off of social media by himself almost and gave license to every eighteen-legged critter to bask in the sun of notoriety. That the more discerning among us were horrified is exactly what should not surprise. We live now in a world where, thanks to the amplifications of digital media, we have Trump-style accusations that a "Jew" (George Soros) controls a "black" (Manhattan DA Alvin Bragg) so thoroughly that together they managed to indict Trump for paying off a porn star just before a national election. We live also in a world where Trump rages against judges, attorneys general, special prosecutors, and even court employees in a whirlwind of witness intimidation that has earned him at least a couple of different limited gag orders.

All along it was Donald Trump who paved the way for the accepted practice of tremendous lies, repeated over and over to a large audience—enabled and amplified by digital technologies in ways that no other media could hope to equal.[4] And thanks to Trump's groundbreaking efforts, every hater in the United States now feels comfortable spewing lies for profit (or for kicks). More importantly, the big digital platforms continue to accept no responsibility for any of this. They accept no responsibility, even as at the same time they rake in billions of dollars while promoting, for their own profit, said hate via "you-might-like-this" algorithms.

Today our era can be defined as a time of digital enablement: where platforms give license to every type of true-believer to spout incoherent nonsense to the world. But not just to the world randomly. To a world of people that have been targeted and selected, with the aid of the platform's own proprietary recommendation engines, because those people would be more likely to accept, understand, and promote messages about Jewish Space Lasers, Pedo-pizza parlors, and how vaccinated Americans are a mortal danger to the unvaxxed. These messages go viral not by accident. They are crafted, targeted, and promoted with the aid of the platforms that supply market velocity to the idea (no matter how heinous)—while taking all the profit and none of the responsibility.

In 2015 we were talking about "content marketing" as if it were a silver bullet. We were deluded into thinking that if we posted enough rational discourse, if we put the work in, if we wrote about what really mattered to us, then it would result in followers, result in positive change, perhaps even make the world a better place! Today, if you can find links to any number of old content marketing sites (often called "blogs"), you will notice that many of them had gone *kaput* by 2019. That's just about when we came to accept that only three things really got you anywhere in digital media: sex, or outrage, or advertising dollars. Despite knowing how more than one celebrity was launched because of a sex tape, most of us were not going to take that road. And only corporations can spend the kind of money it really takes to advertise effectively across a broad spectrum.

Many gravitated toward outrage. This is because outrage seems to sell best, and seems to generate the biggest result with the smallest effort. According to researchers at Yale, "Social media platforms like Twitter amplify expressions of moral outrage over time because users learn such language gets rewarded with an increased number of 'likes' and 'shares.'"[5] In September 2022, National Public Radio published a story called "Does Social Media Leave You Feeling Angry? That Might Be Intentional." The story claims that "[social media] algorithms consistently select content that evokes anger and outrage from its users to maximize engagement. And sometimes, those extreme emotions turn into extreme actions."[6]

Therefore we cannot be surprised when it turns out that these algorithms are *not looking out for the interest of the subscriber*, but for the bottom line of the advertising platform (Facebook, X, Google). And it turns out that what gets recommended is what the algorithm "believes"[7] will deliver more engagement (a.k.a. more time spent eyeballing ads). At the bottom of this is the sad fact that what seems to generate the most engagement is outrage. So outrage is what often gets recommended. And civil discourse be damned. Damned for profit!

A NEXUS OF PROFIT AND HATE

I'm not against profit. But I am against profiting very obviously off of hate. And I am against the idea that these digital platforms such as Facebook and YouTube and X enjoy both immunity and the right to "censor" on their own platforms.[8] As noted above, they are protected by a law known as Section 230. Section 230 creates an enormous free-money loophole for any company that wants to publish, *without* the responsibility of a publisher; for any company that wants to provide a digital dialtone (a.k.a. a social media platform), but *also* retain the right to shut off your dial tone if it's bad for their business.

Yes, in the United States we try to be accommodating to businesses. No, I don't think that is a terrible idea.

But if any one thing can be said to drive us closer to the digital cliff, it is Section 230. This carve-out has created a new class of uberpowerful, non-responsible parties that collectively have been eating the brains of humanity for many years now. It is my contention that without Section 230 we would have no nexus of hate and profit to speak of, because traditional publishers can and would be held liable for amplifying (in other words, publishing) the hateful rhetoric that is the bread and butter of social media platforms.

Important to note that I have compared two words here, *amplify* and *publish*. In many ways, there is between them a distinction without a difference. Publishing is a fairly well-known and time-honored practice. A "publisher" owns a means of production. Until digital came along, they would have owned a means of production that took the form of a printing press. Their assets also included large publicity departments, editorial departments, and distribution channels. If your work was published, the publisher invested money to edit it, print it, and distribute it. They would make profit on sales, and the author would enjoy royalties. The publisher, right along with the author themselves, owned liability as regards any statements made in the publication. Hence, there was little tolerance for lies, especially not ruinous, insulting, violent lies of a type that we unfortunately must take for granted today as they come to us via social media.

Digital platforms will want you to believe that they are not publishers, but merely that they provide a mute, inconsequential, even a *trivial* (according to them) form of amplification for an author's work. They provide a vertically integrated environment for the acceptance, distribution, and promotion of content that, in fact, has better reach and more market velocity than any traditional publisher. It is true they spend little to no time at all on "editing." They do not "accept" or "reject" manuscripts (or posts) in the same way a traditional publisher might; but they exercise control over what gets on the platform in some way, shape, or form, and at their own discretion—which looks to be, if you strip back the rhetoric, quite a bit like what a publisher does all the time. But rather than deploy an editorial department, a printing press, and a publicity department, they simply provide all of the necessary technology such that the author can upload what they want to say at the click of a button, and they also provide the visibility and the recommendations to the public that drives virality. At the same time, they sell ads around all of this content and make billions of dollars in profit.

They will claim that this amplification is by nature entirely unlike publishing. But the only thing that's truly different is that they have made much more money than publishers typically do. This they have done while owning exactly zero responsibility for helping amplify thousands if not millions of hateful messages every single day of the year.

This cannot be permitted to continue.

My contention, and I hope it is not a great surprise, is that digital businesses are not natural forces. Just the same as every other business, they do not have a natural right to exist. I am also not saying they ought *not* to exist, nor do I suggest they ought not be profitable. Let them profit—enormously if they can!—just not off of hate and lies.

The main argument that digital publishers will make is that to get rid of Section 230 would very possibly mean the end of their businesses. As mentioned before, Google successfully defended itself in the Supreme Court against a wrongful death lawsuit that wanted to pierce the Section 230 veil, and bleed out some of their profit. The plaintiff in *Gonzalez vs. Google* claimed that Google's YouTube algorithms promoted ISIS videos that depicted beheadings and executions. And that eventually (according to the suit) those manipulative, promoted videos led an ISIS terrorist to kill an American.[9] Google's defense was that, should it lose its protections under section 230, it would be "a horror show" for its business. Perhaps predictably, in May 2023, the US Supreme Court said that most of the claims in the suit were barred by Section 230—no surprise!

Forgive me for the cynic's chortle right about now. My personal opinion is that "bad for business" is not a cogent legal defense. But the US Supreme Court largely is constituted of justices who many have said represent the people of the United States almost not at all. And in a business-friendly world, Google skates away with impunity, while the hateful content just keeps getting posted.

Does 230 comport with any sane notion of accountability versus power? It does not. Does 230 provide any net benefit to humankind, or is it merely a crutch for easy profit? I say it is the latter.

One of my goals here is to give us all space for a rethink of the entire digital enterprise. And that includes bedrock assumptions like the efficacy of Section 230.

THE BLASTED HEATH

In 2015 I wrote about how "a new, rather eye-catching garden is sprouting upon the blasted heath" that was the digital landscape back then. I was talking about things like GPS, like streaming content, like automatic scheduling, like realistic animated renderings. Today I would offer a different slant on what grows upon that blasted heath: it is the notion of the small mammal, hurrying about the field gathering seeds and nuts while dinosaurs thunder overhead. It is the notion that despite all, human ingenuity will not see itself done in by an arrangement of silicon circuitry. It is the notion that as smart as our software gets, we will remain a little bit smarter. And that upon that blasted heath, truth shall prevail, and perhaps even shall justice.

I remain optimistic about this, and about our long-term prospects.

But only if we can figure out a way to keep the raw sewage of hateful disinformation from flooding into our houses—and about this prospect, I think we do have a lengthy and uncertain fight ahead of us. For today the constituency for meaningful regulation of the worst of social media is, admittedly, small. We must in any case dedicate ourselves to growing this constituency until common sense overwhelms even the Supreme Court.

3

RELATIVISM AND OTHER PEOPLE'S TRUTHS

The truth is we may be much less interested in hearing what our fellow humans have to say than we might have imagined.

Or at least some of us are.

I am, personally, more than tired of seeing pictures of people's dinner plates on my iPhone. And their misbegotten gender-reveals. As well as the repetitive memes that feature Marge Simpson, or Jesus looking disgusted, or invitations to join yet another networking app where everyone recommends everyone to everyone else in a vast exercise of unearned, value-free praise. Never mind that all advertising now has taken on the aspect of the small-print pages of an old *Popular Mechanics*, where you can get rich, see through solid objects, and discover the true cause of diabetes that no one had ever known about. That said, I still cannot seem to get enough of cat videos, but that is another topic.

Worse, I still scroll through my social media apps as if I am expecting them to reveal something fresh, even though the last time that happened was probably 2017. That one's tendency to "doom scroll" through an hour's worth of bad news contributes to a soul-crushing sense of existential horror is, unfortunately, hardly news in 2023.

We are flooded with other people's truths these days. Much of it can be depressing. Occasionally there are nuggets of wisdom gleaming out from the muddy expanse that comprises most of social media. But these are as rare as a garnet in the sand.

I have already laid in a few observations about how the notion of truth itself is called into question in a digital information matrix. Now I plan to add in a concern that the weight of humanity's collective truths has in no way increased our ability to seek truth, nor confront our own, and may in fact contribute to a sense of separation and loss. I am not a psychologist and have no theory as to how this works in the brain. But I can attest that for me, anyway, I long ago reached my limit of "understanding" when I started seeing videos of people eating tarantulas. Perhaps that makes me small-minded. Or perhaps it means we all live in a bubble, and that this is okay. Much the way the entire earth is a bubble of sorts, a bubble of air and water floating like a blue miracle in empty black space. And upon the skin of that bubble, we live out our days shielded from the "truth" of cosmic rays and the absolute zero of interstellar vacuums. Indeed we need our bubble in order to survive.

But even as I switch metaphors from stones to bubbles, we should look again under that big flat rock I mentioned in the last chapter.

In what possible way did we ever think it would be desirable to see what everyone else was thinking? Did we imagine there'd be some kind of liberation? That we would gain a positive understanding about our co-inhabitants upon the surface of Gaia? Instead of discovering enlightenment online, we more typically find blindness, blood, and petty grotesqueries. Social media has done more than its share to destroy the possibility for accepted truths in the world and has only succeeded in increasing general discord to a deafening pitch.

TRUTH, AND THE RISE OF ALTERNATIVE FACTS

A set of definitions are in order. I am taking up the cause of truth, without claiming that I know the truth. Only that I recognize there is a thing called truth, and that it represents a form of reliability in a world of relative factors. I am willing to promote the primacy of truth because we require truth as a navigational aid. We are temporal travelers always, and while we can see behind ourselves, we are blind to the next instant in time. We must, if we are not to crash continually upon rocks, have some way to navigate the next several minutes of life, the next hour, the next year. Our only useful tool in this navigation is what we call "fact," which is a more granular form of the more atmospheric "truth."

And yet, even as truth yields more truth, we are swamped by wave after wave of digitally driven untruths. Witness the digitally manufac-tured furor over the 2020 election, where a large constituency believes, against all evidence to the contrary, that there was massive fraud, that

Trump won by a landslide, and that Joe Biden is not only improperly in the White House, but that he may in fact be a three-dimensional deep-fake while the real Biden is imprisoned upon the island of Cuba in an American prison camp.[1] Witness the Q-adjacent fascination with "medbeds," a futuristic fantasy where "the military" secretly has created a type of hospital bed that, by a type of mysterious action that can only be characterized as magic, cures almost any disease in two shakes of a lamb's tail, including COVID and cancer, but unfortunately not, apparently, mental derangement.[2] And then there are the old, foundational untruths that have found new life because of digital evangelism: race-hate, homophobia, misogyny, and the worship of automatic weapons.[3] These old lies have been dug out of the closet, dusted off, sent to the digital cleaners, and repackaged as "freedom" and "patriotism" in a particularly shallow, self-serving, and nation-destroying manner.

Perhaps social media has not so much failed to deliver any truths as instead delivered an avalanche of other people's truths, and we know already that personal truths often have only a tangential relationship with any particular set of "facts." And yet it may also be the case that we never needed all these random truths but only needed access to the facts.

Facts are more important to decision-making than truths. You can build your own truths out of facts if you care to. Facts are like navigational aids, where truths are like vacation brochures.

I like to deploy metaphors about digital that take digital out of the picture and re-propose the question as if computers had no part in the process, as I believe this helps illuminate the underlying principles with a smaller load of jargon.

So here is an example of how facts are like navigational aids:

A traveler in a pre-digital age is hiking a trail through a little-known wilderness, trying to reach a town on the other side of the woods. The trails are not clearly marked. The traveler must rely on a combination of facts and technology to make it across safely. There are two modes of fact in this scenario: one is static, one is adaptable. The static set of facts is called a "map." The adaptable set of facts is called a "compass." The map is nothing more than a set of geographical facts laid out in a visual format that attempts to mimic the contour of the geography itself. Despite any challenge that, in fact, "the map is not the territory," the traveler knows that the map is the best tool available for figuring out which way is the cliff and which way is the gully. There is no assumption that the map is accurate down to the last detail. But there *is* an understanding that the mapmaker was not intending to strand the traveler in quicksand, nor see them lost in a circular march of death. At the same time, the traveler might supplement the map with real-time navigation in the form of a compass. The compass, too, is an imperfect instrument, prone to influence by magnetic forces, never presumed 100 percent accurate but nonetheless demonstrably useful because it had proven it could point north reliably over time.

With these tools, and a native ability to discern obvious differences between raw data and the actual land to be crossed, a reasonable traveler should have no trouble breaking out of the woods and arriving in town before dark. They have made their way forward in time and space by relying on certain things as accepted truths, or at least they relied on them provisionally because they seemed to work, without evincing any belief in electromagnetism or the sextant deployed by the mapmaker. Of these "facts" the traveler was certain: that the compass generally would point north, and that the mapmaker would not long be a mapmaker if their maps were found to be so faulty as to be detrimental to the fate of the traveler.

But now we have a different type of traveler—one who is especially susceptible to propaganda. One who might be waylaid on their travels and misdirected by liars who want to extract some value from the traveler that can only be obtained by misdirection. So, once they are abroad in the wood, that traveler is now accosted by loud-talking players who claim that mapmaking itself is a falsehood, and that magnetism is the devil's work.

These liars might include personages like Donald Trump, who insists he ought to be president but for the perfidy of millions of voters who went for the other guy. And Tucker Carlson, who says he hates Trump but laughs in public at Trump's jokes told at Saudi-funded golf tournaments while also lying about the election.[4] And Steve Bannon, who openly deploys digital media to spread slander and disinformation in an effort to undermine all other narratives but his own.[5]

Soon our hopeful traveler is circling the terrain, emptying their pockets of change to Trump and other grifters-of-the-wood, who claim they need the money to "keep fighting for lost hikers." At a certain point, the cynical manipulators will have collected enough of these wanderers that they might imagine they have assembled an army.

An army of liars? Or an army assembled out of lies, at least.

Of course, propaganda is not a new thing in the world, nor does it have a history of abject failure. But it has always run up against a natural limit where belief meets skepticism. As noted in the case of Steve Bannon above, one of the chief goals of the propagandist is to surround the media landscape with enough disinformation to create an atmosphere where all statements are made equal: nothing "truer" than the next, regardless its relationship to fact.

This has always included attempts to make ideas and trends seem to rise up naturally from "the grass roots," even though there may be no grass, or roots either, but only a carpet of plastic fringe that was manufactured to look like grass. We have come to call this type of effort "AstroTurfing," in honor of the original fake-grass that was laid down in Houston's epochal but now derelict Astrodome, the first domed stadium in the world but unfortunately not one where grass would grow. So in order not to play major league baseball on a dusty brown lot in an auditorium, it was necessary to invent a semi-convincing type of grass that needed no watering or sunlight. The result was a carpet of AstroTurf.

Grassroots activism—truly grassroots as opposed to AstroTurf-like, manufactured activism—has a long history. The website Streetcivics cites nine historical instances of grassroots activism, including movements against nuclear weapons, the so-called "Arab Spring" that never flowered, the United Farm Workers movement (Caesar Chavez), and even the American Anti-Nazi boycott before World War II. More importantly, we can point to the civil rights movement of the 1960s and even the rise of rock and roll which, as may come as a surprise to many, was seen as an act of liberation in and of itself during the Beatles era and sometime after.

But even before there was AstroTurf, there was AstroTurfing. In a pre-digital age, some attempts to influence the grass roots took on a tone of farce. For instance, during the Kennedy administration, there were notable efforts to win back Cuba from Castro. Overseen largely by Robert F. Kennedy (at that time attorney general), this operation was code-named "Operation Mongoose" and included plans to work with the mafia to murder the Cuban leader in any number of creative ways, all of which of course failed. But according to Laurence Leamer, in *The Kennedy Men*, Operation Mongoose also included a primitive form of AstroTurfing. There were plans to explode rockets above Havana while claiming that the Resurrection was on its way. The idea was to inspire a popular uprising among a putative religious population, but the effort was as naive as it was nefarious. Both Kennedys are gone, as is Castro. And Operation Mongoose shows us that influence does have its limits, especially when it runs up against counternarratives.

In an earlier day, and concerning a much more damaging regime than the Kennedy administration, Adolph Hitler, in 1933, burned down the Reichstag (German Parliament), blaming Jews and Communists in a way that convinced absolutely nobody but that provided a springboard for his murder and destruction of European Jewry.

Propagandistic stunts have a long history, and a good record of success. But propaganda in the past has never succeeded the way it succeeds today.

That is because digital technologies have enabled propagandists finally to crack the code for what results in a *convincing atmosphere of lies in a media-rich society*. Essentially it is a combination of effective audience targeting, persistent messaging, and a high volume of phony digital "sources." None of these techniques were possible before digital technology paved the way for the type of massive brainwashing we see today.

THE SCIENCE OF DIGITAL AUDIENCE MANAGEMENT

Digital platforms control the lion's share of advertising dollars in 2023. According to Statista (among others), digital advertising enjoys 67 percent of all advertising revenue globally, and will control 70 percent by 2025.[6] Thirty years ago it was almost nil. It's been a rapid revolution, and the reasons are easy to understand, from an advertiser's point of view. For not only is it plain that digital platforms are where the eyeballs are, it is also plain that digital advertising, properly executed, can be demonstrated to work! Whereas in the past, all advertising was more or less a guessing game that involved studies, focus groups, ratings, and any number of proxies that stood in for the measurement of real engagement in real time.

The most well-known example of this pre-digital type of audience measurement probably is the Nielsen ratings, which were developed as a way for television advertisers to understand the reach of a particular television show as expressed by "market share," in addition to total viewership and overall popularity rankings. This ratings system was of paramount importance in television advertising, and low ratings would almost always spell doom for the unlucky television show. But it was not as if Nielsen, or anyone, ever actually *knew* who was watching, nor how many watched nor what they watched if they did watch television at all. What Nielsen did have was a small group of purportedly representative households.

According to Study.com, "Nielsen works by providing devices called audimeters to its panel households. These devices collect viewership data from the households' televisions and send it back to Nielsen. Nielsen then uses the panel viewership data to estimate overall ratings across the US."[7] Today there are approximately forty-two thousand Nielsen "households" who have agreed to allow Nielsen to audit what they watch. In order to generate national statistics, the activities of these households are extrapolated using statistical models that yield what at least are meaningfully representative results. In any case, they are deemed suitable enough to drive the spending of advertisers everywhere.

Another example of this "proxy" measurement, pre-digital, is what is called a "focus group." Focus groups are comprised of members of the public who, for a nominal fee and a box lunch, agree to attend a session where they will be shown products or ideas for products and are asked to tell the sponsors what they think of what they have been shown. This, too, has long been a large part of the business of marketing and merchandising, and even with digital measurement in hand, they still are used today. The allure for the advertiser is that they get to hear from real people in real time about real things—quite an advantage, these days!

However, in digital advertising, these proxies are largely superseded by a discipline known as digital analytics, which, at its most basic, measures audience engagement with digital properties. It does this by recording and graphing the "page views," "click-throughs" and overall media consumption of the audience, which groups are referred to as "users." Almost any website owner can review these statistics by adding a line of code onto their web pages—invisible directions given to the computer to record the activity of whoever visits the site. Google provides a basic, free tool for this purpose, and it is widely deployed.

The strength of digital analytics as compared with proxy ratings and focus groups, is that it is an impartial, *uninterpreted* record of actual activity; and that there is so much of it, about so many slices of engagement, from so many sources, that it has given rise to entire enterprises devoted to nothing but audience measurement, audience development, and messaging. It is also the case that digital analytics requires a great deal of technical expertise, and a great deal of testing before it can be relied upon as an accurate depiction of audience behavior. When it works, the results can be revelatory in the best way, but it can be frightening for the marketer who finds their effort suddenly measured *in real time* and possibly found wanting.

It is a singular feature of the digital measurement landscape that, occasionally, and very mysteriously in some cases, the tracking code that fuels the measurement somehow "cannot work on the page," or is stuck "at the developer" for an unlimited amount of time. Very few will sign up to have their own personal ideas and works measured in real time, and this may help explain the occasional roadblock—and the occasional management headache when trying to figure out if a campaign really did as poorly as the analytics tool seemed to have suggested.

To be fair, digital analytics is hardly a science without its drawbacks. It is difficult to get it done properly, and perhaps even more importantly, while most advertisers find digital analytics reporting interesting enough, they also find it not particularly actionable.

In other words, they often stumble when attempting to figure out what to do next. They know that folks seem to like the page with the chameleon video (for example), but they don't know how to boost that into more views, more engagement, more sales.

Truly successful digital advertisers take this to another level, and they succeed by adding "recommendations," and more surreptitiously, by simply showing more keyword-associated content to a user based on what they have already shown an interest in. That said, advertisers don't do the recommending themselves. They only place ads around recommended content. And the recommendations of content come from the platform, which deploys recommendation algorithms in order to keep the user engaged on the platform. This is done in order that the platform can put more ads in front of the user. The big platforms are well suited for this kind of real-time recommendation, because they are the only ones that can supply almost limitless content to millions of users at a time. With unlimited content and vast audiences, they can recommend suitable content for every conceivable sliver of any given demographic. Therefore, if the rise of insane fabulisms seems in lockstep with the rise of powerful messaging platforms, it can be no surprise.

Audience Targeting

Audience assembly and audience management are the heart of the profit engines of social media sites like X and Facebook. Their entire enterprise is focused on identifying the preferences and proclivities of users, and delivering those self-selected audiences to advertisers. We will elsewhere talk about the specific types of engagement involved in the destruction of truth, but let's be clear, this audience-assembly is not solely the domain of the cynical manipulator. It is the hope and dream of every advertiser. It's just that some advertisers are trying to sell more widgets. While some other advertisers are trying to overthrow Western democracy.

Also it is important to keep in mind that advertising does not necessarily look like advertising anymore. Especially where politics is concerned, the focus may never be on literal ads, but on the promotion of posts that present one viewpoint or another. This is especially the case in the realm of digitally driven disinformation, where, rather than ads, the persuasion is driven by thousands or even millions of social media messages from hackers, bots, and influencers on the various platforms.

When you propose to advertise, for instance, on Facebook, you can "buy an audience." On its advertiser introduction pages, Facebook directs the advertiser to "choose the demographics, interests and behaviors that best represent your audience." This type of deep, accurate choice would never have been possible without digital analytics and the science of audience measurement. The granularity of it is what makes digital advertising totally unlike any advertising that came before, and what can make it so much more effective.

Let's say, for instance, that you wanted to find an audience that would be receptive to the message (a lie) that Trump won the 2020 election. You already have some notion of who those people are, most likely. And Facebook has invested billions in gathering data about all of its users precisely so they can sell those audiences to you in ever more exacting slivers. So when you work closely with them, you can specify that you want to target, for instance, older, rural Americans who have shown an interest in tax cuts, birther theories, and the collected master-works of Bill O'Reilly. The Facebook business model makes this easy.

Message Selection

Once you have identified your audience, your next challenge is how to deliver content that they will find actionable. Mostly, this is done by trial and error. With the help of an array of capabilities often referred to as "ad tech" (advertising technology), different types of messages can be tested out on different audiences. With enough time and money, dozens or even hundreds of different messages can be tested. A continuing comparison between marketing options (the generic term for this is "a/b testing") often delivers the most effective result. In other words, the advertiser quickly knows which version of the message drives the most engagement. What that content may be is the subject of another discussion. Here we are only talking about the method of audience targeting, and the technology that drives effective messaging.

Keep in mind that audience targeting is an iterative science. Once the target is identified, there is no end to the amount of microtargeting that an advertiser can deploy, nor any limit on the volume of messaging aimed at the target.

Persistence Advertising

Here is where the winners begin to pull away from the pack. Because when you have both the science and the resources to make the science actionable, your accomplishments will outstrip those who lack the focus or the resources to carry it out. We talked earlier about Astro-Turfing, and here is where it plays out especially well when you are looking for broad, deep influence on large topics like "election fraud" or "anti-choice candidates." Unlike a company selling a product, the political manipulator has more variety available in his arsenal of content. And remember how we said that advertising does not necessarily look like advertising anymore. It can look just like the rest of the content, especially when the product is an idea (for instance, election fraud). In this space especially, we look to a sheer volume of messaging—some human, some not—to surround an audience the better to convince them of the advertiser's argument.

According to the Brookings Institution, digital media is especially suited to AstroTurfing via the generation of bogus messages. Brookings conducted an experiment in 2023 where they asked a well-known chat technology to generate a right-wing-slanted letter about gun control.[8] They sent it to over seven thousand state legislators. The response rate was a typical 2 percent, but what is plain to see in the article is that legislators totally failed to notice that the letter was *generated by a computer*, nor had they any idea this was not part of a cadre of unique individuals—Brookings had sent about five emails per legislator. The conclusion reached by Brookings was that a combination of massive volume plus bot accounts plus chatbot content can make it seem as if one cause or another has actual human support, when in fact it may not.

Above I have used the term "chatbot," which has, until recently, defined the type of online help you get when you log into your insurance account. Companies have long determined that the lion's share of questions coming through to a help desk are routine and easily answered, and that they can use a robot to generate textual conversational replies and suggestions. But, as I will get to in a later chapter, chatbots have taken on a new importance with the advent of a chatbot that is hooked up to a large language set, no less voluminous than the entirety of online information, and that leverages that information to answer random questions from random people. I am talking about OpenAI's product Chat-GPT, which is headlining globally as I write this book.

Can chatbots become part of an ad campaign? Yahoo News is also talking about politically motivated chatbots—as an "imminent threat." According to a recent article there, "An informational cacophony could emerge from competing chatbots with different versions of reality, undermining the viability of artificial intelligence as a tool in everyday life and further eroding trust in society."[9]

And why not? The advent of social media, as Eric Schmidt has said, puts publishing power into the hands of the general public. And if it gets into the hands of the general public, that means it can get into *anyone's* hands—including the hands of someone who is designing a chatbot; and they can give their chatbot a particular slant in any way they choose. Some will say this wide availability of advanced technology can only be a good thing. To them I say: if nuclear power had an open-source interface, everyone would have their own atom bomb, and wouldn't that be peachy!

But there are more layers to unpeel here at the influence desk. For a campaign may or may not start with a human, or a chatbot, but by deploying audience targeting plus known human weakness, we can even recruit the unwitting to spread our message. Here we will go right to the heart of the challenges associated with universal empowerment: an enormous majority of people—your guess is as good as mine, but probably upwards of 90 percent—are not interested in writing or publishing anything at all. What they are interested in, and what they do all the time, is to attempt to influence their contacts by deploying thoughts and observations written by others. This is called "forwarding." There are entire online communities built around the observation of the type of clueless forwarding that seems to run rampant among a legion of ill-informed armchair warriors. Witness "r/forwardsfromklandma," a group, or "subreddit" on popular social media hangout Reddit, where boomer-aged power-forwarders are revealed as cat's paws for the KKK and the Neo-Nazi movement.

The decentralized world of right-wing, AstroTurf-building, cynical media manipulators relies on this army of forwarders to amplify its message. We are well into this age, and the proof is that millions of Americans have been enough surrounded by, and enough preached-to, and entirely lied to for long enough, that they believe Trump is secretly president, that Hillary Clinton was executed at Gitmo, and that the long-dead JFK Jr. is alive and directing the white-hats against a horde of homosexual predators looking to groom children via the reading of inclusive children's books at public libraries.

Further proof is that, in some jurisdictions, a vocal segment of the local population thinks these fabulisms are tantamount to a hanging matter. There is no shortage of anecdotal evidence of school board meetings now attended by fully armed men in tactical gear, observing silently and with obvious malice aforethought. There is no shortage of evidence that school board members have received death threats from brainwashed, violent actors who consider themselves upstanding pillars of the community. In fact the Department of Justice in 2021 issued a letter to alert local authorities that school boards may be under threat from armed constituents. That many of these armed constituents are associated with law enforcement makes the entire proposition that much less manageable.

Clearly the types of criminal intimidation that are being undertaken in gun-happy districts, where teachers, librarians, and other public servants are made to feel as if their lives are in danger, are almost entirely digitally driven. Again, it is not merely that the organizing has taken place digitally, because there is nothing unique in that. What is unique is the amount of brainwashing that has taken place via audience selection, message targeting, forwards from clueless constituents, and persistence in digital media. The brainwashing has succeeded so well that librarians are learning the hard way that not all information, having been freed, would be guaranteed not to come back in the form of election-denying, sidearm-carrying nincompoops who think Harry Potter was born of Satan. It has gotten so bad that in September 2022 the American Library Association wrote a letter to the FBI expressing concern that librarians were no longer safe.[10]

Worse, there is little to no mechanism in place whereby threatened librarians can be protected. What with police departments focused on traffic stops, so-called street crime, and militarized protest-suppression, they have little taste or any plans to combat crimes rooted in hate speech and direct, digital threats. One wonders what would happen if a truckload of handwritten threats to individuals, with return addresses, were dropped off at a local police department. My guess is that it would get the force's attention. But it's digital, and therefore, because of the wonderful magic of Internet Fairy Dust, these threats are deemed inconsequential and that everyone can go on about their lives, threatened, unprotected, and perfectly free to suffer. You are on your own because digital.

It is evident to me that, in general, the public can expect no protection from evildoers if those evildoers are white, gun-toting, and married to mindlessly backward viewpoints that barely survived the Enlightenment. The perfect example of unequal protection lies in a comparison of the US Capitol on January 6, 2021, with the Tennessee State Capitol on March 4, 2023. In the former, an army of white, conservative thugs raided the seat of government, smashed violently through its minimally defended perimeter, wrought havoc inside, then marched out quietly into the night. Many of these good folks were indicted later, but the fact remains that the seat of government was breached with just one shot fired at one insurrectionist (Ashli Babbit, who, as a criminal trespasser and a violent revolutionary, does not deserve recognition as a martyr).

One might argue that the major surprise was that the nation's Capitol was not defended with machine-gun fire, but this is yet one more lament in a sea of woes that has descended upon the United States.

But back to our comparison.

On January 6, the Capitol was violently overtaken by an enemy brigade. They were never fired upon, except for the abovementioned dead insurrectionist. Now let's make a contrast. On April 4, 2023, anti-gun demonstrators peacefully protested (loudly) at the Tennessee State Capitol, led by three Democratic members of the House. There was chanting, there was singing, there were signs. There was no violence and no attempt to shut down the government. They did not force their way in. They did not claim to want to hang anyone, nor did any of them bring zip ties to bind victims. Nonetheless, a GOP legislature kicked out two of the three Democratic legislators—both, of course, African American. This made these two legislators immediate heroes on the left, and they were soon returned to the statehouse by their constituents. But regardless of whether this may have helped a couple of nascent political careers, what's clear is that the law looks differently on the same behaviors when performed by different groups. Evidently this difference usually plays out as a matter of race, class, and political preference.

Put another way, law enforcement too often seems to smash the left and the darker-skinned reflexively, while at the same time kissing the ring of the tired, Christian, old white male in charge. So it would stand to reason that antiquated forms of racially motivated policing would ignore online threats, because the vast majority of threats are coming from Christian whites and are thrown in the direction of the left, people of color, and other marginalized communities. The police in the United States have a long-standing reputation for cruelty toward the marginalized and a history of kowtowing to the powerful racists who run their departments and who determine their budgets. Bottom line: never look to the police for policing online threats.

THE NATIONAL DIVORCE AND A MEDDLING IN-LAW

The massive forwarding of half-truths and lies is foundational to the distribution of hate-memes. It is also a key component of the emerging desire for a National Divorce. It can be no surprise to the observant that the nation has become divided along roughly religious fissures, and that these fissures are getting wider every day. We already discussed how churches are literally engines of alternative facts, and I am on record for saying that anyone can believe any set of statements they want, and that they ought to be allowed to worship even falsehoods to their heart's content, in their places of worship. But unfortunately, these alternative facts, as promulgated chiefly by Christian churches, too often include the usual zero-sum equations that call for the eradication of other belief systems, the physical destruction (a.k.a. murder) of nonbelievers, and the supremacy of the narrow stripe of coreligionist who votes for the likes of Donald Trump (who is, according to some of these churches, Jesus). It's apparent that now they are so fed up with the rest of us that they are proposing a separate Christian nation. Perhaps this is a better thing than to have them trying to make all of us into Pentecostals. But it is a new thing in American political discourse, that elected officials such as Marjorie Taylor Greene are calling for this National Divorce, which is a different way of saying "sedition."

My own opinion, for what it's worth, is that I would much rather divorce than give in to a gaggle of performative, starry-eyed Christers, if it came to that. Maybe this is because I am ensconced in one of those big, blue states that seem, to my surprise, islands of sanity in a Red Sea of preacher-inspired lunacy. Perhaps it is merely good fortune for liberalism, but the lion's share of the gross domestic product is in the blue states: New York, California, and beyond. For instance, the New York City Metropolitan Area GDP is almost $2 trillion in 2022. The entire United States is rather more than $20 trillion. Which means the New York City metro area *alone* delivers almost 10 percent of the total, even if its geographical area is less than 1 percent of the nation's total landmass.

Just by way of comparison, the NYC-Metro gross domestic product (including parts of Connecticut and New Jersey) is as large as the entire GDP of South Korea. It is almost half of the entire nation of Japan. California, meanwhile, delivers over $3 trillion in GDP, roughly comparable to the United Kingdom and sneaking up on the entire nation of Germany. And while it's true that Texas (red) equals Canada; and Florida (now red) equals Mexico, there really is something less than a dynamic economic base in the GOP states beyond these two, and certainly very little that does not depend on selling natural resources or agricultural products to the Northeast and beyond. Finally, it is no secret that states like New York and California are net donors to federal coffers, where nearly every red state is a net beneficiary.[11]

So on a purely economic basis, any National Divorce would leave the GOP states impoverished, and would see Texas and Florida much more heavily taxed because New York and California would no longer be bailing out, for instance, the Huckabees in Arkansas.

In any case, the assembled army of forwarders has been successfully directed by right-wing media manipulators for several years at least. The concept of a National Divorce—essentially the end of the United States—would seem to be the kind of proposal that would absolutely delight a global enemy that wanted to supersede the United States in dominating the world stage. And we don't have to dig very far to see how it's been done. That is, it's been done, openly, with the help of digitally powered foreign influencers.

For it is not just a domestic cadre of cynical manipulators that trouble us today. No, it is also a *foreign influence* that attacks us. According to *Business Insider*, Elon Musk (X) is now promoting Russian propaganda, where Twitter had restricted it before.[12] Meanwhile, US intelligence confirms that Russia tried to influence the 2022 elections and that they will try to influence 2024.[13] While the enemy may lack the nonnuclear weapons to destroy us, they certainly have the tweets to poison our national discourse.

While Russian efforts to undermine the United States is nothing entirely new, it is a different type of enemy and a different type of influence than we had before the fall of Communism. There, the competing narrative was capitalism versus collectivism. Now it is Western participatory democracy versus fascism. The Russians may have spent twenty years figuring out how to get back at us for beating them in the Cold War. But with the advent of digital anonymity, and the arrival of cost-free hate mongering, plus the apotheosis of one of their intelligence assets inside one of the two major political parties in the United States, they were able to mount a surprisingly effective assault.

When Paul Manafort became Donald Trump's campaign manager in 2016, he brought with him a unique type of connection to the Kremlin. PBS News reports that, as long ago as 2005, "Manafort pitched a plan to Oleg Deripaska, a wealthy Russian business leader and close ally of Russian President Vladimir Putin. Manafort's strategy was to 'influence politics, business dealings and news coverage inside the United States, Europe, and former Soviet republics to benefit President Vladimir Putin's government,' according to the Associated Press, which obtained documents from that pitch as well as later contracts."[14] According to the same source, Manafort won the business and began to implement his plan.

During Trump's victorious 2016 campaign, Manafort delivered to his Russian contact, Konstantin Kilimnik, secret polling data about Republican Party voters.[15] According to NBC News, Kilimnik "may have helped coordinate [a] hack-and-leak operation that delivered private emails between Democratic politicians to Wikileaks." But that wasn't the most important part of the operation. This detailed polling data also enabled Russian bots to microtarget Americans the GOP determined were especially susceptible to the type of madcap, paranoid lies that would fuel just enough outrage to tank the already faltering Hillary Clinton campaign. According to CBS News in an article from February 2020, "Intelligence officials have been suggesting publicly and privately that Russia and other adversaries have been refining their disinformation methods, working to spread and amplify their messages through 'authentic' US sources, rather than creating personas that can be flagged by social media companies as fake identities."[16]

No doubt in 2023 that data has been improved upon, and the duplicitous liars that run the GOP, in their blind pursuit of power, have, in effect, sold out the American heartland to the unkind ministrations of Russian propagandists who are attempting to destabilize the nation the better to beat us permanently on the global stage.

That this is known by all and acted upon by no one, that Trump is not already in prison for colluding with an enemy state actor, and that Russia remains a paragon for the army of haters that fuels the Trump base is all we need to know about how far down the road to perdition we have come as a nation. Despite numerous court actions that may hobble any attempt at a Trumpian dictatorship, we are left with the strong suspicion that, despite valiant efforts among the judiciary, we no longer have much in the way of social guardrails; no very strong mechanisms in place that might halt our slide. Some might say it is a lack of will. Even as Trump has been indicted for buying the silence of a pornstar in order to cheat his way into the White House, even as he is accused of stealing nuclear secrets and is on trial for trying to overthrow the government, the 2016 chapter of his Russian collusion has gone unpunished. The once-vaunted "Mueller Report" was, we can now say, nothing but a poultice to cover a grievous wound, still not healed.

Personally, I found it ludicrous that anyone would think that Mueller, a career Republican, would do anything that resembled the more forceful type of righteousness that the situation clearly called for. Instead he delivered milquetoast and a nothing-to-see-here conclusion that left Trump disastrously in office even through two attempts to impeach him.

My personal belief is that Trump's days as a free citizen may be numbered, even as the trials have only just begun in earnest. No doubt by the time this book goes to press, we will know far more about where Trump ends up with his almost uncountable indictments. But for the present, Trump's behavior is unchanged. Even after Trump was indicted in New York for paying hush money, we saw where Trump flew back to Mar-a-Largo to give an incendiary, taunting, quasi-violent speech that ought to have seen him dragged back to court for contempt. Under indictment in Manhattan, he had gone so far as to have posted a picture on social media of himself holding a bat near the head of Alvin Bragg, the African American district attorney who charged him with a campaign finance–related felony. Later he made defamatory statements about a court clerk in another trial, and received a limited gag order from a frustrated judge.

We are forced to ask ourselves what other possible defendant could ever remain free having widely proposed violence against the prosecutor, and having attacked a court functionary? At this moment, I would say there are no others besides Trump. Perhaps his misbehavior in Judge Engoron's civil court trial or his misbehavior in the January 6 indictment will soon catch up to him. But it is a slippery slope, and since he has not been immediately detained for an open threat against law enforcement, we can expect little meaningful pushback against right-wing terror, or at least not very swift or very effective pushback.

Not long after he was indicted by Bragg in New York, Trump was sued by E. Jean Carroll, also in Manhattan. Carroll claimed Trump raped her and then defamed her. It took three hours for a jury to agree that he sexually assaulted and then defamed her. Immediately Trump was back on his Section 230-protected "Truth Social" defaming her. And then he made the mistake of repeating the same defamatory lies on a town hall at CNN not thirty-six hours after the verdict in *Carroll vs. Trump*. Carroll sued him again for further defamation, and won again.

I believe we are well into a state of digital fatigue—where regulators and managers in every tradition have thrown up their hands for lack of guidance, lack of tools, lack of jurisdiction, lack of understanding, lack of any meaningful attempt at management of anything that touches digital. For if Trump had published his Bragg-baseball-bat-threat in a newspaper, my bet is that he would already have been in handcuffs. Or if he had phoned in the threat: same. But because it was put up on a public, digital platform, the attitude is, it's "hands-off" the perpetrator, at least partly because the liability of the "platform" is ill-understood or at least nominally protected under the aforementioned Section 230.

Digital, here as elsewhere, gets a free pass because there is a pervasive sense that humans really have no control over these complex systems. This, of course, is a convenient misapprehension.

PERSUADABLE POPULATIONS

Woe betide the people who fail to govern their strengths, as they quickly fall victim to their weakness. I say this in relation to the way in which the United States, having invented the internet, now begins to falter under the weight of its own invention because we have not had the sense to create advantageous laws to keep the internet functional, or at least society functional in the face of the new technology.

We have established that "forwarding" is a key element of the neo-fascist communications engine. And that this army of forwarders has long been identified and targeted by Facebook advertisers, criminal organizations, political parties, state actors, and thousands of devious hackers everywhere. Once these hacker-ideologues have identified a vulnerable party, they pile on with an incessant flow of messages that seem to come from everywhere.

Not to say it's all directed by Dr. Evil in his underground lair. It isn't that simple.

But it is an efficient engine. Microtargeting represents one method by which vulnerable populations are surrounded by messages that are so voluminous, and that come from so many sources, that they seem to be organic. According to Wikipedia, "Microtargeting can . . . be used, sometimes by foreign actors, to spread disinformation about political candidates and events among target groups. For example, during the 2016 US election, Russian disinformation campaigns targeted Facebook followers and now-defunct Cambridge Analytica exploited their data."[17] And yet, according to the *Washington Post*, "Facebook knew ads [and] microtargeting could be exploited by politicians. They accepted the risk."[18] And according to one study, political microtargeting (PMT) attempts to "assess the persuasion effects of personality-tailored ads on social media."[19]

Worse, at a certain tipping point, and we have certainly passed that tipping point, the wish and hope of the manipulator is granted: there are enough actual true believers pumping out enough balderdash to vulnerable populations that the vulnerable targets begin to feel there is a real movement to support claims that, to an outsider, might seem madcap at best.

How did millions of Americans end up believing the 2020 election was stolen from Donald Trump? Sure, the ex-president talked about it a lot. But that would never have been enough. It required an orchestrated, digitally powered, PMT effort, carried out by a decentralized, QAnon-like cadre of fellow travelers. The intent was to build out a carpet of AstroTurf that was convincingly natural in appearance. Never mind that the cynical manipulators themselves (some of whom have already pleaded guilty in a Georgia RICO indictment) knew the claims were false. The digital audience targeting was so effective that millions of Americans believed an obvious lie.

The lie was accomplished by a constellation of efforts. Among these, perhaps the most important was the assertion that certain types of digital vote tabulation machines were not only inaccurate, but were manipulated such that literally hundreds of thousands if not millions of Democratic votes were tallied where there ought to have been many fewer. The most famous example of this, of which we will have more to say later, is the assertion that a voting machine company called Dominion was in league with Venezuela and an unnamed, mysterious Democratic cabal that, despite being comprised of people of obvious inferiority, still managed to somehow produce more than enough "fake" votes to win a presidential election.

Reuters reported on February 16, 2023, that Fox News knew the claims against Dominion were "crazy" and "shockingly reckless." But they trumpeted the fraudulent claims regardless. Dominion, predictably, sued Fox. In the end, Fox, not a digital platform, paid Dominion over $750 million to settle before trial. The digital connection, as we will note further on, was that the chief source for these claims was an attorney named Sidney Powell, a Trump legal adviser. She relied on a digitally sourced story of unknown provenance that made certain claims that no one ever checked, that could never have been checked, and that were false on the face of it. But again, because it was an internet thing, Internet Fairy Dust was sprinkled, and the information passed muster at the nation's most-watched television news network.

It is fascinating how time can decay Internet Fairy Dust in some cases, as attorney Powell has since pleaded guilty in Georgia, where she admitted she was wrong, knew she was wrong, and had to cooperate against other defendants.

I am absolutely not a fan of digital vote counting for the very reasons cited above, but I am coming at it from the other side of the table: the fact is, millions of people don't trust digital voting because it would be possible, unlike with paper ballots and more primitive, mechanical voting machines, to actually manipulate the vote surreptitiously; and that if carried off with enough sophistication, this would be near impossible to detect. That said, I do not believe there was fraud in the 2020 election, and I don't think Dominion has participated in anything questionable. But I do think that in 2004, it is altogether possible that another voting machine company—Diebold—did, in fact "deliver" (as they said they would) the state of Ohio to George W. Bush, thereby handing him a victory over Democrat John Kerry.

The challenge here is that we are expected to trust our voting systems, and digital does not make trust any easier than it would have been otherwise. In fact, it opens up the door to exactly the kind of wild, unsupported claims that have been made about the 2020 election simply because it is plausible. It is plausible because, while switching millions of paper or mechanical ballots would be virtually impossible, it would be not very hard at all for some bad actor to change digital votes and not get caught. It did not happen in 2020, but digital voting may leave us forever questioning whether votes are ever really properly tabulated.

The social media landscape today is defined by the above sorts of manipulations. Ridiculous, unsupported claims about voter fraud are only the most salient example. Propagandists have used digital advertising technologies to assemble, message, and control the sentiments of millions with lies coming from every direction and in such volume that the victim must, at some point, believe that the whole world must agree with the lunatic assertions that we hear coming out of the right-wing echo chamber; and that those who don't accept these calumnies must be Hillary-worshipping, Satanic infantophages who must be wiped off the face of the earth.

I would like nothing better than to examine the psychological sources of this hate, but that is another topic and beyond the purview of a book concerned with digital technologies. Suffice it to say digital's contribution is much less about the content itself—there is nothing new in hatred!—and much more about the infrastructure and message delivery that makes massive amounts of hate and alienation possible in what had been a pluralistic, relatively tolerant society.

Our enormous burden is to manage and control fast-changing, powerful technologies before we allow them to drive us right off the cliff. What we experience today is the near total lack of government willpower to rein in, regulate, and refine digital content such that it does not constitute a universal blast of the collective, society-destroying Id of humanity.

THE ID OF HUMANITY

When I say "Id," I mean that dark underbelly of the human system that essentially houses all of the basest, most animalistic urges that trouble us as a group. We can debate Freud in another context, but it's probably safe to say he did identify a thing called "the subconscious," and that this entity holds remarkable sway over what we do as individuals, and what we don't. And a significant inhabitant of that unseen world is the abovementioned Id.

Some say that the suppression of the Id is coterminous with the advance of what we call "civilization." For instance, in a society of laws, you can't attack your neighbor just because you were feeling it that day. This is a succinct way of saying that the notion of civilization must include trade-offs of freedoms, rights, and responsibilities. It necessarily requires the suppression of the lizard-like Id that lurks abroad in the human subconscious. But it is a delicate balance. The wrong mix one way and you have an uninhabitable chaos. The wrong mix the other way and you've got lockstep, robotic fascism. We have been living in a sort of rationalistic sweet spot for a couple of hundred years now, or at least some of us have been. And that rationalistic civilization now is under threat of dissolution, perhaps soon to be burned away by the torches lit by digitally enabled fabulists aligned with Christianity and White Supremacy.

Our civilized world, where, presumably, the worst instincts are suppressed in favor of cooperation, has brought forth nearly everything we take for granted today: from plumbing to pension funds. Much of the things we take for granted in civilization are based on what is also known as "trust." For instance, only in an atmosphere of relative trust can one live in a place where the municipality provides your drinking water. By and large, cities and towns have, over the course of decades, and with the exception of Flint, Michigan, perhaps, proven at least trustworthy enough so that you will probably drink the water coming out of your tap without a second thought, or at least you are comfortable that you will not soon die from drinking it. Retirement funding represents another form of trust—and here we can say that the government certainly has earned the right to be trusted at least to deliver as promised. For your entire working life, you pay into Social Security: an insurance program that promises you an income once you retire. And, incredibly enough, once you reach retirement age, the government actually sends you a check every month.

It can reasonably be asserted that satisfied trust results in a recognition of responsibilities toward the trust others have also placed in the body politic. From this proceeds a set of rights and responsibilities: tradeoffs of some freedoms for some security.

That is the kind of world we live in today. It took centuries to build these institutions of trust. These institutions—water and sewer, medicine, insurance, banking—provide real benefits. Kick out the underpinnings of trust, and it all begins to fall away. Minus a viable alternative, it falls away into chaos.

But the destruction of trust is, in fact, the plan and the goal of the cynical manipulator. We have already noted that the Steve Bannons of the world have professed that their goal is to fill the public sphere with so much disinformation that trust is impossible. Only by harnessing a broad array of digital communication platforms, and via persistent disinformation attacks, can trust be eroded. And this is what the Bannon types have done: they have deployed digital media to flood the conversation with disgraceful, murderous propaganda. They have done it in high enough volume, and for a long enough time, that they have at least partially achieved their goal. Hence, it can be no surprise that the ill-informed "patriot" trusts nothing. The very rights and responsibilities that form civil society is questioned by digitally influenced "patriots," who would have you believe that freedom really is absolute, and that a properly ordered society is merely one in which the most powerful are permitted to do exactly as they please, with no repercussions whatsoever.

Let us take this moment to point out that this is a recipe for fascism. I say this because I believe the roots of fascism lie not in oppression but in freedom. A common fallacy is that fascism operates by depriving others of freedom. In fact, there is never any such plan in the fascist playbook. The only thing the fascist really cares about is the satisfaction of their own personal desires. That the satisfaction of these desires may be enormously costly, or ruinous, or murderous to others, is of no consequence. If a fascist could gain all they want in the world by sitting in an easy chair, they would absolutely opt for that. Because few things characterize the fascist other than laziness and a lack of self-control.

History shows us that the horrors of fascism are rarely by design and almost entirely accomplished by satisfying the whim of one psychopath or another. The cruelties heaped upon innocent populations are not necessarily a benefit to any group of fascists, but only the whim and the determination of any particular empowered fascist who desires to hurt or destroy another.

In this manner, I say that fascism is much more about giving license to psychopaths than it is about any particular doctrine. Fascism gives license without responsibility, but only to the few who charge in to claim their license before anyone else can object. And a fascist system rewards the most aggressive as they exercise their perfect freedoms, even as they exercise those freedoms—often perversions—upon the weak and the innocent.

Digital media technology, with its anonymity, its power, and its remove, represents a perfect tool for the impulsive fascist. In their hands, digital media (as well as digital surveillance) can be deployed to kick out the Lally columns that hold up the pier of civilization.

Once digital makes all things possible for all people all the time, it simply means that the most aggressive, the most psychotic, the most impulsive among us will take the lead. Once that happens, we can only expect a total destruction of trust, civility, and cooperation in favor of an impossible stew of mutual loathing, war, and the triumph of the strong at the expense of the weak. Or should I say, the triumph of the gun-carrying simpleton over the more civilized type that would rather read a book than murder a librarian.

WE DON'T LIKE US VERY MUCH

I'm already on record for being bone-tired of most social media posts; and I recommend to all that setting the phone aside for hours at a time is bound to be salutary. But let's peel away another layer of social media's patina to see what lies beneath.

Social media posts can range in a spectrum from enlightening to disgraceful and beyond. But I believe a convincing case can be made that the overall character of most social media posts amounts to nothing better than "too much information." These are the inconsequential overshares about dining incidents, the recorded behavior of toddlers or significant others, or examples of an expansive set of accepted witticisms. Worse, the posts that qualify as benign but "TMI," as useless as they may be, comprise the *most benign* part of the spectrum. At the other end of the objectionability spectrum are videos of people being beheaded. And lest we are tempted to think these are cost-free aberrations, we know that recently in Israel, actual beheadings took place at the hands of an invading army of terrorists who attacked a music festival.

More practically, is there any reason why we should welcome the insipid idiocy of the typical social media post? Are these not cringey at best? Occasionally amusing? But mostly dreadful. Perhaps they are useful to the individual as a form of therapy or self-actualization. But the benefit to the public is negligible. No, it's worse than negligible. It is detrimental. It may even be ruinous.

Do social media represent, then, a self-validated verdict on the collective soul of humanity? Do they tell us we are quite as petty and as silly as the latest Tik-Tok video would lead us to believe? Have we stumbled on a sad, inconvenient truth about people in general? If social media today represent the collective soul of the human project, then we will have to make our excuses. For it is a poor showing.

Here are examples of how social media platforms push the ersatz over the real, where appearances come before substance, where it's just too easy to post nonsense, where it's just too easy to consume nonsense; indeed, where you can do very little except move your thumb and be flooded with madcap messages about White Hats in the Military who secretly installed Trump in the White House while having already executed Nancy Pelosi such that the Pelosi that walks the halls of Congress must be a living clone, or at best a Christian-baby-adrenochrome-fueled zombie.

Even the more benign forms of digital advertising are a form of flummery.

These days we are beset by a class of individuals who call themselves "influencers." These folks claim to have scads of "followers," presumably such that they can tweet out or Tik-Tok or otherwise disseminate some cultural choice or some product in order to drive sales or adoption of one thing or another. Somewhere in this equation, there is a kickback to the influencer. It may be a direct payment based on eyeballs.

It may come in the form of nonmonetary compensation, such as a free lunch for a positive post about "my latest fave brunch," or a free hotel room in exchange for a gushy endorsement of that Lucky Hideaway a mile from the airport.

However, the standing of the influencer is, too often, yet one more shifty, insubstantial truth-fail somewhere in the vicinity of mis-representation. A particularly juicy example is the story of Chinese streamers under a bridge in a rich neighborhood, which recently was the subject of a dystopian viral video.[20] It seems they were camping out under a bridge in order to game the algorithm into believing they lived in a more prosperous area than they actually did; thereby increasing the likelihood that their stream would become more "recommended" by the algorithm that governs recommendations to visitors to social media sites. Another example shows a woman doing a podcast, but in front of several dozen smartphones trained on her as she spoke. Presumably, this was her "starter" audience. If you're going to be an influencer, you've got to get those numbers up!

Influencers are nothing without digital followers. We can suggest that they are perhaps engaged in a subterfuge, and that they don't really support personally all of the brands they claim to support. We can say they indeed do trade off mentions and endorsements for perks and other forms of payment in a relay race of disingenuous posturing. We can even say what they are engaged in is a form of AstroTurfing—a time-honored public relations technique that did not come along with the internet.

If you understand the history of publicity and public relations, you know that planting stories and generating "support" with a fistful of dollars is as old as influencing itself. Today there is pushback against the influencer, where some restaurants, it is said, are banning them, or at least refusing to offer any sort of free-lunch compensation.

But internet influencers hardly invented crafty manipulation techniques. Even *elections* were manipulated prior to the internet—shocking as that may be! When Senator John F. Kennedy ran for president in 1960, he had a tough fight on his hands in the West Virginia Democratic primary. The Kennedy family delivered cash to West Virginian sheriffs and other local pols in order to literally buy the election. His opponent, Hubert Humphrey, knew he hadn't enough cash to do the same, and conceded the state and probably the nomination. He did not try to say the election was stolen. He knew how elections had always worked. He just did not have enough bank to compete.[21]

That may have been bad enough. Today it is almost universally understood that a large percentage of followers on social media are either fake, were purchased, or were gamed and manipulated much as described above. The fakery involved in declaring followers is one of the dirty, not-very-secret secrets of digital marketing, and every influencer knows it. They know it so well that when Elon Musk was buying Twitter, he originally tried to cut the deal in half by claiming that half the accounts on Twitter were fake. While it is a curiosity that he tried this, let's say here that the real story is in why there'd be so many fake accounts to start with—for even if it were nowhere near half, even 15 percent would be a statistically disqualifying amount. I would posit that the reason there are so many fake accounts is twofold: one is that they are sold over and over again to influencers who want to increase their "following." The second is that they are bot accounts deployed by cynical manipulators who want to push stories from so-called "sources" that never existed outside the manipulators' own plan.

These techniques make it so that the best grifters get to tell the most stories. Nowadays, it's not what you write, or even who you know. It's how many ways you can trick the public into believing you've got a following. And if you get good enough at that, then, in the spirit of faking-it-'til-we-are-making-it, you will at some point, presumably, have an actual following in the form of actual possible buyers of products and services.

As it turns out, we may wish we had never disintermediated those gatekeepers. You know the ones: editors, literary agents, publishers, and the like. In their world—the real one that most of us live in—you must take some responsibility for what you have a hand in making public. Some of that responsibility is self-imposed due to a natural tendency to non-embarrassment. Very few publishers would agree to print and distribute something that they felt would diminish their reputation. And some of that responsibility is in place in order to avoid suits for libel. For publishers are, in fact, responsible for what happens in the great wide world if such happenings can be traced back to their publication of, say, naked, obvious, pernicious falsehoods that result in violent behavior.

But in our brave new digital world, where our communications are all coated in a thick mantle of Internet Fairy Dust, where IFD obliterates all rules, responsibilities, and guidelines, where all is possible and none are accountable, we can only expect a general course of societal decay. The chief culprit, as I have mentioned earlier, is an environment of untruth. And the environment of untruth can be traced back to the mechanics of a particular law (Section 230) that exempts the amplifiers of hateful, untruthful messages from any and all responsibility for the harm these messages cause to society.

FANTASY AND THE DIVORCE FROM FACTS

Under the auspices of Section 230 of the Communications Decency Act, social media platforms like Facebook (Instagram) and Google (YouTube) are immune from liability for anything posted on their platform; *and* immune from any complaint that they are unfairly blocking any content they don't want on their platform.

The result is an atmosphere of fantasy parading as fact.

This double whammy of no responsibility plus untrammeled rights, is, in my opinion, *the fount of alternative facts* upon which public discourse unhappily rests today.

Often the fount of irresponsibility reaches out beyond digital realms, and into more traditional media formats—although, as shown below, it seems that the most damaging insanities stem from some kind of anonymous, untraceable, unverified digital source.

As noted earlier, Fox News in 2023 was sued by Dominion Voting Systems for billions of dollars, essentially for defamation. They ended up settling for three-quarters of a billion dollars—largely because they were not a digital platform.

We have talked about how trust in digital voting has been seriously questioned by what are called "election deniers," mainly in the form of die-hard Trump supporters who cannot accept that their Great Leader was not the preference of the majority of voters. And although it has already been revealed that Fox News knew the claims were bogus, they did not report on any stories about bogus claims of fraud. Instead, Fox repeatedly claimed, minus even a shred of credible evidence, that

Dominion helped steal the 2020 election for Biden. Dominion sued, claiming Fox News damaged their reputation and therefore owed them $1.6 billion in damages plus an unlimited amount of punitive payment. Before the settlement, many legal analysts had already noted that, in a world where libel is hard to prove, this case was, for all intents and purposes, already proven. In short: being non-digital cost Fox nearly $1 billion. The same lies continue to be amplified on social media, because the social media giants, protected by 230, have nothing to fear from the courts—as demonstrated by the SCOTUS decision in *Gonzalez vs. Google.*

The Dominion settlement did, however, result in the firing of Tucker Carlson, Fox's most popular talking head. Perhaps this is partly because the testimony in Dominion revealed that senior journalists at Fox News texted one another to the effect that they knew for certain that Trump's election fraud claims were bogus.[22] Tucker Carlson, whose segment was, until his firing, the most popular show on cable news, texted to his colleagues that Trump "could destroy us" if Fox did not go along with the lie. And so they continued to report 2020 fraud claims as if they were legitimate. According to Dominion, Fox openly lied to the world, over and over, in a pernicious, deliberate, and damaging manner.

They did so by interviewing guests like Sidney Powell, an attorney who has since pleaded guilty to a number of election-related offenses. Where did she get this so-called evidence from? She claimed that some of it came from a "decapitated time-traveler."[23] Yes, you read that correctly. In other words: Fox News put a manifestly insane person on the air and promoted what she claimed as fact. Remember the movie *Network*? Where Howard Beale, a "manifestly insane man" was made the anchor of a tarted-up "news" show? It was, at the time, a form of satire that seemed cynical.

Now that looks quaint. All Howard Beale did was tell people to stick their heads out the window and shout. He did not tell them to kill transvestites. He did not call women who needed an abortion murderers. He did not badger people into voting for a hateful simpleton. But Fox News did. And they did it by weaponizing lies in a way that no one in this country has ever done before.

But wait, what has this got to do with digital? Isn't Fox News a cable outfit?

Yes, they are. But they live within a media ecosystem that includes a heavy dose of social media influence. Again, let us emphasize: it turns out the foundation of their lie was a *digital post* from a probably fictional character. Sidney Powell herself was never the source, she only presented it. It is this sleight-of-hand that I find most troubling: by piggybacking on generations of the relative trustworthiness of things that find their way into print (with notable exceptions), Fox, leaning on convenient, untraceable digital sources, deploys a "people are talking about it" approach to putting ideas into their viewer's heads. When, in fact, "people" are *not* "talking about" anything. What Fox came up with was a lame smidgen of madcap extemporization, presented by a brazen liar probably also mentally unstable, as a stand-in for some actual, legitimate claim of fraud.

Another example on a smaller scale goes somewhat as follows:

According to Influencewatch.org, "America First Legal Foundation is a right-of-center nonprofit organization formed by former senior Trump White House advisor Stephen Miller and counselor to the Attorney General Gene Hamilton in February 2021. It aims to use litigation to oppose left-of-center policies enacted by the Biden administration."

Here we have a former Trump advisor starting a political action committee disguised as a "foundation." Among the efforts mounted by this organization is an "investigation"[24] into the Department of Justice's documents raid on Mar-a-Lago, where, famously, hundreds of sensitive intelligence documents were found illegally in Trump's possession, including in his office and in his desk. Based on their bogus investigation, they tweet out their "findings." In no very long time at all, and as is no surprise, Jim Jordan's House Judiciary Committee is citing these findings as a reason to ramp up their own utterly bogus investigation based on zero evidence but lots of wild claims. These claims are reamplified by official tweets. Finally the Trump family—in this case son Eric—tweets out news of the bogus Jordan investigation as "vindication" and "victory."

This is a complete cycle of nonsense: from nonsense generated, to nonsense amplified, to nonsense injected into an official investigation, to nonsense proclaimed as fact by those who will most benefit from the nonsense. And it's all digital, and it has never been fact-checked by anyone in the process.

How did digital become literally immune from fact-checking? What created the environment in which a Network of Liars could not merely exist, but thrive and profit and build an audience of millions?

We will get to that in a moment.

But first, let's rewind to a pre-digital time when a different Republican media-star was in the White House. His name was Ronald Reagan. He was famous for calling ketchup a vegetable when it came to cheapening school lunches, and for selling arms to our enemies if they would only keep our hostages until he was inaugurated. Many say he was a thoroughgoing traitor and most likely one of the dumbest men ever to sit in the Oval Office. But more importantly, for our purposes, he ended what was called the Federal Communications Commission's Fairness Doctrine.[25] This required that broadcasters *had an obligation to fairness and relative objectivity in exchange for their having been licensed to use public airwaves in order to sell advertising.*

Fox News, in this environment, would have been impossible— although some have said that, as a cable company, Fox News would have been exempt. My position is that Fox News may or may not have found themselves exempt, but that they would have been singled out much more quickly as a platform for liars had the general trend been toward truth instead of lies. The disappearance of this law made it easy for liars to claim a right to lie as a form of free speech. To be plain, lies *are* protected speech, as long as those lies are not written down, for instance, on a loan application.[26] That said they are, nonetheless, abhorrent in and of themselves.

And it is this *environment of lies* that gives Fox News the power that it has. Let's picture a world where *only* Fox News was spewing election lies. Let's further suppose they had to answer for a published source of information rather than a tweet or email from a murky, digitally sourced wack-a-doodle. How long could that gambit have lasted in the absence of fifty thousand bot-driven Twitter accounts spouting the same type of ruinous diatribe? One of the least welcome developments that I predicted in my old book is the notion that "nation will hack at nation" in an ugly cyber war.

Make no mistake: there is a cyber war being fought today, and it isn't being fought with drones and smartbombs. It is being fought with influencers, liars, bot-accounts, and hackers funded by enemies of the

United States—Russia, for instance. Or the Republican Party, which has become, largely speaking, a fifth-column of the Putin regime. We have already discussed how the consulting work performed by Trump's 2016 campaign chairman, Paul Manafort, led him to contract with Russians in order to influence public dialogue in the United States. Manafort has been convicted and has served out a sentence for, more or less, treason. And if he had sold us out to Communists, or if he were nonwhite, or non-male, I submit that he might have fared much, much worse. Remember that Julius and Ethel Rosenberg were, in the 1950s, *executed* for selling state secrets to the Soviet Union. Today, it seems, because Russia is no longer Communist, and because the Manafort brand of treason shares the larger part of a Venn diagram with the hopes and dreams of tired, racist old white people, we settle instead for a slap on the wrist and a prayer they don't try this again. Of course, they *will* try again, even if several leading Proud Boys are recently convicted for seditious conspiracy. For selling out the presidency to a sworn enemy of the nation, the sentences to date have been much, much too short. After all, wasn't Hitler in jail for a few years?

We have talked about how nation would hack at nation. This type of hacking was exemplified in the matter of a company called Cambridge Analytica—now defunct, but very much alive during the lead-up to the 2020 election. Cambridge Analytica specialized in identifying and delivering audiences to advertisers. They were embroiled in scandal once it was revealed how they were going about identifying audiences. Simply put, they were accused of collecting and keeping email address data from over fifty million Facebook users without their permission.

Chief among their collection techniques was the surreptitious collection of data via an app called *thisisyourdigitallife* that was created by the company. Over three hundred million Facebook users downloaded it. The app allowed Cambridge Analytica to collect data on not only the person who downloaded it but all of their contacts as well (it may shock you to know that this is a common technique deployed by many apps). Cambridge Analytica was then hired by the Republican Party to help them target their advertising much as many advertisers do every day of the week. However, this was not a soda pop company looking to sell more sugar water. By 2016, the GOP had, under the auspices of Trump and his campaign manager/Russian agent Paul Manafort, become at least partly an intelligence asset of the Kremlin. As such, they relied on Russia for the technical knowhow and hacker wherewithal to target the audiences that Cambridge Analytica had assembled. And with Russian bot activity and Russian-invented stories designed specifically to destroy Americans' faith in their own electoral system, they deployed what amounted to a surrounding ecosystem of lies and fantasies to an audience that proved far more vulnerable than anyone might have guessed.

A UK government watchdog called the Insolvency Service investigated Cambridge Analytica and found that "the unethical services offered by the companies included bribery or honey trap stings, voter disengagement campaigns, obtaining information to discredit political opponents and spreading information anonymously in political campaigns."[27]

With the data Cambridge Analytica collected surreptitiously, they were able to help the Trump campaign, and the Russians thereby, deploy a vast customer database to fuel the crafting of misinformation and disinformation to help get Trump elected. Trump's brand has suffered mightily since those heady days, but in 2016, these efforts were a ringing success!

Not least among the accomplishments of Fox News, Cambridge Analytica and its fellow-travelers on the QAnon side, is that millions of Americans now actually believe, and more importantly vote as if they believe, that so-called "liberals" like Tom Hanks and Hillary Clinton murder Christian babies in order to feast on their adrenaline-rich blood. Again, this is not a story out of the murky, ill-informed infancy of the human mind. It is ripped from yesterday's headlines. Not only that, but millions believe that they ought to be able to kill these liberals. My contention is that the liars *and the enablers that own digital platforms* to spread these lies are absolutely responsible for the creation and continuation of this dreadful ecosystem of falsehood and hate. For how can it be that the billion-dollar corporation that creates the environment, owns the technology and the promotion engines—indeed, the billion-dollar corporation that controls the entire process except for the creation of the content itself—how can it be that this wealthy organization owes nothing to anyone?

Partly through the offices of Manafort in 2016 but now through the offices of members of Congress (like Ohio's Jim Jordan), Russia has played a role in the destabilization of truth, especially where they can inject targeted misinformation into the American mindscape. But there are other players!

DIGITAL RELIGIONISTS

It's not just Fox News, of course, and it isn't just Russian bots. It's also the evangelical Christian community. We have already talked about how churches are engines of alternative facts. But they are also increasingly deploying digital methods to spread not just "the word" about their savior. They are using it to spread slander and hatred in ways that must surely damage those they needlessly target. Journalist Sarah Posner writes about a Christian nationalist boot camp called the Statesman Academy that is pushing anti-trans laws across the nation: "The Statesman Academy elevates the profiles of right-wing lawmakers and helps them promote legislation rooted in baseless distortions of science and medicine."[28]

Let me say, for whatever it is worth, that I am not an atheist. My own personal feelings about matters of the spirit are probably not worth discussing, as I am sure they are neither original nor enlightening. I do feel that there are more things than meet the eye in the great wide world, but I am also pretty sure I don't have a good grasp of what they might be.

Nevertheless, and unlike me, there is a large contingent of American citizens who seem to believe they have found the answer. Not just part of an answer. All the answers. In one book. They call it "the Bible." And under our system of government, and indeed under any system designed for freedom and fairness, they have every right to believe they have done so.

But we find ourselves now at the confluence of two phenomena that, together, form a poisonous compound that, injected into the public discourse, has made for a generous helping of hateful self-righteousness and even violence. One might call it the Digital Jesus movement.

Yes, the evangelicals have discovered technology. I'm sure a nimbler observer than I am could fill a bookshelf with scornful examples of how ironical this is—because, of course, evangelical Christianity (and fundamentalists in both of the other Abrahamic religions) have placed themselves in opposition to science—of which technology is the adept brainchild.

According to National Public Radio, more than half of Republican voters support Christian nationalism, "a worldview that claims the US is a Christian nation and that the country's laws should therefore be rooted in Christian values."[29] As mentioned above, Congressperson Marjorie Taylor Greene has openly embraced the idea as part of her proposed National Divorce. Also, according to the article, roughly 40 percent of Christian nationalist sympathizers support the idea of an authoritarian regime in order to enforce this unconstitutional plan.

It would be bad enough if the Christian nationalists held beliefs that were in some way rational.

But the real problem comes with the *irrational* claims they make. And it pains me to say that too many religionists have decided that their chosen faith also needs to be *your* chosen faith, and mine. And that if we don't like that, then we are not simply going to hell, but we should be made to kowtow to priests and pastors in this life as well.

It all becomes so much worse when the evangelicals can "paper the house" with Christianized digital messaging—targeted (as per Cambridge Analytica) at the most vulnerable populations. Sourced from nowhere, supported by no evidence but their holy book, yet amplified by the power of (Christian-abhorred) science, the science-deniers rely on digital technology to spew their dark across a spectrum of light.

Christian nationalism only gives a more cohesive plan to what has long been held dear by evangelicals. These evangelicals are convinced they have the answer for all of the world's troubles, that it is all found in their holy book, and that there are no other books or belief systems that are in any way legitimate. These self-appointed saviors will claim that there is no law of the land, that government is of relatively little importance, and that what truly matters is whatever they determine their one true book says about, say, whether a raped teenager can get an abortion in Mississippi.

Again, it is tempting to spend more time on the grotesque hypocrisy involved in all didactic religion. Especially upon those religions who believe it was all written down in one book. Especially upon the adherents of that book who say that one need look no further for answers to great questions, and who also want to claim that they are not, in fact, among the laziest and least discerning "thinkers" the world has ever known.

But our task here is not to describe the threadbare, depressing lack of curiosity on the part of the self-satisfied, tongue-talking evangelical. It is more about an attempt to show how digital technologies have been deployed by even those who would question the methods by which digital technology was developed, and how the deniers conveniently have metastasized their pernicious messages by leveraging technology the underpinnings of which they openly deny.

One radical I know has said he thinks anyone who publicly professes to believe obvious fantasies as fact should be prohibited from partaking in taxpayer-funded discourse (according to his theory, this would include voting).

In fact, this is technically already the case, in law. Churches, as we all are given to understand, are nonprofit organizations and are tax exempt. And therefore, as non-taxpayers, they are prohibited, as organizations, from making political contributions or political recommendations. This is a nicer way of saying what my radical friend also indicated.

There is also the matter of the United States Constitution, which can be read in any number of ways other than the orthodox manner to which we have become accustomed. Let's try an exercise. We all know that the First Amendment says that "Congress shall make no law regarding an establishment of religion." Incredibly, this has been extrapolated to mean that religious institutions, while they may own real estate and conduct business just like anyone else, cannot be taxed. Is this not a giveaway that directly contradicts what the Constitution says? If we cannot make any laws regarding religion, is not a law that forbids their taxation prima facie unconstitutional? Is that not a law regarding the establishment of religion? For how could these religions remain establishments if they had to pay taxes?

Churches are already neck-deep in politics, even as they pay zero taxes. Indeed, insofar as they have influenced voters sufficiently, they enjoy representation without taxation. And the poster-child of this nexus of hypocrisy is, as noted above, Christian nationalism.

And Christian nationalism, I contend, would never have gained traction if not for the way it's promulgated by a network of live preachers, cable channels, traditional publishers, and now most importantly, social media accounts often driven by bots and hackers. This digital component is the key to Christian nationalism's newfound currency. It is therefore not likely a coincidence, given what we have said about "nation hacking at nation," that *very often, Christian nationalists find themselves rooting for enemies of the United States.*

Largely this is because Russia has been neck-deep in right-wing extremism, and especially digitally powered extremism, for years. Andrew Torba, CEO of Gab, a social media site popular in conservative circles, tweeted "Putin is brilliant," and added, "I hope the Globalist American Empire gets humiliated from all angles. Ukraine needs to be liberated & cleansed from the degeneracy of the secular western globalist empire."[30]

Torba is also author of a book called *Christian Nationalism: A Biblical Guide for Taking Dominion and Discipling Nations.* In it he proclaims, "This world belongs to Jesus Christ" and designates "the word" as "our most powerful weapon." As noted above, Torba's right-wing social media site is called Gab, a self-important enterprise comprised mainly of puffery and questionable claims of censorship. The censorship they claim to have fallen victim to is also known as "content moderation"; and it is practiced, for example, by X where, by the way, the lion's share of Christian nationalists continues to post their maniacal claims. So it doesn't matter that Gab itself has a tiny usership—the message will get amplified later on the big platforms like X.

Despite X's recent travails (they have lost considerable advertising revenue since Elon Musk purchased it and gutted its content moderation teams), the platform still has over sixty million weekly users in the United States. There are easily more than a hundred million weekly users of Facebook in the United States. These are tremendous numbers. This kind of reach is stupendous, and almost unprecedented.

And because of the combination of absolute rights and zero responsibilities enshrined in Section 230, *any message of any kind* has a chance to reach and be seen by all these millions of users. In digital, it is apparent that no media can die but to be resurrected, propped up, passed around, and transmogrified into a perverse form of media-immortality via the machinations of what some have called the "right wing echo chamber."

The University of Texas says: "A social media echo chamber is when one experiences a biased, tailored media experience that eliminates opposing viewpoints and differing voices."[31] Social media sites are designed to increase engagement. In designing their recommendation algorithms to offer "more of the same," they have, perhaps intentionally, created an atmosphere where we can easily be surrounded by messages that confirm our beliefs so that we never see any information that does not comport with those beliefs. That small universe of like-minded digital buddies, assembled, preached to, and manipulated en masse by those who know how to craft and disseminate messages, is the essence of the echo chamber.

And this "echo chamber" is among the most important factors in the era of social media.

Say what you want about the old, top-down news media paradigm. It may have been biased. It may have been secretly directed, or at least manipulated. And it may have fostered its own form of echo chamber because so few voices were in the chamber. But one thing it was: universal. If you were in Coeur D'Alene or Conshohocken, and you turned on the television at 6 p.m., you were going to see Walter Cronkite. And Walter Cronkite, a journalist who took his job seriously, would tell you what the big headlines were for that day. You may not have liked what he was saying, but you knew that everyone else was hearing the same thing. It gave everyone a baseline about which to disagree.

That baseline is shattered by digital media. It has been atomized into millions of shards of bizarre, irreconcilable memes that are dumped out upon your laptop every day.

Thus, even the very crankiest and least well-supported diatribe can have the power to convince. This power to convince is amplified across social media channels, from one hustler to the next, until it assumes hurricane-force. We have discovered, just as we might have suspected, that the dissemination of beliefs is only partly a matter of conviction. It is very largely a matter of reach. Of eyeballs. And of getting attention by any means necessary. And one of the ways that messages gain reach is that they must have a certain amount of throw-weight coming out of the barrel. That throw-weight is comprised mostly of perceivable outrage. As we have suggested earlier, outrage generates engagement.

Stanford law professor Richard Thompson Ford calls it "The Outrage-Industrial Complex."[32] He says, "It is our civic duty to be outraged . . . by the appalling lack of outrage demonstrated by other people." And while it's true that outrage is a natural human instinct, it is a very nonhuman set of recommendation algorithms, designed for the purposes of maximizing profit, that stoke, very much on purpose, the fires of outrage. For the hotter burns the outrage, the more advertising dollars that flow into Facebook's coffers. The outrage is not naturally occurring. The outrage is manufactured for profit. The benefit goes to Facebook shareholders (and Elon Musk if he can figure a way to make X turn a profit). The rest of us are left with a nation that resembles more a night at WrestleMania than it does *Mr. Smith Goes to Washington.*

4

DISINFORMATION IN CONFLICT

Perhaps nothing focuses the mind on the deleterious effects of disinformation more effectively than to see its deployment in a bloody upheaval. I am, most unfortunately, referring to the way disinformation has become a weapon in the grenade-belt of the common terrorist. And specifically, to its deployment in companion with a grotesque and disqualifying attack such as was perpetrated by Hamas terror cells against Israelis, most notably at a music concert. At the same time Hamas evildoers, disguised roughly as humans, shot, raped, and murdered their way through a music festival, a fresh avalanche of disinformation crashed down from consequence-free platforms like X;[1] from where it proceeded to swamp the international dialog with confusing, often inaccurate reports. These I will describe shortly, along with what I hope will be a helpful analysis.

First, let us say with no equivocation that, for many observers of the Hamas October 2023 attacks, a part of us has officially died having seen the insufferable atrocities they have committed. Suffice to say a certain low type of individual associated with religious jihad and, more specifically, anti-Semitism, has outdone itself in an orgy of hate. The details are well known and do not bear repeating here. But I will not be the first, nor by far the most important person to say this reminds us too, too terribly of the literal Holocaust itself.

Second, let us say that we don't know where this goes from here. I had advanced a disclaimer at the beginning of the book about how events might overtake the narrative before publication. Now I must redouble the disclaimer, because it's not outlandish to suggest we may be in the grip of a global conflict before you have a chance to read this.

And at least part of the problem will tie back to disinformation and the constant repetition and wide distribution thereof.

It's long been a maxim of war that the first casualty is truth.

Perhaps we have all been remiss in failing to notice that when untruth rises as dramatically as it has of late, it is not simply a sign of malaise, or of errant business practices. No. It is actually a sign that we are at war. Orchestration of detailed, continuing lies does not take place except where a war is already upon us. Disinformation has long been a weapon of war, and we might as well get comfortable with the idea that we are all at war against an enemy that wants us to believe dangerous, even murderous fabulisms.

And much as we are tempted to blame the right-wing ignorance of the Netanyahu anti-democratic juggernaut in the nation of Israel, we must at the same time admit that the scope and bloodthirstiness of the attacks render any discussion of internal Israeli politics almost beside the point. Because what we know is that Israel is a small country in a region where a well-organized faction of monsters wants to murder every last Jew in the world. And we know too that at the very least, Israel is a pluralistic enough nation such that a music festival can take place there—and I was tempted to say "unmolested," but we are no longer afforded that luxury. Whereas we can be quite certain that in any world where Hamas makes determinations, there would be no music, nor any festival, nor dancing, nor joy in anything except, perhaps, the taste of a victim's blood.

I am no friend of radical religionists under any flag, and will continue to contend that religion hardly qualifies as a benefit to humankind given its history of blood and rage. But frankly, we are no longer at a stage where we can talk about such finery as the difference between one nation's god-head and another.

What we are confronted with, instead, are the screams and cries of murdered innocents, slashed and raped in their tents at a dance festival. What we have instead is the very likely possibility that a disgraceful band of anti-Semitic terrorists committed all of the above and more: according to some accounts, they also committed beheadings, perhaps even of children or babies. We have the data to show they intended to attack schools, especially to torture and murder children.

Safe to say it is a major turning point much as was 9/11, much as Kristallnacht was in Hitler's Germany, much as the election of our

American homegrown fascist in 2016 were extremely negative turning points in world history. It is difficult to remain thoughtful and analytical in the face of such awfulness. It feels like arguing about iambic pentameter before the gas chamber, or some such other offensively callow pursuit.

But we are here to talk not so much about an army of jihadists. Instead we are here to talk about that global Army of Liars whose job it is to destroy facts with persistent lies; and who would like to drag us back not so much to an earlier era as to obliterate history and culture altogether in a fit of nihilistic, blood-soaked madness.

One is tempted to contemplate the nature of evil itself, and where it lurks. But that is for another time. We can say for certain that where evil finds a home, it cannot be in the light of day, nor can it ever be limned in the brightness of truth, nor supported by justice, nor can it ever survive a free and fair discussion of issues. No, it continually must seek the dark, and the death of hope. Evil, much as Hamas does, much as the MAGA crowd does, looks to be diametrically opposed to any project of clarity and fairness. Evil remains the enemy of any free air of debate in a functioning civilization.

If anyone might have wondered what it looks like once you have demonized your opposition with murderous calumnies, how it plays out once you have internalized hate for the vulnerable, once you have run roughshod over every societal norm and have abandoned basic decency in public life, we now know. We know it looks like monsters in hang gliders with machine guns murdering festivalgoers, raping and humiliating the innocent at every turn.

That Israel has probably exceeded already the limits of an appropriate response, and that many innocents in Gaza have been killed, is only an artifact of the plans well-laid by Hamas. Even as it may be wrong for Israel literally to overkill in Gaza, it is exactly the type of response that the leaders of Hamas had hoped to elicit.

And yes, it *can happen here* in a gun-crazed United States.

We can no longer say we don't understand what it means when a Greg Gutfeld on Fox News talks about an armed civil war.[2] We can no longer say we cannot see the bloody splats of humanity that drip from the wall where Sarah Palin has lined us up for her "at some point we might need guns" shenanigans.[3] We know for certain what Donald

Trump means when he says, "If you come for me, I am coming for you"; and when he calls Hezbollah "smart" and the Israeli defense minister "stupid" as his backers sport swastika tattoos and as they hoot and holler for the death of their perceived enemies. We know what it could look like, not long into a second Trump administration, where Trump has praised a Chinese dictator who rules "with an iron fist."

If anyone doubted what we now confront in blood, sweat, and tears, and in case anyone doubted a link between disinformation and war, we can now say the argument has been made. And woe betide us if we cannot grasp what may be one of our last opportunities to turn away from a hateful, gory future.

For we are in the thick of a war against fascism, a war in which disinformation is a key battlefield. And in case we had thought it overwrought to suggest we might be in real peril, Hamas has reminded us that we have been naive in believing in the triumph of the human spirit. Naive too, to suggest truth wins, without an enormous effort to fight off lies. For Hamas, if anything, is only the intestine-garlanded shock troop of this global Army of Liars.

In the wake of their atrocities, Hamas was not without coconspirators in the spread of propagandistic falsehoods. We shall have a look at some of the fruits of those labors of untruth in a moment. But we must also admit that disinformation seems to come from all angles in this kind of war, not unlike shrapnel flying from multiple explosions.

Here are some of the most notable, in these early days of conflict.

According to the *New York Times* on October 11, 2023, "Graphic imagery and footage has flooded social media since Hamas terrorists attacked Israel" and that "bogus claims are also circulating." They identified a number of instances, and I add them in here without attempting to discern their source, their purpose, or their effect.

First there is a report, with video, claiming "Hamas militants started a new air assault," but the supporting video was from a video game. Next, we cite "a woman being lit on fire," putatively at the ill-fated festival; except that the video came from Latin America in 2015. Then there was a fake White House memo about providing Israel support to the detriment of Ukraine. The White House never issued the memo in question. Yet another bogus account wanted to say that the BBC had reported NATO weapons from Ukraine somehow in the hands of Hamas—even though the BBC never published any such report. Another video seems to show Israeli warplanes bombing the largest Christian church in Gaza—but church officials denied the report. Finally, there was a claim that the Israeli Defense Force bombed a hospital in Gaza, complete with video and global condemnations. But analysts have since proven this was not the case, and that the explosion was probably a misfire coming from somewhere inside Gaza.

This war, like others before it, spills forth a cornucopia of lies. It seems we now have only a right to slog through mountains of trash information, shamelessly amplified by above-the-law platforms who claim they are providing a valuable, humanistic service in a world longing for connection. It is quite possible there are some who continue to believe Facebook connects us; or that the posting of beheading-videos on YouTube is acceptable for any reason; or that X is a legitimate "town square" where free and open discourse is not merely a smirking joke. But I don't think any of those people would care to meet for a non-smirking debate on the topic. Because if they say they believe it, they are most certainly a member of the Army for which this book was named.

According to NBC News, "Researchers have uncovered a propaganda network on the X social platform that is coordinating a campaign of posting false, inflammatory content related to the Israel-Hamas war."[4] The article goes on to say that "the research is believed to be the first concrete evidence that deliberate propaganda to mislead people about the conflict has gone unchecked on the platform." To anyone who has been watching the unsettling corybantics of this odd duck called Musk, this can come as no surprise. As is clear to anyone who has eyes to see, Musk very likely bought Twitter with an eye to either destroy it completely, or to turn it into a council for hate and violence as perpetrated by a certain type of right-wing, "free-speech-absolutist" authoritarian.[5]

Can there really be much debate on this topic, where the richest man in the world buys a microblogging platform called Twitter, fires all of its content moderation teams, and then renames it "X," a moniker that could hardly be less like the Twitter brand, but that instead hearkens to crosses and perhaps even crooked crosses and perhaps, with exactly four little right turns, an actual swastika. We went from a happy bluebird (rather a phony little critter as it has turned out) to a symbol that looks as if it came, at best, out of a dystopian cartoon; and that promises to give a Nazi a warm and runny feeling for the similarity to his own form of cross.

And because he's richer than many nations and cares not at all if Twitter makes a nickel, he is continuing to drag it down into pure propaganda even as advertisers have fled in droves. Perhaps grasping that he really ought to spend more time at Tesla HQ, Musk in 2023 hired what looks to be a most uncomfortable Linda Yaccarino (ex of NBC) to add what amounts to a professional face to the regime. I am not sure if Yaccarino took this job for the money, or the recognition, or both, but one must wonder whether she feels any compunction to serve society in a way less damaging than to shill for Musk's openly fascist gambit. It's difficult to imagine that any professional media executive would imagine that NBC was remotely in the same industry as the feverish X product, and I have been known to be too trusting at times. My guess is that she sleeps like a baby, but I could be wrong.

But we don't have to blame X for all the trouble. We can point to any number of GOP politicos who have already suggested that what triggered the Hamas attack was a $6 billion tranche of aid that was (it is claimed) "turned over" to Iran by the United States as part of a prisoner exchange wherein several trapped Americans were reunited with their families by the Biden administration. But of course the aid was never turned over to Iran in the first place. All along it was sitting in escrow at a bank in Qatar, awaiting distribution to vetted aid societies who would be granted the money for specific humanitarian purposes in Iran. The money would never have gone to the regime. What's happened now, of course, is that the tranche is on hold in Qatar, will probably never get to Iran at all, and moreover could never have been part of the attack because it happened only weeks ago, while the operation obviously was in the works for much longer than a few weeks. The impossibility of this claim did not slow its dissemination; and only now, perhaps, will the producers of this calumny be forced to recant. Or not! They will call the truth fake news.

Meanwhile, it begins to emerge that X may be the winner in the disinformation sweepstakes. The Associated Press reports that "the platform has deteriorated to the point that it's not just failing to clamp down on misinformation but is favoring posts by accounts that pay for its blue-check subscription service, regardless of who runs them."[6] This means there is no meaningful attempt at content moderation. X simply sells its audiences to the highest bidder, no matter who that is. It might be the very hand that slaughtered an innocent at a music festival—does the platform formerly known as Twitter seem to care? No, in fact it seems to welcome this as part of its newfound affection for chaos. Some have suggested there's even a whiff of the anti-Semite about all of this, much as there is the stench of it clinging to all manner of right-wing media stars.

What can be done to make X care about disinformation that helps a murderous attempt to destroy Israel? Today, nothing—at least not here in the United States. Here, a combination of extraordinarily broad free speech laws that protect lying as a matter of course plus the added cushions of Section 230 immunity means you are absolutely powerless to stop X. We have zero ability to keep X from spreading lies even during a time of war. Perhaps this could change if the United States *declares* war, but this is an awful thing to contemplate. Perhaps we would be more likely to avoid war if the likes of Musk and his mainstream-ish CEO took even a small chance on decency in the public sphere. But I think we ought not hold our collective breath.

That said, in the EU things relating to free speech are different, and not just as relates to this challenge with disinformation on the platform called X.

In the United States, the first amendment says, "Congress shall make no law . . . abridging the freedom of speech, or of the press." This, of course, is foundational to the American way of life, and it sets us apart from governments where the right to free speech is more or less granted rather than required. For instance, the constitution of modern-day Germany provides for free expression, but refers to criminal codes that describe certain limits. Under German law, "insult" is not permitted although "satire" is. "Malicious gossip" and "hate speech" or "incitement of popular hatred" are not permitted. Please note "incitement of popular hatred." I state elsewhere that Germany is probably the most instructive example of a nation that has learned the very hardest lessons about the limits of free speech where such free speech includes blood libel. By the time the free speech of the Third Reich was silenced, an entire nation and much of the rest of the world was a smoking ruin.

Take heed, America.

No one in Germany today is complaining about their inability to speak out, and certainly there is no call there for anything resembling a "both sides" argument when it comes to anti-Semitism. In fact, we feel compelled to call out a recent act of goodness that may be emblematic of just how far Germany has come since the era of the Hakenkreuz. According to an article in the *Messenger,* Berliners on a recent Hamas-proclaimed "Day of Rage" surrounded a group of Jews praying at a synagogue in that capital city.[7] You can be forgiven for suspecting that this tale will soon turn dark. But it does not. The citizens of Berlin were there, in their hundreds, to protect the Jews as they prayed in front of their house of worship. This is what ought to be happening all over the world. But it happened in Germany in October 2023. As for "freedom of speech" in Germany: of course the literal Nazis are not happy, but that's because they, and all of their diatribes, are pretty much outlawed in that nation. And perhaps we should take note of what makes Nazis unhappy, as most of us would be glad to live in a world where Nazis can't seem to make any headway.

Germany is a large industrial nation with a Western tradition. But we in the United States don't identify that much with Germany beyond a taste for their ultimate driving machines. What about something closer to home?

How about the United Kingdom? We share a parliamentary system roughly with them, and then there's the whole "language" thing. You would imagine we might trust they are muddling along okay with their collection of rights, might we not?

In a land where they had long said, "Any man who sets foot on English soil is free" (as opposed to enslaved), what do they say today about free speech? The fact is, there are more laws restricting free speech in the UK than any that openly support it. Custom and practice are enormously important in the UK—their equivalent of the Bill of Rights is called the Magna Carta, and it dates back to King John in the thirteenth century. It's well known that the UK enjoys broad de facto freedoms of the press, but UK law provides significant restrictions, mostly in ways that would likely be found unconstitutional here in the United States. Wikipedia points out that, in the UK, there are restrictions against "threatening or abusive words or behaviour intending or likely to cause harassment, alarm or distress or cause a breach of the peace, sending another any article which is indecent or grossly offensive with an intent to cause distress or anxiety, incitement, incitement to racial hatred, incitement to religious hatred, incitement to terrorism including encouragement of terrorism and dissemination of terrorist publications, glorifying terrorism." And yet we also know that the British tabloid press is among the least accommodating to the distress or anxiety of its targets. So we can suggest that British case law likely broadens protections for speech; even as they actually have no Bill of Rights as we know it, nor even a Constitution as we understand it in the United States.

What neither Germany nor the UK have is any law that even begins to resemble Section 230 of the United States Communications Decency Act. It's safe to say an X-type company would have a great deal of trouble operating in a nation where "free speech absolutism" was a nonstarter. It is also safe to say that neither Germany nor the United Kingdom has been free of disinformation and prejudice regardless of their free speech laws. We know too much about how Nazi propaganda drove the world to ruin. But we can also point to disinformation in England *about Germany*—in World War One. It was widely claimed in England and in other Allied countries that German soldiers in World War One impaled Belgian children on their bayonets. It made "the Hun" a monster. It was not true. Later it would pale before the encyclopedia of atrocities committed under Hitler.

In the end, the anti-Semitic attacks perpetrated by Hamas have their roots in disinformation. In an article published by *Politico*, "[In] Trent, Italy, on Easter Sunday, 1475, a child had gone missing, and a Franciscan preacher . . . gave a series of sermons claiming that the Jewish community had murdered the child, drained his blood and drunk it to celebrate Passover. In response, the Prince-Bishop of Trent . . . ordered the city's entire Jewish community arrested and tortured."[8] Hamas's own foundational document—often referred to as "The Covenant"—refers to the anti-Semitic, discredited "Elders of Zion" protocols where it is alleged that, as it was in Trent in 1475, Jews drink the blood of non-Jewish babies for sport. This is foundational disinformation. It also contains the following passage: "The Day of Judgment will not come about until Moslems fight Jews and kill them. Then, the Jews will hide behind rocks and trees, and the rocks and trees will cry out: 'O Moslem, there is a Jew hiding behind me, come and kill him.'"[9]

None of this purports to excuse Israeli political maneuverings or the frankly illegal placement of settlements in the West Bank. Look not here for support for the bulldozing of ancient olive trees so a family from Brooklyn can set up a home in a disputed land. It must be recognized that Israel is not a blameless entity that has never given anyone cause for offense. But I am unaware of any Jewish or Israeli foundational text that claims anyone in particular ought to be killed. So in this regard, we must accept that Hamas is founded on the notion of atrocity and upon blood-libel and disinformation.

I include them in this narrative only in part because the October attacks are of timely importance. I include them because they show very clearly how disinformation begets hate, and that hate begets murder. It's what any Army of Liars would be striving for, and it's what they will achieve if they cannot be stopped.

5

ATTACK OF THE LIARS

It may serve to remind ourselves here that on January 6, 2021, our nation's Capitol was invaded and overtaken by *an army of liars*. They didn't get there because of a few handbills posted at the Grange Hall. They got there because of the outrage-industrial complex. They got there because of the echo chamber. They got there because the president, on Twitter, told them to be there, and that it was going to be "wild."[1] He was able to send a direct message to millions of willing followers to show up at a certain time and a certain place, and once they had shown up, he then exhorted them to "fight like hell" or "you won't have a country." That last bit he said live to a well-armed audience. They left his rally and went straight to the Capitol, ostensibly under his directive, where they smashed their way in, threatened to hang the vice president, and delayed the tabulation of the 2020 election result for several hours. Turns out Trump might have gone with them, but his chauffeur wouldn't take him.

The confluence of cable news (full of lies as we now know because of the Dominion lawsuit), live incitement in the form of a raging loser in a red hat, and most importantly, the constant barrage of micromessages to an eager, hateful population, led, on January 6, 2021, to a near-successful attempt to violently overthrow a legally elected government.

Assembled by digital analytics, profited off of by the likes of Facebook, an aggrieved, essentially racist segment of the population was digitally directed to cause mayhem at what passes for the font of democracy in the United States: they crawled all over the Capitol like a horde of vermin. Taking selfies all the while and posting these across every digital channel, they marched with a Confederate flag inside the Capitol, they taunted armed guards with impunity, they smeared feces on the wall, they stole what wasn't nailed down. If we are to believe the videos, these nation-wrecking insurrectionists were comfortable enough, during this unlawful, violent incursion, to loiter casually and choose what they might thieve. In fact, a certain young, dark-haired hellion named Riley June Williams saw fit to steal a laptop belonging to Speaker Pelosi. Riley was convicted in March 2023 for same, and sentenced to prison.

In addition we were all treated to the sight of a half-naked shamanic figure, heavily tattooed, with a scepter, clad in a buffalo robe, literally howling as he brought a particularly brain-dead strain of paganism to the halls of Congress. Jacob Chansley in his buffalo robe became the face of the lunatic insurgency, was sentenced to prison, and more or less admitted he'd been sorta kinda brainwashed and could he please just move on from this mistake. Having completed his brief sentence, he repudiated his culpability and said he would still vote for Trump.

The last time anything of this type happened in the United States was in 1968, when dozens of college campuses were overtaken by leftist students as they posed, at least in one famous photo, with cigars in the dean's office. And what we observed then, we also observe now: a certain preening, privileged attitude on the part of the rioter where it seems they are gambling with house money and will never suffer the real consequences of their actions. Many have already speculated that had the Capitol rioters been people of color, or had they been aligned with today's left, they'd have been fired upon and there'd have been a massacre on the steps of the Capitol. It did not happen. It did not happen because these white conservative marauders were treated with *an unwarranted amount of deference* by those tasked with defending the seat of government.

Many want to glorify the Capitol police, but the fact remains they left themselves and the Capitol itself in danger by failing to carry out their duty in a manner commensurate with their mission. It is safe to say the Capitol police behaved in an anomalous manner at best, and have handed the nation a shattering crisis that ought to have been solved by their simply doing their job. Their job was to prevent insurrectionists from getting in. Never was there a caveat to "keep them out as long as you don't hurt them."

The protection of the Capitol was a near total failure, although at least no legislators were harmed. In fact, except for social media, the revolutionaries might have gotten away with the affair almost entirely. We know the faces and the details of many of these wannabes because the grossness of their ineptitude was matched only by the callousness of their political goals. In the commission of treasonous acts, they felt comfortable enough to post pictures of themselves on the internet.

Make no mistake: the selfie-posting was part of the allure. One might say they hadn't done anything at all until they posted those selfies. For nothing reeks of self-aggrandizement like posting pictures of yourself rampaging through halls of government while wearing a buffalo robe. This ability to immediately gratify a self-identity urge is part and parcel of the digital allure and should not be underestimated. In fact, selfies are one of the only reliable "truths" in social media.

LIES PIGGYBACKED ON TRUTH

But why does anyone believe anything they see in their X feed? In their Parler screen? On Facebook?

It's because the grounds for belief had been long prepared by more careful scribes.

Long before section 230 protected platforms like Facebook from liability while at the same time protecting their right to profit, generations of traditional publishers sought to deliver their version of truth to a content-hungry nation. Again, I am not going to pretend these news sources were transparent, accurate, and free from agenda.

The media certainly had its role to play in promulgating naked untruths. Remember that mainstream media were all in on Vietnam, until they weren't. Throughout the 1960s we saw innumerable stories of upstanding American advisors helping a smaller, darker people as purportedly they struggled toward some slipshod version of the American Dream. We had mountains of printed propaganda where American soldiers faux-repeated their World War Two role as liberators, but in Vietnam. Unfortunately for the myth makers, Vietnam was where no one had asked us in, and from where our national security was never threatened. And then came the day when *Life* magazine had pictures of dead babies on the cover. I am referring to pictures of dead babies that had been killed by American soldiers in the village of My Lai at the direction of a certain Lieutenant William Calley, who went on to conviction at court-martial for his behavior.[2] From that day onward, media and government parted ways, perhaps permanently and probably for good.

Prior to the late 1960s, the big media were expected to play along with the government on the most important issues, and largely they did. They were fine with military adventurism. They touted the benefits of nuclear power as if they had gotten a tip at the dog track—nuclear power would win, and it would mean free electricity for all! At the same time, they were comfortable that regulations on fossil fuel emissions represented the benighted un-American equivalent of collectivism not unlike the dehumanizing tropes of George Orwell's *Animal Farm*, where everyone was equal, but some were more equal than others. Forever and a day, big American media—newspapers, magazines, television and radio—presented the picture of America as Andy Griffith's Mayberry, where cops were good-natured, if bumbling; where coal was king, where the Soviets were outgunned, and Aunt Bea would have warm soup for Opie on a cold day.

But even as they indulged in propaganda, they did not engage in *the promotion of falsehoods with no tether to reality whatsoever.* They did not claim that pizza parlors were fronts for pedophilic human trafficking operations run from Hillary Clinton's basement in Chappaqua north of New York City.[3] They did not claim that the world belonged to Jesus Christ (although they were very, very fond of Christmas and Easter specials that gave them ample excuses to contribute to the hagiography of church elders). Absolutely never ever did they dare to suggest a foreign enemy might in some way be more correct than the policymakers in Washington, D.C., and on Wall Street. Their fealty toward the powerful was not to be underestimated; and I am certain the public trusted the media far too readily back then. But as I have suggested earlier, it is one thing to support one or another type of political narrative, and quite another to claim that the president is engaged in the live-skinning of children and the wearing of those children's faces as a mask while committing other bloody atrocities.[4]

Thus, digital has donned a costume knit out of decades of good-faith, if flawed, efforts at actual news reporting. They have donned it and then marched around in the mask of truth, lying that the sky is falling.

Digital media have usurped the reputation of print media in order to push naked falsehoods. Again, we are not talking about hiding a president's physical infirmities, or even supporting a war of very questionable importance. No, this is truly a different space and a different scale of lying.

For where media may once have conspired to keep the public from seeing Franklin Delano Roosevelt in a wheelchair, now digital media conspires to convince millions of poor saps that Trump is secretly president in 2023 when he is not; that President Biden was already executed at Gitmo; that "the military" will soon let everyone know that it was all for show and that, indeed MAGA rules the land along with a sideshow full of Christian nationalists.

They are going at this propaganda with dedication and resources. Their figurehead remains Donald Trump, recently indicted in several jurisdictions for a long list of felonies. And Donald Trump continues to make the tiresome claim that the 2020 election was stolen—an obvious lie. But his digital fellow-travelers nevertheless pound home that message and more. Some of the claims by Trump supporters are even more wild than claims made by Trump himself. Also, much like Andrew Torba and Donald Trump, the MAGA crowd have keen affection for brutal, murderous despots like Vladimir Putin of Russia. They seem to feel as if they would be immune from harm, if only there might be a dictator.

This is not mere coincidence.

Russia is engaged in a prolonged, dedicated, post–Cold War battle against the United States wherein they have attempted all manner of inversion and subterfuge. To an extent that can hardly be imagined, they are very close to accomplishing their goal. If recent GOP bat-meepings are to be believed, considerable numbers of Republican legislators and their misinformed constituents are openly rooting for Russia to defeat Ukraine—and, by proxy, "woke" America. The words of Mr. Torba are again duly noted. But Torba did not convince all these MAGAs to want the end of America all on his own! No, the goal was achieved largely through persistent, targeted messaging from Russian hackers to vulnerable populations in a manner unlike any the world has never seen before.[5] I'll get to this more in-depth in another chapter about Russia and the digital apocalypse. But it's a safe bet that we have not gone *by accident* from "The Greatest Generation"[6] having beat the pants off

Nazis, to a world where the presumptive GOP nominee for the presidency sits down to dinner with openly anti-Semitic neo-Nazis like a hooded Ye (music celebrity) and his Nazi-curious Ray-Ban-wearing buddy Nick Fuentes.[7]

Very much by design, the Russians and the Christian right form a mutual admiration society that makes common cause to destroy liberal Western democracy and, in its place, install a form of fascism that would not be out of character with the benighted state of government in, say, fourteenth-century France or Italy, except with computers and nukes. Together they are on record for racism, intolerance, misogyny, and homophobia. They espouse any number of implausible beliefs (see QAnon), as well as throw support behind antidemocratic forms of government that criminalize women's right to control their own reproductive systems, oppress marginalized communities; and that aggrandize preachers, sex predators, and haters of every Christian stripe.

Even as Russia works toward the ultimate defeat of the military forces of the West, including that of the United States, they are mired in an attempt to destroy a democratic nation called Ukraine. Here in the United States, by comparison, it can be fairly stated that in this particular mutual admiration society, the Russians provide the technical and propaganda chops, while the Christians supply the intolerance and the vitriol to sell the program through to the voting public.

I have stated already that there's a case to be made that Section 230 provides legal cover for all who would amplify hate speech otherwise unprotected by the United States Constitution. And in fact, there is a case to be made. This case, the aforementioned *Gonzalez vs. Google*, made it all the way to the United States Supreme Court. As stated earlier, the plaintiff's argument was that Google was a proximate cause to a wrongful death, having helped radicalize a murderer. SCOTUS rejected Gonzalez's claim. They leaned heavily on Section 230 to deliver their verdict. But let's look at some of the dynamics of this case in detail.

NEWSSTANDS AND MURDERERS

The lawsuit before the Supreme Court regarding Section 230 was constituted as follows, according to *Time* magazine, "*Gonzalez v. Google* . . .

argues that YouTube's algorithm helped ISIS post videos and recruit members—making online platforms directly and secondarily liable for the 2015 Paris attacks that killed 130 people, including 23-year-old American college student Nohemi Gonzalez."[8]

That liability was, in May 2023, denied by the Supreme Court. In ruling for Google, the court cited Section 230 as the liability shield. This is the same Supreme Court, by the way, that already had signaled it did not feel quite qualified to understand such matters! It was one of the liberals on the court (Elena Kagan, an Obama appointee) who said, hearing arguments in the case, "We're a court. We really don't know about these things. These are not the nine greatest experts on the internet." A shocking admission, and proof positive that Google has succeeded in sprinkling just enough internet fairy dust about the highest court in the land to keep them flying above the law and any liability.

Again it seems that one's jaw must, almost by law, *drop* to hear such an admission from someone whose job it is to adjudicate on behalf of all of us on matters of utmost importance. My comment to Elena and any of the nine who care to listen: "If you don't know what you're doing, you need to resign."

Doesn't matter to me whether they are liberal or conservative. The notion that this, of all issues, would bring someone with a reputation for probity to say something as nitwitted as what she said, must make all of us feel that we are served, when it comes to all things computational, by a gang of incompetents who can barely forward an email, never mind help us outlaw the avalanche of hate speech that threatens to crush society flat.

Or better yet, Dear SCOTUS: I think I can do a better job here than you can. So how about it?

In the vain hope that a SCOTUS judge needs a wee smidgen of clarity about exactly what is going on here, let us again perform an exercise I like to call "remove the computer." I find it helpful to deploy this analysis when trying to understand the dynamics of a digital activity in terms of what it would look like if you did not have computers. Sometimes it can reveal some amazing anomalies!

Gonzalez vs. Google is a perfect example. As mentioned above, this case was argued before the Supreme Court on February 21, 2023, and then essentially dismissed by SCOTUS in May 2023.

SCOTUSblog said the issue at hand was as follows:

Whether Section 230(c)(1) of the Communications Decency Act immunizes interactive computer services when they make targeted recommendations of information provided by another information content provider, or only limits the liability of interactive computer services when they engage in traditional editorial functions (such as deciding whether to display or withdraw) with regard to such information.[9]

So this case was focused on recommendation algorithms—in other words, not the mere posting of information on the platform, but the platform's way of providing market-velocity to a particular message. This is the "you might like this" aspect of the business, and the one that makes all the money. For this is what separates digital from traditional publishing: digital domains can, in real time, discern what you seem to be interested in, and make recommendations to you before you make your next click. No nondigital advertising medium has ever come close to this. It's why the lion's share of all advertising these days is digital.

My assertion is that the SCOTUS ruling in *Gonzalez* is a disaster, and bodes ill for any attempt to limit hate speech going forward. And to illustrate just how erroneous their determination really is, allow me to continue with my "remove the computer" exercise.

Our exercise finds us at a newsstand. A newsstand, for those who have forgotten, or who have never seen one, is a retail operation, often in the form of a sidewalk booth, where a variety of news-oriented, printed publications are displayed. Once upon a time this would have included several newspapers, dozens of magazines, a number of books and special editions, and, in addition to printed matter, a lot of gum and candy. Often there was an individual in the booth, making change and small talk with regular patrons.

By what stretch of the imagination could this purveyor of publications be held responsible if one of the magazines had an article in it titled "We Must Kill Big Bird," when that magazine was found to have influenced a bird hater who ended up killing Big Bird? I say, by no stretch of the imagination. The newsstand operator would likely not have been aware, nor should they have been aware, of the contents of what they were selling. Truly they are just a sales platform. And in any case, the publishers of these magazines had their own standards, because they certainly could be held responsible, as publishers, for printing and selling a call to kill Big Bird, that resulted in the murder of Big Bird.

That the publications for sale at the newsstand would already have been published in an atmosphere where there are such things as liability does, I can promise you, weigh into the business model of the newsstand. Many of these stands, at least in recent years, are owned and operated by corporations (like Hudson News); and there is no doubt in my mind that the attorneys for this corporation would be looking more than a little askance at provisioning the public with murderous claptrap. This is because they operate in a world *not* sprinkled with internet fairy dust. And in that world, the publishers of these magazines also exist in a world where you are *not* allowed to scream fire in a crowded theater. But on the other side of Alice's Looking Glass, in a bizarro world where hate can generate billions in profit and zero liability, we have the likes of Google and Facebook looming not even in the shadows but front and center, daring you to hold them responsible for anything at all.

In this bizarro world, where everything is backwards from where it would be in a world of common sense, publishers are not publishers and newsstands are not newsstands. The definition of publisher needs to be understood here, because this is where the platforms want to make a distinction. What social media platforms say is that they are not publishers, but only newsstands (or maybe even mail carriers who simply drop printed matter into mailboxes).

In the real world, a publisher would have been a business that wrote (or hired writers to write), edited, printed, and distributed physical copies on paper of language-based materials (with pictures) to newsstands and bookstores and also mailed physical copies of same to people's homes. They were always free to publish whatever they wanted, as long as they did not specifically target anyone for violence or engage in any form of widely recognized libelous speech that would include obvious, pernicious lies and especially hate-speech that would, without evidence, destroy a person's reputation or perhaps even result in their harm.

In a world coated by internet fairy dust, that type of publisher does not exist. The IFD crowd wants you to believe that a publisher is now *anyone who writes anything and then clicks a button.* Never mind that this publisher, who might be the Chinese Communist Party or a four-hundred-pound loser in his mother's basement (we can thank Trump for that locution), is not, in fact, a publisher most typically, or at least not of the type we have come to recognize. They *can* be a *New York Times*–like publisher, of course. But 99 percent of the time they are not. They are just a person or an agent or a hacker or the technology equivalent of a guerrilla army, but they are largely untrackable and, as it has turned out, almost entirely irresponsible. And yet their output has proven irresistible in aggregate. The world has become addicted to what these random agents are saying. The world has become addicted to it because the platforms (Facebook, YouTube, Reddit, Twitter, Parler, Gab, and beyond) have provided a global distribution network that amplifies whatever anyone posts and makes it available globally to anyone with an internet connection. Intertwined with this content are ads that make billions of dollars for the platforms, not unlike the way a traditional publisher would make money off of the ads in their magazine.

Minus the formatting and distribution afforded by social media platforms, these so-called publishers have no presence whatsoever. You would not know what Ye was thinking without Twitter, unless perhaps he were interviewed on a news program. You would absolutely not know what Charlie Noteworthy was saying, were he not on Twitter with a bizarre claim, because Charlie Noteworthy really is a four-hundred-pound loser, has not left his mother's basement in ten years, and without the good offices of Twitter has no reading public whatsoever.

Now, back to our newsstand. let's say the newsstand operator was incentivized to sell more magazines, and, in order to accomplish this goal, they deployed a system of magazine-recommendation. Not content to just accept what people were buying on their own, this newsie—let's call him Sandy—decided to get to know the customer more thoroughly. By some sort of mental trick, he was able to understand not just what magazines a customer was buying, but what articles in particular that they spent the most time looking at. This form of recommendation, of course, is what really and truly makes social media platforms that much more powerful and, in my opinion, at least *as* liable if not *more* liable than a traditional publisher. I have just described the mechanism of "recommendation," a feat that no publisher of print has ever had the power to deploy; and which, in my opinion, buries the platforms very deep inside a stew of liability.

Let's say that one of the customers at our non-computerized newsstand was a member of ISIS. ISIS is a radical Islamic terror organization that specializes in the murder of innocents in the West. ISIS in November 2015 perpetrated a hateful attack at a Paris nightclub that killed over a hundred revelers. In 2022, fifteen murderers were convicted of these crimes. For the purposes of our exercise (and also according to the SCOTUS lawsuit), at least one of the customers of the newsstand is an ISIS adherent. In our newsstand model, they are seen perusing magazines at the newsstand. Sandy, the owner of the newsstand, notices that Mr. Isis is looking at a magazine that contains hateful messages and images of beheadings.

Sandy may or may not agree with Mr. Isis, but it doesn't matter. Sandy's natural tendency is to increase sales. And thus Sandy begins to look for other beheading-related content that might capture the attention of Mr. Isis. Sandy finds magazines of a particularly gruesome nature, with bloody tableaux and the celebration of murder. The next time Sandy sees Mr. Isis, he says, "Mr. Isis, I see you are interested in magazines that show beheadings. I have several magazines that show beheadings. Would you like to see them?"

Of course the answer is "Yes."

And Sandy shows Mr. Isis the magazines that specialize in beheading techniques. Mr. Isis buys the magazines.

A few days later, Mr. Isis is back for more. Sandy obliges. Sandy suggests, in addition, magazines of shooting, hangings, and poisonings. Mr. Isis is very interested!

This cycle is repeated. Each time Sandy says he's got more pictures of brutal murder for Mr. Isis to enjoy. Sandy has these magazines ready for Mr. Isis every time Mr. Isis wants them. Sandy does not recommend them to everybody, but only to Mr. Isis and others like Mr. Isis, because it was Mr. Isis who seemed interested in the murder of innocents.

A week later, it turns out Mr. Isis has shot several people at a cafe because their behavior offended him. When they search Mr. Isis's apartment, they find not only the many magazines, but also lists of recommended magazines that were given to him by Sandy. It turns out that Sandy was Mr. Isis's only real connection with these magazines.

When they ask Sandy what he knows about Mr. Isis, Sandy openly admits having made these recommendations. But Sandy claims to be not responsible for what Mr. Isis did, because Sandy did not publish the magazines, but only recommended them. Did Sandy know they were violent, extreme images? Yes!

But Sandy's defense is that others had *also* sought recommendations—about flower arrangements and such—and that therefore the recommendation technique is content-neutral. And that if the technique itself is neutral, then it must also remain unconnected to Mr. Isis's bad behavior. Sandy's other defense—similar to Google's defense at SCOTUS—is that if a newsstand could not make recommendations, it would be very bad for the newsstand business.

My contention is that everything becomes so much clearer when you stop sprinkling internet fairy dust on the subject. Once you take away the computer and lay out the behavior in human terms, the culpability becomes obvious. For it is one thing to let people post what they want on your platform. It is quite another to *have an active hand in what users eventually see.* Further, to have a hand not just in what they see, but the collection of billions of dollars from ads that the platform sells around this content. It is this act of targeting, selection, and content delivery that creates what I believe is a significant, inescapable liability.

But regardless of my point of view, the Supreme Court has ruled that 230 rules.

Again, it is Section 230 that permits and enables the dissemination of hate, while allowing for both massive profit and zero responsibility on the part of those platforms that disseminate it: chiefly Facebook, YouTube (Google), Twitter, and a handful of other global platforms.

The Paris attack took place in France, but the *Gonzalez* case was filed in the United States. However, Europe may yet prove to be the rocks that break the social media ship. For in Germany there is also a case that poses a great threat: Twitter has been informed that it is on the hook for a massive fine that is almost as much as the net worth of the entire company—$20 billion. CNBC notes that "as per a report by Techcrunch, more than 600 cases regarding hate speech on Twitter are pending before German courts . . . 'under the country's hate speech takedowns law.' . . . The law, known colloquially as NetzDG, allows for fines of up to 50 million euros per case."[10]

If all of these cases were to go against Twitter, and they might, it would mean that Twitter would owe up to $30 billion in fines. Musk bought Twitter in 2022 for about $40 billion. He says it is worth half of that (which means the entire company is not worth as much as they might be fined). And in his blinkered, billionaire, free-speech-absolutist mania to remake the world in his image, Musk decided that X could get rid of nearly all of their content-moderation teams that might have helped prevent the appearance of some of this hate speech. Further, Musk, apparently, and in a manner that must strike the observer as obtuse, seems to have forgot that Germany is not the United States. It happens to be a large, industrial nation with its own laws, and, as noted earlier, those laws do not comport with the United States Constitution. Instead, the post–World War Two German constitution insists that the job of the government is to protect human dignity regardless of any notion of free speech. And they ought to know! After all, where was it that hate speech took control of a large industrial nation, nearly destroyed the entire earth in the process, and left that nation in rubble?

If you don't recall my earlier assertion, the answer is "Germany, because of Nazis, during World War Two."

Of course, we don't know the outcome of this case. We can say, however, that Section 230 helps the platforms not at all in other countries.

In the end, would the possible gutting of 230 mean an overhaul, and possibly the end of social media as we know it? Yes, it certainly could! But unlike the way it is portrayed in the mainstream media, social media does not have an inherent right to exist. Nor, I say, do social media companies have a right to poison the moral atmosphere of the entire world simply because it's pretty good for the stock price.

It is ironical in the extreme that I find myself looking for government regulations in a way that puts me in common with any number of right-wing politicians who also want to do away with Section 230. They profess to hate big government, except when that big government can be directed to destroy content moderation and open the floodgates to more and more hate. And they tend to confuse "social media" with "government" and consider editorial discretion an illegal form of censorship. They want to argue that any utterance, no matter how hateful, must be as amplified as the hater wants, otherwise that utterance, unamplified but also unpunished, amounts to government censorship that penalizes thinkers and writers by law.

Very simply, content moderation is not censorship, because only a government can censor. Non-acceptance by a publisher, or by the public, is not censorship. Opposition is not censorship. *Only governmental suppression of content and the punishment of content providers equals censorship.* And for the record, I am not in favor of censorship as defined above. Nor do I believe every injury ought to be traced back to a prompt, digital or otherwise. But over the years we have proceeded rather successfully with our combination of press freedom plus restrictions on hate speech—and I am 100 percent certain that the digital platforms can, if they must, develop ways to provide plenty of leeway for every man woman and child's one million selfies, while still severely curtailing blood libel.

So I may have a narrow agreement with some of the right wingers about one-half of the law called Section 230. But unlike them, I am against Section 230 because of the *combined totality of rights and protections* afforded digital platforms, as if they were, indeed, a special case and somehow above the law. Section 230 is a law that places them above the law.

Might social media come to an end if they no longer are permitted to recommend hate for profit with impunity? Certainly it is possible. And if social-media-as-we-know-it were to disappear, would we still see phenomena like digitally prompted physical attacks upon politicians and their significant others? We might, but I suspect there'd be less of it.

A GAMER'S HAMMER ATTACK

Paul Pelosi, the husband of Nancy Pelosi (at that time Speaker of the United States House of Representatives), recently was the victim of a nearly fatal hammer attack. The attack was perpetrated by an outraged male who claimed he was doing the bidding of . . . well, we are not certain, exactly. But we do know that he made a number of statements to the media, as follows:

> [The suspect] said there was "evil in Washington" and he was looking to harm Pelosi because she is second in line for the presidency, a

San Francisco police investigator testified Wednesday. The suspect, David DePape, broke into the couple's San Francisco home Oct. 28, seeking to kidnap the speaker—who was out of town—and instead beat her 82-year-old husband, Paul Pelosi, with a hammer, authorities said.[11]

According to the *New York Times*, DePape began his descent into misogynistic hate via a phenomenon known as "Gamergate." The *Times* article goes on to say that DePape had at one time been attracted to progressive causes, but that over time he became increasingly isolated and gravitated toward such theoretical constructs as Gamergate, Qanon, and Pizzagate. It turns out that Gamergate might as well be called Hatergate, or at least it seems to be a gateway to hate.

According to Joan Donovan, the research director of the Shorenstein Center on Media, Politics and Public Policy at Harvard University: "In recent years, it has not been uncommon for Gamergate to become a gateway for disaffected men to discover conspiracy theories like Pizzagate and QAnon, two subjects Mr. DePape wrote about, and to become wrapped up in right-wing Trumpian politics."[12]

As alluded to earlier, QAnon promotes the fallacy that a cabal of Democratic pedophiles are working secretly to undermine Donald Trump. And Pizzagate claims that Hillary Clinton and other liberals are trafficking Christian babies through pizza parlors tied to underground tunnels where these children are hidden, and where their blood is sucked for its healthful benefits. These are ancient, blood-libel tropes, and bear a chilling resemblance to the bogus Elders of Zion documents, wherein the Nazi Party found "documentation" that Jews were, as always, plotting to foment evil and especially that they would murder non-Jewish babies for ritual purposes.[13]

Gamergate, according to right-wing pundit Steve Bannon, is a great place to find the angry young men that the right-wing, outrage-industrial complex requires.

According to news site Quartz (Go Media) at qz.com:

> The Gamergate playbook is simple and direct. First, identify a vulnerable target—usually a woman, person of color, or a member of the LGBTQ community—and then highlight their vulnerabilities so that disaffected, mostly white young men can attack them. Continue

the attacks until someone pushes back, or the platform of choice shuts it down.[14]

USA Today reported that Bannon, observing Gamergate participants, "became intrigued by the game's online community dynamics. In describing gamers, Bannon said, 'These guys, these rootless white males, had monster power.'"[15]

The plan, of course, was to weaponize these angry, rootless young males and direct their anger at profitable targets. For if they could be directed to actively hate an innocent victim in Gamergate fashion, they could also be directed to actively hate political figures. And, in the case of Nancy Pelosi, what better than to target that hate at a powerful, progressive female politician?

So Mr. DePape, like so many others, began consuming hateful content online. It began with Gamergate, which proved only an anteroom to the Great Hall of Hatred that is social media today. According to the Associated Press, DePape, in

> an Aug. 24 [2022 social media] entry titled "Q," displayed a scatological collection of memes that included photos of the deceased sex offender Jeffrey Epstein and made reference to QAnon, the baseless pro-Trump conspiracy theory that espouses the belief that the country is run by a deep state cabal of child sex traffickers, satanic pedophiles and baby-eating cannibals.[16]

Clearly DePape was already troubled. Apparently, he had a connection to a certain brand of nudist, nominally progressive, conspiracy-minded protest in the City of San Francisco, where he was often seen at rallies filming his girlfriend, who was fond of stripping down in public as a way of demonstrating opposition to one thing or another. Also he was morbidly afraid of strangers, according to a number of stories, and over time had become a recluse. This type of citizen: young, male, unconnected, disaffected, angry, digitally aware, has long been identified with trouble. In some countries they are taking steps to bring groups of them back into society. South Korea, for example, has recently instituted a $500/month payment to young men isolated from society, in order to reintegrate them.[17] No word yet as to whether it is a success, but it's a good start, because these young men can cause real trouble in a society armed with hammers, rifles, and bombs.

Historically they have been called "lone nuts," and the United States has seen a plague of them. In fact, we have seen so many that it begs the question how "lone" they can really be. It started with Lee Harvey Oswald, the lone nut who in Dallas in 1963 shot JFK but in my opinion never delivered the kill shot. Followed by another lone nut named Jack Ruby who shot Oswald on live television. Followed by James Earl Ray, the lone nut who shot Martin Luther King Jr. And Arthur Bremer, the lone nut who shot George Wallace. And Sirhan Sirhan, the Palestinian lone nut who shot RFK. And Squeaky Fromme, the lone Manson nut who would have shot Gerald Ford if her gun had not jammed, followed close on by Sarah Jane Moore, another lone nut who also couldn't fire the gun at Ford. Followed by Mark David Chapman, a lone nut who murdered my favorite musician, John Winston Lennon in front of his New York City apartment building. And John Hinckley, the lone nut Jodie Foster acolyte who shot Ronald Reagan. There have been others since, but after a time I lost track.

All of the above were pre-digital, and there is no way to suggest that digital technology or Section 230 had anything to do with their possible recruitment and the commission of their crimes. What even a small amount of research will reveal, however, is that they are all cut from the same patch of threadbare cloth: white, disaffected mostly males with wacky grievances and no shortage of ammunition. Kind of like Steve Bannon has said, they do seem to have "monster power," if by "monster" you mean "sick and twisted."

A companion narrative would suggest that all of them were directed and groomed in some way by some intelligence agency somewhere. Truly these are hidden narratives, not at all accepted by the mainstream media, and unproven. But the sheer number of the lone nuts, and the sameness of their approach, begs the question how come only the United States has these by the dozen, while other countries almost never have them?

Against this type of background, it is not hard to imagine that propagandists with access to the most robust propaganda tools in the history of humankind may have figured out that they can launch a thousand lone nuts without trying very hard. Gamergate, as we will see, is nothing more than an excellent example.

Like many who never commit any type of crime, the Pelosi attacker was interested in computer games. This is where he discovered the troubling dynamics of Gamergate, essentially a community of digital trolls targeting vulnerable individuals out of a manufactured sense of outrage at who-knows-what. It would be only a matter of time before this free-floating anomie found its manipulator.

These manipulations came in the form of digital messaging: QAnon, Pizzagate, and the constant hate blasted out by any number of right-wing platforms. Among the messages? Nancy Pelosi was part of the (literally) blood-sucking Democratic elite, was a "repeat liar," and was the local face of the "evil" that pervaded Washington, D.C.[18]

Make no mistake, DePape's induction into the fever-swamp of hate and hateful behavior was facilitated by digital technologies. The argument can be made that the earlier lone nuts (Lee Harvey Oswald) got their inspiration without the aid of digital, and this is obviously true. But DePape is only an example of what looks to be a rising tide of lone nuts shooting at schools, shopping malls, movie theaters, and banks. A stochastic army of inspired lunatics, armed by the NRA and prodded to action by Gamergate.

Not just Gamergate, of course. It is difficult to support the notion there cannot be any link between a rising tide of random gun violence and the rising tide of digitally promoted hate. Because the digital manipulation plan has many touchpoints and no central clearing house, it can be said that if the hate is directed, it is not directed by one person or one authority. No, instead it is ginned up generally and aimed generally, kind of the way a madman would plant bombs that blow up the good and the bad at the same time. You might also call it a shotgun approach: blast out hate, blast out violence, and pick up the spoils the way any terrorist would love to do. Because, as we already know about the Q-nut nihilists, their goal, first, is to destroy the civilization we know, and then replace it with Christian nationalism during what they imagine would be a season of chaos that would lend support to their authoritarian dreams.

Worse, DePape was hardly condemned universally. On the contrary, many on the right sought to dignify him, or to direct attention away from him in an act of journalistic legerdemain. Particularly grotesque were the conspiracy theories bruited about by right-wing pundits after the attack. Some said Paul Pelosi was having an affair with his attacker.[19] Some said he at least must have invited in the attacker. Or perhaps it was staged! They all had to backtrack once the video footage was released, revealing that it was an attack by a person unknown to the victim.

THE MAGIC OF SECTION 230 AND THE COMMODIFICATION OF HATE

But the most important question here is: why was a DePape able to connect with so many conspiracy theories, and why with so many that were obviously false, and what kind of help did he receive in finding all of this hateful content?

The answer is simple: we can trace nearly all of it back to Section 230 of the Communications Decency Act. For in a non-digital legal framework, a printed publication might want to consider whether it ought to entice, promote, and direct a member of the public to murder. The traditional media publisher would find themselves liable via libel and hate-speech laws.

But digital, as if by magic, removes any of these liabilities and permits the amplifier (X?) to assume no liability just as if X were no more than a stranger standing at a bus stop. With such digital protections, it only makes sense that the savvy manipulator will rely on digital anonymity, misdirection, and subterfuge in order to influence the disaffected male that ends up doing the damage. The Bannons of the world do not, ever, write any of these hateful messages themselves. Instead, they know there are reservoirs of hackers and haters that will anonymously launch hateful attacks online that can be targeted by digital analytics and recommendation engines at the same targets they identified by using, for instance, Cambridge Analytica data.

Those vulnerable populations are targeted by the digital equivalent of a shaped explosive,[20] so that eventually, at least some of the members of these populations will go off and commit an act of stochastic terrorism.[21] Doesn't matter so much exactly what it is, as long as the victim is not a white, right-wing male, and as long as the message itself causes maximum discomfort to the body politic.

There are those who will go so far as to say that the NRA is in on it, and that school shootings are a form of intimidation as a precursor to routine shootings and concentration camps. Regardless of whether that is true or not, it can be safely said that there are significant efforts to shape social media hate to target the vulnerable (DePape), in the hopes that those vulnerables will go out and commit atrocities the quicker to destroy civilization as we know it.

Section 230 was enacted in 1996, and it was designed to protect computer bulletin boards from liability for what some user might post. It's important to recall that in 1996, the internet was the electronic version of the automobile market in 1906. In 1906 there were mere thousands of vehicles in the United States, few passable roads outside towns, no highways, and certainly no superhighways. And if you could travel at twenty miles per hour without being tossed out of your open car into a ditch, you were doing pretty well.

Nowadays we are on an information superhighway, and we're in the equivalent of a supercar with all-wheel drive.

But what's really changed is the digital technology driving social media. Today, analytics, recommendations, and the packaging of audiences for advertisers (who may be criminals) are at the heart of the paradigm. Without targeted recommendations, there is no audience assembly, no meaningful targeting, and therefore no digital advertising to speak of. Without recommendations, there really is no advertising model for social media. And hence no social media business model.

And it is absolutely the case that this profitable focus on recommendation is where the culpability lies. Section 230 created the possibility for a hybrid business that enjoys both zero responsibility plus boundless freedom. Zero responsibility means that, under present statutes, they can't be held responsible even if they promoted your name to the nearest psychopath and provided them with techniques to murder you in your sleep. These techniques would have been uploaded by a member of the public. *But your murderer would never have seen them without the recommendations of the social media company.*

Boundless freedom, as granted by section 230, means the platforms still have the right to decide what they want and what they don't want on their platform. They have the right to take your content off their platform, and because of the End User License Agreement you agreed to before posting, you have no legal recourse against them for doing so. This makes them the equivalent of a publisher. But wait! The platform—having worn the "publisher" hat for an advantageous moment—also wants to say that at the same time, they are in no way *obligated* to do anything in particular about hateful content because, much as the phone company cannot monitor all phone calls (indeed the dial-tone provider is prohibited from doing so), they are also *physically unable* to remove enough of the hateful, libelous content to keep their sites wholesome.

In terms of traditional media, this means the platforms that call themselves Facebook, YouTube, Twitter, or whatever have both the rights of a publisher when it comes to providing a forum (editorial) and at the same time the protection of a carrier (like AT&T) when recommending content. And if this were a private space, we would have no objection. But it is the public sphere, and the entire enterprise is built to influence the public for a profit using a classic ad-supported model. Frankly, this public-facing, hybrid model is *natively* hypocritical, and in any form of just society, it cannot be permitted to continue.

Let's take this question out of the digital realm. Is it okay for a publicly traded company to profit very directly off of hate? I ask this obvious question because it does not seem like anyone is asking it. Again, let's sweep away the IFD and look at another type of company, and how they would fare under the same rules. Let's say there was a big soft drink company that sold a brand of soda that somehow was found to cause its customer base to spout hate speech, and that then could be traced as a source of real violence in the real world—and I don't mean the type of idiocy associated with alcohol, but the type associated with digital media—that is, targeted hate, harassment, and assassination. Would it not be that company's obligation to shut down that product regardless of shareholder value? Would it not seem the only right thing for them to do so that their shareholders would not be obvious profiteers off of hate and murder? This matter seems not to have occurred to platforms or their shareholders, but I am throwing down the challenge directly.

Perhaps any self-aware shareholder of a Google or a Meta might consider whether they really can relax by the pool, knowing how much of their wealth relies on the murder of innocents and the sale of advertising around same.

More importantly, and as I have mused earlier here: would the end of 230 also mean the destruction of social media?

It might!

Could it mean the end of the internet as we know it? Possibly!

Might it cause a massive economic upheaval? It certainly could.

But if Section 230 remains, then we will be trapped in a world where every insanity becomes your daily feed; where mad bombers build communities of bombers; where you become a victim of a crime that was directly encouraged by persistent recommendation of pernicious content. And senior executives at Facebook all get their bonuses meanwhile.

Here is an appropriate analogy, again using factors in the real world to disperse the fairy dust. Today the internet is the equivalent of an open sewer. An open sewer in the middle of the street. Flowing from the street through your front door and into your living room. It is the equivalent of a smoke-belching factory next to a nursery school. It's not that we have no regulations to prohibit such a monstrosity. *It's that we have regulations that promote this kind of sewage.* That regulation takes the form of Section 230. It is fouling your town, your home, your life every day, all day.

Finally, it means that lying liars will continue to lie with impunity on social media. It means that every lie gets metastasized and promoted until lies become the law of the land.

In order to restore sanity to the United States of America, Section 230 must end.

6

INFORMATION OVERLOAD AND THE DESTRUCTION OF BELIEF

M any people can't handle the truth.

Philosophers have long held that the face we present to the outer world, *and* the face we present to our inner world, are both fabrications, thin tissues meant to display rectitude, doughtiness, and compassion. But much like what Abraham Lincoln called our "integument" (skin), that facade covers a much more complex and less savory prospect. We are naturally made with a facade. All creatures share this trait. A creature's own skin may be smooth, or furry, or hard, like shellac. But the skin always hides the squishy, unappetizing interior where blood pumps, foods are digested, and waste is stored until evacuation. It's no wonder nature has chosen to promote good optics!

Software is made this way too. The interface is that skin. Programmers call it a "presentation layer." The user interacts with buttons, icons, pictures, and words that seem like two-dimensional simulacrums of objects in the real world. We like to think of this graphical interface as intuitive, and largely this is the case. But it wasn't very long ago that there was no presentation layer in software, and we were more exposed to what was actually going on inside the processors.

This paradigm deployed what was called a "command line" interface, because you needed to know the commands and you needed to type them in so that the computer would know what you wanted. Even today, if you're using a Windows machine, there's still a kernel under there where the original Disk Operating System lurks, an ancient command-line infrastructure that is now completely hidden behind large graphics and badges. Not to say Apple hasn't any programming behind its products. It does. But from the start, Apple wanted their computer to work "for the rest of us," and that meant a graphical interface almost from the inception. Certainly a robust presentation layer was and remains the hallmark of the Macintosh line of products, now about forty years old.

I will admit that the first Mac was a revelation to me, and was my gateway to harder stuff. It taught me about what you can see versus what you cannot, and how an effective interface drives adoption of otherwise unapproachable processes. I had a friend who got hold of an original 128K Mac in 1983, and he insisted that I type something using his graphical interface. I typed my name. Fine. Then he switched the font to Olde English, and I was never the same again. For it was immediately apparent to me that if you could make a computer screen show any font at will, you could make any pixel on any screen behave in any way you wanted, so long as you had the software and the processing power to command it.

What has this got to do with truth?

It's about what's hidden, and what's been told, and how when some people learn too much, they don't know what to think, and they become frustrated. And soon they decide to trust nothing.

The knowledge and the power that is resident in any networked computer these days represents the kind of communication power and access to information that surpasses that of all humanity's ability in aggregate before, say, 1990. This graphical interface has opened up new worlds for all of humanity. But many say it has resulted in unhelpful overload.

You have access to all the world's knowledge. Are you prepared to deal with it?

Very likely you're not.

It's like when you go to a diner and they have a menu with twenty-five different pasta offerings, twenty sandwiches, and one hundred types of omelets. What is the percentage of orders for bacon and eggs? It's not just that diners must always want bacon and eggs. It's that they don't know anything much about the kitchen, have learned that large menus suggest mediocrity in general, and out of a sense of self-preservation and an inclination to not waste time, they just don't believe in the chicken cordon bleu.

And what is the percentage of folks who would really rather have a menu of limited choice to start with? My contention is that it is much larger than we are prepared to confront.

EXPOSURE TO HIDDEN HISTORY

Presentation layers or interfaces or facades or pretenses very often may prove key to public acceptance of difficult ideas. But some ideas, as I will point out, cannot be sufficiently simplified without contravening the purpose of the idea in the first place. Which is why some knowledge is called "esoteric." It's not meant for all. In a more circumspect time in history (all of it until digital), it was generally accepted that some knowledge might be better left undistributed. We can talk about state secrets, bomb formulae, and the like. We can also talk about cosmology, and the head-scratching weirdness that attends thereto, and about arcane science, where category-defying phenomena like viruses are neither plant, nor parasite, but deadly just the same.

In a less media-centric world, people didn't get much information, and they didn't question that much of it either. There was a time, of course, when there truly was no media. There was word of mouth. There was the town crier. There were the king's edicts. At church, a preacher. But his news was old, typically. And there was no such thing as professional journalism or fact-checking or any notion of the greater good or even freedom of speech. What you did have was the town commons, where everyone went to meet, greet, and argue, in the absence of an evening newspaper or a TV dinner in front of the boob tube.

Some say that social media has resurrected the town common even as it has summarily executed the titans of old, big media. But if we had any small amount of trust in the newspaper, flawed as often they were, there was a sense that they could only get away with so much before another news source canceled them out. This balance is completely gone because there is no counternarrative to anything. In the new digital commons, everyone whispers in everyone else's ear, and it's all got the same level of trustworthiness as the spew from any gossipmonger. However, as a visitor to the town common, you might have had the good sense to ignore the spittle-mouthed madwoman pointing fingers at people who wronged her at the shops. Nor had you any good reason to trust your local gossipmonger any more than you would trust a cow to do the grocery shopping.

Does this lack of trust sound like good advice, if it is not eerily familiar, in a social media environment?

One day approximately in 2014 in Kingston, New York, there was an earthquake. I was there speaking at a conference about Twitter, which at that time was new in the world. I had yet to go on stage when the building shook, a light crashed down, and chairs were disarrayed. It was nothing much on the Richter scale, but we all felt it. And then I went on stage and told everyone how I thought Twitter would destroy trust in communications, and that it would be "the equivalent of the town commons," where all was rumor and nothing was proven and there were no authoritative truth-tellers. I am pretty sure the local Tweeters, digital boosters all, were less than thrilled at my takedown of their new pet tweety bird. The director of the forum practically cut off my mike. It did not bother me, and I had a strong feeling I had already got their number.

Today, the owner of Twitter, Elon Musk, is calling it the town common as well. But where he doesn't see it as a problem, I do. I believe social media is part of the *architecture of untruth*, and a major player in the destruction of trust generally. And it isn't just about lying, although that is a major component.

During most of the nineteenth century, journalism was shamelessly partisan and there was little consideration given to facts and whether there was anything resembling a public good. The US State Department says: "Yellow journalism was a style of newspaper reporting that emphasized sensationalism over facts. During its heyday in the late 19th century it was one of many factors that helped push the United States and Spain into war in Cuba and the Philippines."[1]

But by the time we found ourselves at war in Europe with tanks and biplanes (1917), American newspapers and magazines had determined there was a loyal readership for what would turn out to be at least demonstrably true. In an uncertain world, people naturally hungered for facts. Facts about the weather. And about science. And politics. And about business. It would help them determine where to live, where to travel, what to buy, and what to do in an emergency. Newspapers were printed several times a day! They arrived damp from the press and often had to be ironed dry.

In the 1920s, radio made for a new entertainment medium, and while it offered plenty of news, it remained an adjunct to the newspapers that flourished then. In New York City alone during the 1920s and 1930s, no less than six major newspapers were published every day, and dozens of smaller ones as well.² Today there are three in New York, and one of them is the *New York Times*. The *Daily News* runs on fumes and memories. The *Post* seems a labor of hate, if you will, and in all likelihood a loss leader for its owners, the Murdochs of Fox News infamy.

As for the rest of the country, many big cities have hardly any newspaper at all. For example, The *Columbus Post-Dispatch* in 1980 had a weekday circulation of over two hundred twenty-five thousand. In that year they became the first newspaper to publish electronically by delivering news through an online bulletin board called CompuServe. In 2022 the newspaper's circulation, in a city of nearly one million, is about twenty-six thousand, not including its online readership.

Before television, the American public listened eagerly and with naive belief to radio. A famous incident about fiction and belief involves the great Orson Welles and his *Mercury Theater* radio program that was broadcast nationally. On Halloween night in 1938, he broadcast a dramatization of H. G. Wells's *War of the Worlds*, which told the story of a Martian invasion. So convincing was the program that thousands of panicked Americans, especially in the New Jersey corridor where the story took place, thought there really was an invasion. They took to the roads, they called the police, they prepared for the end. Only to find it was all just a story. I'm sure many listeners were chagrined when they were told how the show had *started off with a warning*, and that they rightfully could claim no overriding reason to think the fantasy was true, except that they may have been extra wary in those days just before the start of World War Two.

World War Two, no doubt the most cataclysmic event in history, can also be summed up in three words: we beat fascism.

After World War Two we saw the rise of television news, as discussed earlier: the Walter Cronkites of the world, who were tasked with giving us our national narrative for better or worse. It was the same crew—Cronkite, Dan Rather, and the like—who announced, for instance, that President Kennedy was dead, and then, seventeen years later, that John Lennon was also dead of an assassin's bullet. In those days it was taken for granted that the news media did not invent stories out of whole cloth.

But we seem to have lost any faith we might have once had in broadcast news. And many of us have found ourselves suspecting we are being lied to, generally, and that these lies are meant to manipulate, generally. And so we have a new basis for disbelief: we don't want to get caught out again like we did with *War of the Worlds*. We don't want to believe what we hear, see, or read in the news. It might be fiction!

Facts are inconvenient, and many would be thrilled never to have to deal with any.

To be sure, the QAnon/Trump/Russian propaganda project is designed to have millions reject all messaging as fake, except for the substitute messages provided by the Q-adjacent propaganda consortium. The extent to which this is true can be exemplified by a study conducted by Reddit user u/Trash_man_can. This Reddit user created a chart showing all the times that a Trump tweet contained the word "fake."[3] As the visual shows (see link in end notes), the frequency of his use of this word can be described as both overwhelming and continuing. Each "fake" generates a red dot, and you can see that the chart is literally covered in red dots.

These Trump-inspired attacks upon information are both unprecedented and effective. Largely because of these, what we confront today is a combination of paranoia, narrative selection, and misbelief that would have been alien to any mainstream American of an earlier generation. But today, skepticism is also layered with blanket, largely unjustified rejection of inconvenient truths and their substitution by comfortable myths and self-aggrandizing fables.

Some of these doubts succeed because the world has come to understand, unfortunately, that the "official word" too often is almost beneath consideration. I say this as a natural skeptic and a nonbeliever— in what the authorities say, in what anyone says—without some shred of fact or truth being presented.

The cynic's goal is not to claim that *all* official words are worthless. But instead, they want to say that *just enough* of the official words are incorrect as to be disqualifying. The cynic wants to make sure that the target audience never believes any information disseminated by "experts" and "the government." Indeed, the two are linked, in "fake news" parlance, as if these two were in a kind of lockstep march toward convincing the populace of one giant lie after another.

Armchair skeptics in the United States have convinced themselves that because the government *has* lied, they must then be liars about *all things*. And here is where we begin to explore an atmosphere that persists not because of digital, but beside digital, with its own tortured history of official misinformation, coverup, and exposure. I believe it represents an obvious example of how a government can, just as the cynic would have it, deploy decades of ham-handed lying and obfuscation, only to lately admit that those decades of official pablum were, for all intents and purposes, misdirection.

An obvious example is the UFO phenomenon. For decades, the official stance of the US government was that UFOs were a joke. Now, after seventy years of lying, the US Navy has admitted that it is in possession of hundreds of credible reports that unmanned, non-aerodynamic objects are playing hob with our most advanced military installations. Is it any wonder, then, that large numbers of people on both sides of the political divide see a large credibility gap in the official stance of the US government? We have so much doubting to fall back on! From UFOs to Saddam's nonexistent "yellowcake," the United States has openly misled and lied to the public. It's a virtual playground for the cynical manipulator. The government has made it all too easy for a Jim Jordan (R-OH) to claim, in an atmosphere where we have been lied to repeatedly, that the government, in the matter of Donald J. Trump and his election-related misdeeds, is, once again, lying.

He may not be explicit about it, but he is relying on the seeds of doubt sown by years of misinformation: that UFOs are fake, that Lee Oswald figured out how to kill JFK all by his lonesome, that we were winning in Vietnam when we were losing, that Saddam Hussein had something to do with 9/11. Trump leveraged this history of untruths when he first said his crowd was bigger: they lied before, why not now? The anti-vaxxers leveraged this history when they turned against the COVID vaccine—for we must now be led to believe that the United States officially is injecting people with chemistry that turns them into nonhumans and allows them to be controlled by wireless radio waves much like cell phones.[4]

But for me, it is the now long-standing UFO misinformation campaign that really sets the stage. UFOs are officially called UAPs now (Unidentified Aerial Phenomena). Regardless of the name, no doubt this challenge has been lurking in the back of the public consciousness since at least 1947 when pilot Kenneth Arnold first reported a string of peculiar, saucer-shaped craft skipping alongside him near Mt. Rainier in the state of Washington. Soon after Arnold, the world saw a more alarming headline about a crashed saucer.

In July 1947, a New Mexico rancher named Mack Brazel discovered what looked to be a massive debris field on his property. It was enough of a wreck that he reported it to the local news station, who alerted the US Army. The Army permitted a headline to cross the wires that admitted they had captured the remains of a flying saucer. A few days later, that story was retracted and in its place was an ill-supported cover story that featured a smirking intelligence major and a few shreds of tin foil as from a kite. The difference between this paltry array of sticks and balloons, and what was originally reported by people who had no good reason to sensationalize, is the difference between a dinghy and a fifty-foot yacht. One of the claims is false.

The United States went on to officially unrecognize any and all UFO phenomena. Instead they characterized each and every sighting as something like foolishness, and the United States officially went out of its way to make any investigation into a matter of glowing gases, misidentified stars, and reflective birds. It was considered a matter of national security that the government deny the existence of anything that left it a possibility that the United States did not have 100 percent control over its own airspace. Other Western nations were never so dyed-in-the-wool as the Unites States about denial. The French and the Belgians especially have given credence to any number of sightings that the United States would have called unverifiable.

I have never seen a classic UFO, although I have seen, on a couple of occasions, things in the sky that did not comport with my understanding of aircraft that humans fly. But my observations, and indeed my own personal opinion about UAPs are not relevant even remotely. What is important is that by the 2020s, the United States now officially says they have evidence of craft that cannot be made by any technology we know of, nor any technology we know the Russians or Chinese to possess, nor do these craft behave in aerodynamically consistent ways, nor do they behave in ways that would permit the survival of any human occupant. Some of them travel at several thousand miles per hour, and have been tracked at those speeds on radar. They have been observed by trained military pilots. Some of these pilots have claimed to observe how UAPs stop on a dime and change direction again at several thousand miles per hour. Prior to digital media, pictures of UFOs (never mind videos) were only to be found in esoteric magazines and were known only to those who bothered to investigate. The number of interested parties was tiny. But after the Google machine made it so that any casual researcher can see more pictures and videos of UFOs than can even be digested, this of course changed. Now the history of government misinformation and disinformation lay exposed for all to see—that and, of course, the baffling pictures of the crafts themselves, if they were crafts.

My contention is that the sudden exposure of the uninitiated to this unsettling information may set off a number of unintended reactions. Chief among these may be a blanket rejection of all government information (including vaccine recommendations, by the way); and at the same time a growing sense that very few things we thought were bedrock truly are bedrock. We might, in fact, be under an invasion threat from an army of little green men.

All of the above notwithstanding, the United States has more or less admitted they'd been lying all those years. The Navy has even provided video of non-aerodynamic orbs in the sky that behave very obviously unlike any known craft.

In a timely twist, it also turns out that, at least in the winter of 2023, there were certain objects in the sky over the United States, and that at least one of them was a Chinese spying platform attached to a balloon that was shot down by the US Navy. And if that is not enough of a twist, it turns out also that on one subsequent weekend, the United States also spotted a handful of other drones and balloons in the air, all unidentified, all of them shot down or neutralized. And then totally forgotten. And no balloons prior and none since. It's almost enough to make a total disbeliever out of even the most trusting citizen.

So the United States has handed the cynics all the weapons they need. But what's clear is that right-wing propagandists are leveraging general doubts in the population to promote theories even weirder than that there might be aliens in the sky.

Other facts about the nature of reality and existence are equally difficult to understand, and many influencers have leaped to take advantage of the sudden shallow skepticism espoused by otherwise clueless armchair warriors who may believe the government lies, but also believe that the NRA and Donald Trump do not. Some of the disbelief, arguably, can be traced back to the availability of advanced cosmological and physical theories that, until the advent of the Google machine, would have been almost impossible for the casual news-consumer to locate.

Today's skeptic is in fact an incurious sort, who cannot be bothered to seek in good faith and to follow facts to their conclusion. No, today's skeptic is much better at finding what breadcrumbs have been placed in his path on purpose. That these crumbs might lead to his own bewitchment and imprisonment may not have occurred to him! But he is quite certain that Antifa operatives got all dressed up in confederate flag costumes and stormed the US Capitol in a convincing cosplay of bigotry.

There are other levels of strangeness that can affect belief systems. A particularly troublesome line of inquiry involves the indeterminate nature of reality, and how it turns out that science must freely admit the limits of its understanding—which limits, for the naive recipient of tainted information, must mean that science is not only imperfect and admittedly fallible, but that such limits must proceed from a fundamental lack of soundness. This, of course, is a misunderstanding of scientific method.

For science can produce mighty results. Without raw science, there is no technology. Without digital technology, there is very much less access to arcane, esoteric, baffling ideas about time, space, and reality. Discussions of cosmology and physics are bound to confuse the ill-educated, for they certainly can confuse those who consider themselves well read. But science never really makes bold proclamations—only findings that can be repeated by others. The armchair warrior probably is not familiar enough with scientific method to understand that the entire point of scientific inquiry is to locate nuggets of fact, not to self-aggrandize. Science does not provide universal answers, and never claims that it does. Which may make it seem weak and inferior in comparison with righteous Christians and their manly (if bogus) claims about subjects about which they know almost nothing.

Advanced physics and cosmology have provided us with a world of uncertainty. My contention is that most people will find this news unsettling, and that a certain percentage of them will almost naturally proceed to simpler beliefs that savor at least of red meat even in a thin broth of relativity. Many of these troublesome cosmological concepts are at least a hundred years old. They date back to when Albert Einstein proposed the theory of relativity, and the space-time continuum. And yet the armchair skeptic may have only discovered them recently because of the ease of a Google search, and because of the way UAPs are now in the mainstream.

Largely proven over the past century, Einstein's cosmological principles have nothing in common with religious narratives, or at least they don't seem to on the surface. And mind you, the surface is the only place where these Google-surfing armchair warriors can be found, much as pond-scum is where you find all the algae. Where a Christian church will say the Lord created Heaven and Earth in seven days, science gives us a much more credible scenario where, over billions of years, incremental changes have brought us the world we know today. Where the Christian will say you have a reward for you in Heaven, science cannot say anything about any possible afterlife. But that is not even the biggest problem. Science cannot say anything certain about this life either.

As we learn more about the universe, it is plain that we know little and understand less. We may even live in only one of an infinite number of possible universes. We don't even know what it is we are actually made of (as I mentioned in an earlier chapter), nor do we understand any of the sizes and distances at nano- and macroscales. The intersection with digital is this: you can google around and find lots of esoteric claims and counterclaims. Before Google, only physicists and those otherwise interested in cosmology and physics would have even encountered these concepts. But when Bobbie-Ann Forwarder sees it, the result is brain-chaos, and a retreat to a small set of false-bottomed "certainties" about God and Family and whatnot.

Cosmology presents confounding issues where science freely admits no answer, even as religion proclaims that it *does* have them. And to the insecure, to the casual thinker, to the man-who-can't-be-bothered, the intellectual equivalent of a TV dinner is far easier to bear than the pains of having to make one's own eggplant parmigiana. That the TV dinner tastes nothing like the home-made dish, that the received explanations that come from church and the GOP bear little resemblance to any consistent mode of inquiry, means nothing to the lazy thinker. What's important is the comfort of certainty in an uncertain world.

My contention is that prior to digital media, entire lines of scientific and physical inquiry were in essence unknown to the general public, and the public were unlikely to encounter them in any casual setting. They could not google the information, they would have had to register for a class at least, and read thick tomes, and take notes. They'd have needed to be something more than just a surfer with a quick Google-finger. Digital has removed the barrier, and now this admittedly confounding, confusing, unsettling information is flooded out into the mainstream. If the rise of fabulisms in the public sphere is any indication, then the mainstream is not ready to handle any of this. But we now live in a world where the simple can laugh at the complex for its complexity; and where the blinkered certainties of religion and the GOP can be easily slotted in where science seems to have left an opening (even if it really has not).

Simple lies instead of complex truth: a convenient substitution! Where governments and scientists cannot be relied upon for ultimate truth, here comes a demagogue like Trump, alongside a clown-car of quasi-fascist preachers, calling everybody else "fake" and saying that, if we cannot know the nature of the universe, then we also cannot know the outcome of an election unless it was won by a Republican.

These cynical manipulators go to war every day against a world of facts as they try to convince people that their God has the power to heal you instantly if only you would just stop whining.

Preachers and their congregations have been barnstorming the nation for more than a century, and they show no sign of letting up even as church attendance continues to drop every year.[5] One must wonder if the recent Christian vitriol is in any way related to loss of confidence. Perhaps as they lose their grip on the body politic, the more shrilly they must shout.

How has evangelism changed since the days of Aimee Semple McPherson?[6] Now the preachers tweet. Now they have YouTube videos. Now their megaflocks know instantly, across the broad evange-liscape, what preacher bonked which purported cripple on the head and cured them. The targeted, deliberate evangelical message-penetration is far superior to what it was before. And in an atmosphere of misbelief and untruth, we find that many millions of people buy into wholesale folly not just about the structure of a moral universe, but about the Satan-soaked behaviors of people they have never met and know nothing about. I am talking especially about the Christian-borne hatred of LGBTQ folks, the sudden illegality in Tennessee of drag performance (Rudy Giuliani notwithstanding), and the toxic, un-American notion of "Christian nationalism," which is born, bred, and fed almost solely by digital sources.

So perhaps we have established two key drivers of misbelief: first, that there are facts in the public domain that are almost irreconcilable with not only traditional faith, but that strongly suggest nobody really knows how the universe is truly constructed. Second, that there is a "man behind the [media] curtain," much as in the Wizard of Oz (see below).

And if nobody knows the nature of reality, then nobody is an ultimate authority, correct?

Except for the preacher who says he *does* know (he does not) and is an authority because he has highlighted certain passages in a certain dog-eared book. Too bad he's as wildly incorrect as he is relentlessly self-serving.

THE MAN BEHIND THE CURTAIN

For too long, we trusted media implicitly, and the payoff was unhealthy for us all. Media didn't deserve our trust, but we saw the newspapers as authoritative, and the television news perhaps even more so. But as noted earlier, along about the time of the Vietnam war, we learned that media, along with the vast majority of the US government, had been perpetrating what some called a "bright, shining lie"[7] about sending our "best and brightest" to liberate a needy nation of democrats from the clutches of communistic slavery. More than fifty thousand American deaths later, it turned out the government and the media were both wrong, even willfully so. The Vietnam War was started and perpetuated by Democrats, and while Nixon, a

Republican, certainly made it worse, it was an inherited nightmare and not of his manufacture.

Then came Watergate, the exposure of President Richard Nixon as a liar if not a crook, and his subsequent 1974 resignation under threat of impeachment.

By the end of the 1970s, the notion that you ought to trust the government was as dead as John Kennedy himself. It can be reasonably asserted that the injection of right-wing mania into the political mainstream can be traced to Ronald Reagan, elected president in 1980, who famously said that the scariest words in the English language were: "I'm from the government and I am here to help." If Reagan was anything but a big government phony, I am open to hearing about it. But I am pretty sure the objections will be minimal.

However, the general population had stopped trusting government.

Reagan, in his folksy, "great communicator" fashion, channeled government-doubt in a particularly cynical, self-serving manner. Never mind that mistrusting the government was forever and always about taxes, to wit: since the government cannot be trusted, they ought not tax you either. This false equivalency has been the basis of every GOP-led tax cut since the dawn of tax-avoidance. And in the post-Vietnam era, with government mistrust at an all-time high, Reagan struck this discord hard, and from the right. One might as easily have struck from the left, except that then the preachers would not have got on board. At that time there were a litany of official falsehoods that gave government a bad—an awful!—reputation, even as Reagan perverted this doubt for his own narrow purpose.

Among the signal government failures then and now, we can catalog only a few. But I think you will see the point having reviewed the examples:

- the Vietnam War, a nation-breaking catastrophe because of which the American reputation for global righteousness was forever smashed
- Nixon, whose lies and Watergate-related resignation permanently damaged the office of the presidency
- a bogus, and now largely forgotten "war on drugs" that imprisoned the innocent and left marginalized communities with large

percentages of its male population behind bars for smoking and selling weed

- COINTELPRO, a 1970s-era FBI program to infiltrate, target, and destroy what was then called the New Left movement in the United States

In this atmosphere, Reagan perverted the failures and misdeeds *actually* committed by government into a newly formulated, toxic stew of quasi-religious blather and racist sophistries: that government, inherently bad (except, of course, for the government's largest expense, the military), must be held responsible for everything: crime, the existence of "welfare queens," environmental regulations that might keep us in wetlands but might be bad for business—and many others.

These formed the bedrock for what turned out to be today's right-wing discontent. It's based on the incoherent assumption that there are unworthies in society leeching off the hard work of the taxpayer, and that these unworthies take the form of darker-skinned, work-avoiding baby-machines that have gamed the system and get a free pass because they're not white Christian males. Or it's based on another incoherent assumption that another darker-skinned group is actually striving too hard, and thereby taking jobs away from the poor innocent Christian white male who would much rather be picking beans than twirling around in an ottoman with Fox News on the ear pods.

It took forty years, but eventually the right combined digital messaging plus government hate into a surround-sound of faux-revolutionary rhetoric. Any sort of revolution would always include 90 percent of everything already in place, except that it must pass muster under the principle of "small government." Small government is a way of deprecating any program disliked by a conservative. It is a useful misdirection that in no way characterizes any actual GOP policy.

The GOP goal, now and always, is to see that wealthy Americans pay little to no income tax. For that is what it has always been about, that is the only thing it has ever been about, and that is the only thing it ever will be about. All else is subterfuge and distraction. The GOP is a magic act. Look at the top hat! Never mind that it's sitting on a hollow table big enough to hide a small mammal. Out pops a rabbit. And the audience roars every time.

No normal American would ever vote in the interest of no-tax billionaires directly. But they *will* vote for phantoms raised by the no-tax crowd. These include all of the traditional American hobgoblins: racism, homophobia, paranoia, "traditional values" and, just as a trivial adjunct of course, a massive reduction in taxes on the wealthy.

The billionaire-friendly GOP will use any tactic to win the tax war, because that is the entire playbook about how you get and stay wealthy in America—you overcharge on all aspects of your passive income, you skip out on paying bills, you maximize margin by increasing the suffering of your customers and employees, and you reduce all spending including tax. It is time-honored, market-tested; and the present economic system favors this approach.

The nuts and bolts of the program are simple, but sometimes the entire machine can get more sophisticated. The loss of trust in government, once taken rather for granted by conservatives, now becomes a central theme as their arguments become more detached from the needs of the voter. And so we come back again to the ideas and trends that the GOP will cynically manipulate in order to delegitimize the opposition. And much of what they say goes right back to the uncertainties that the honest inquirer must always express. In brief, the GOP has decided they ought to go against science now, because science begins to tell us things unfriendly to no-taxation; unfriendly to fossil-fuel pollution; unfriendly to untrammeled gun mania; unfriendly to biblical, restrictive roles for women; unfriendly to all things regressive and ignorant. As it must!

But science expresses its findings in ways that emphasize the provisional nature of its findings. Science avoids making the kind of literal, global, absolutist pronouncements that make tired old white people feel extra comfortable as they skim yet more cream off the top of the social hierarchy.

Digital has given easy access to all kinds of unusual ideas. I've already suggested that many Americans cannot imagine how a properly ordered world can accommodate uncertainties, seeing as how they've never been forced to confront any. This lack of exposure makes the armchair skeptic prone to false equivalencies. For instance, they may want to suggest that if you believe that humans and apes have a common ancestor, then it might as well be true that millions of dead people voted illegally for a Democrat in a national election.

Before digital, many of these arcane investigations into the nature of reality were found only in scientific journals, where you would not be able to read much of them without looking for answers in a way that was more than merely casual. My contention is that digital search has made it too easy for the unprepared to encounter these unsettling ideas, and that the result has been catastrophic. For digital is the only way for John Q. Farmer, he of little education and little tolerance, to access these esoterica.

Should esoterica have remained hidden, as it was until the "information wants to be free" crowd got wind of it?

Let's look at what science is saying these days about the nature of reality. Because my contention is that, if the latest findings in physics and cosmology represent the truth, most people, as noted above, "can't *handle* it."[8] It turns out, as mentioned earlier, that the universe is much more dodgy, diaphanous, and madcap than the wildest sort of fiction. If you didn't know any better (and a huge percentage of the US population absolutely does not), and you are also bombarded hourly by insane, bogus claims full of lies and slander, you would be tempted to say it's all hogwash; and you would skip the vaccine, drink bleach to cure COVID, claim that six billion people crossed the border illegally from Mexico since Biden took office in 2021[9] and talk about soggy-bottomed real estate moguls as incarnations of Jesus.[10] The deification of Trump represents a telling departure from reality.

The hagiographical treatment of Trump that his cult lavishes upon him closely parallels a type of transference of divinity that marks only the least sophisticated belief systems. It forces us back to the beliefs of marginally contacted tribes, as described in James Frazer's *The Golden Bough*. That there are actual Americans promoting the idea that this poor excuse for a man—let's call him Trump—is an incarnation of Jesus, is one of the key "tells" that something dreadful has happened in our national dialogue. We are no longer working with people who can claim sanity or anything more than sheer idiocy. Some say that the derangement is so thorough in the Trump worshipper that they will go to any length (and I mean *any* length) to keep Trump in the public eye, if not in office. That's as may be, but their elevation of the Loser Cheet-o to divine status is not unlike what Frazer describes here in *The Golden Bough*:

The kings of Egypt were deified in their lifetime, sacrifices were offered to them, and their worship was celebrated in special temples and by special priests. Indeed the worship of the kings sometimes cast that of the gods into the shade. Thus in the reign of Merenra a high official declared that he had built many holy places in order that the spirits of the king, the ever-living Merenra, might be invoked "more than all the gods."

The real world is complicated, and digital exposes us to much more of it than ever before. So much easier for the worshipful to talk about how there's just one book and one Trumpy savior, and that only white Christian males have rights!

THE UNFATHOMABLE IS HARD TO UNDERSTAND

Perhaps the national dialogue would be much the same without digital, but I rather doubt it. I must emphasize again the popularization, or at least the wider dissemination of scientific ideas that might be considered esoteric, baffling, and unsettling. And I'm not even talking about such controversies as to the accuracy of Darwin's theory of evolution, though some very ill-informed folk find this, too, unsettling. We have seen for a hundred years the war against Darwin's theories: witness the Scopes Monkey Trial from the 1920s, made famous by the play (and movie) *Inherit the Wind*, where preachers help convict a man in court for teaching evolution.

Evolution aside, I am talking about two additional phenomena that demonstrate how the general public perhaps ought not be trusted to handle the truth. Or at least it demonstrates that if you keep people in the dark for long enough, you will have reinforced their childishness sufficiently such that you can never expect them to make an adult-level decision throughout their entire lives.

We have talked about certain arcane, even esoteric knowledge relating to cosmology and physics, and how even the well-prepared can come away with a disturbing sense that we really don't even know the ground we walk on. And we have talked about how the United States has, for all practical purposes, admitted that there are, in fact, unknown objects flying with impunity above our fruited plain.

Make no mistake that these trends have undermined the average person's sense of grounding, and that, even for those not especially religious, these physical observations are deeply disturbing. Or at least they erode one's sense that there is an actual truth out there.

My contention is that the presence of these cosmological memes in the population are having unintended effects. That they are part of the underlying lack of comfort in what reality is for many of the more simpleminded, and how that has come to mean, for them, under their heavy burden of manipulated alternative facts, that *all expertise is questionable*, and that if you express uncertainty, you are then fit to be ignored in favor of the loudest, most confident donkey in the stable.

Let's briefly return to our discussion of cosmology, an arcane branch of science that is related to physics, and which has a lot to say about the nature of the universe. Cosmology looks to be in direct competition with metaphorical claims in the Bible, but it also remains at odds with the everyday physics we call "perceivable reality." Cosmology often seems to defy logic. It talks about "quantum entanglement" between distant particles, almost as if by magic. It talks of alternative universes. If you come away from a discussion about the nature of infinity and the universe without a deep uncertainty, you have missed the point. But it doesn't mean you suddenly question who won the 2020 election.

Or, perhaps, sometimes, and for some people, it does mean exactly that.

What many non-scientists don't understand is that science is not about statements of fact, but about a method of demonstrating repeated results that strongly suggest certain approaches are workable until something more refined is discovered. Nor do they seem to comprehend that science will eagerly admit to these changes, because, frankly, this method of search and discovery is foundational to the scientific endeavor. There is no "settled science." No less a person than physicist Niels Bohr said "Physics is not how the world works. Physics is what we can say about how the world works."

This is a demonstration of honesty about a paramount uncertainty. It really may not be suitable for the average person to think much about what we can know about reality, for those esoteric theories about cosmology are not likely to help that person change diapers, for instance, or pick up the dry cleaning. Contemplation of the nature of reality may even lead to some very troubling doubts. More importantly, the widespread acknowledgment that these fundamental doubts exist, and that science does not have answers, makes science seem weak as compared with biblical certainty, no matter how untenable the biblical certainty may be.

Not to revert to Newtonian physics without cause, but in psychology, it is fair to assert that every action gets a reaction. Often the reaction to uncertainty is a retreat behind comfortable certainties. And the more you are bombarded (digitally) with hints of foundational weirdness, the more of a "skeptic" you become, and the more you seek any harbor (church?) in a storm.

As noted above, these days we are beset by armies of people who believe that a Google search is tantamount to doing your own research. This army fails to understand that Google makes no representations that anything you find there has even a shred of veracity. But because digital *usurps the trust* conveyed by older, more sober media empires, an army of ill-informed cybernauts believe that if they read several unhinged diatribes about drinking bleach to cure a virus, then *it must be true.* They think it's been subject to the same scrutiny that was practiced by nearly every journalist and publisher in the nation until digital became a platform for liars.

RETREAT TO SAFETY

Reality, I feel comfortable in asserting, is a shifting set of circumstances and contingencies. Many people, some more desperately than others, long for a few bedrock certainties in a world of flux and nuance. Religionists find it in their sacred books. But even the casual observer can be expected to want to think that solid objects are solid, and that distances can be understood, and that we know how large (or small) we are.

Alas, physics and cosmology have long abandoned those fairy tale certainties in favor of almost overwhelmingly bizarre assertions that, while proven in the laboratory, almost defy description. Having mentioned them earlier, I will describe these briefly here—but my point is that these esoteric understandings were once heard pretty much only in academia and among those who understood enough to know not only that they might not understand, but that *not understanding is acceptable.* Allow me to suggest that it is the immediate availability, via search and via promotion, of these esoteric ideas that has contributed to the loss of belief in authority generally.

I'm happy to be corrected if I've misunderstood, but physicists have been saying for about a hundred years that, unlike death and taxes, the nature of reality is uncertain. Indeed, at the quantum level, Newtonian physics breaks down almost completely.

The famous Einstein equation $E=mc^2$ says that matter is energy and vice versa. This means that what we perceive as "solid" is more likely an artifact related to our sensory apprehension of certain vibratory rates as, for instance, those that generate the appearance of "wood" or "uranium." But the laboratory suggests this basic stuff is not at all solid, but is a swirling mass of charged energy fields (that cannot precisely be measured except to arrest them in mid-flight as particles) in a variety of combinations that form atoms, and that these atoms are combined as molecules that *seem* like wood or uranium. Perhaps as surprising is the indication that the relative size and distance between an electron and a nucleus is such that, much like the universe at large, the nanoverse is almost unimaginably empty.

Until this foundational science became generally available via search, it was the kind of knowledge deemed suitable mostly for those who were familiar enough with the background research to understand the phenomena in context. But digital has placed this, and pretty much all available knowledge, at the fingertips of every person with a Google machine. Which means *everyone.* Including people like Congresswoman Lauren Boebert of Colorado, who has asserted that we ought to "trust the science" as we remove environmental protections for gray wolves who have, according to Lauren, "fully recovered" even as the actual science shows clearly they have not.[11]

If we are feeling a twinge of 2008 nostalgia, we can look back, not fondly, upon the ever-quotable Sarah Palin, who made it known that she held in contempt the notion that tax dollars were being spent to study fruit flies *in France.* For what could be more dreadful than that the nation spend money on scientific investigation? Why, it might result in the development of vaccines against deadly viruses, and certainly we would never want that.

Can we say a little bit of knowledge is dangerous?

Quantum mechanics, or at least the Cliff Notes version of it, is now part of the mainstream in ways it never was before. And to those who struggle to understand that Darwin never said we came from monkeys, the notion that we can say almost nothing with certainty about the precise nature of reality must come freighted with serious concerns that all of science is a bogus game of unsupported assertions and absurdities.

Nothing, of course, could be further from the truth. And no self-respecting scientist will say they have found the ultimate truth. And while this ought to be seen as their partaking necessarily in a well-justified humility, it is often taken as an example of hypocrisy. The confidently incorrect skeptic is likely to say: "You're saying I should trust your vaccine when you don't even know what the basic stuff of matter is?"[12]

Also in the mainstream today are the notions of parallel universes, and the idea that, very likely, the meaning of "infinity" must necessarily include all possibilities and their possible outcomes. Which means that, arguably, every moment we exist causes the next moment to spin off in any number of other directions where, for instance, you did in fact step onto that bus that ended up going off the cliff. I know I cannot spend much time thinking about this without wanting to throw the whole question over into the wine dark sea. And I consider myself an adherent, at least for practical purposes, to the scientific method.

If you think this stuff is too nutty to be influential, you're not reading the kind of head-spinning madness that people are spouting-off about on Q-adjacent forums.[13] One is tempted to conclude that these folks have read a little of this and a little of that, and have heard a preacher or two talk about the easy certainties in a book they call Bible, and have come to the conclusion that science is all bathwater and no baby.

Hence, because the government has lied, and because scientists make baffling claims about the nature of reality, they feel compelled to assert that there are, in fact, certainties in the world. And that they know what these are! They will assert these truths are found either in the Bible or in the QAnon echo chamber, or perhaps even on the deeply troubled Fox News.

UNIDENTIFIED AERIAL PHENOMENA

They used to call them flying saucers. Then UFOs. Now they come in a variety of shapes and forms and often, while they may be in the sky, they don't even seem to be flying in any way we can recognize. As noted above, for decades the US government officially denied the very existence of these, calling them hallucinations or "swamp gas" or "birds" or "Venus."

Of late they have made public any number of reports of non-aerodynamic, apparently unmanned, and mysteriously powered objects flitting about. The famous "tictac" video comes from the US Navy, as recorded during an encounter not far from the USS *Nimitz*, a nuclear-powered aircraft carrier.[14] As does the "gimbal" video (USS *Roosevelt*) where we see what looks like a drone twisting in hundred-mile-an-hour headwinds as if it were stationary in calm skies.[15] These reports are only the most obvious and most well-known. There are thousands of these reports, and now that the "crazy-person" stigma has been substantially eroded, it has come to light that many observers who understand aerial phenomena have testified, to no great personal advantage, that they have seen major, baffling, otherworldly objects in the sky.

My personal theory, for what it's worth, is that these phenomena have been here for a very, very long time, that they may be earth-bound phenomena rather than alien, but that in any case they represent a form of intelligence that intersects with humanity almost not at all. This notion is bound to be disturbing. And the government appears to have well understood this, as they spent nearly a century attempting to debunk reality. Presumably, this was because it was determined early on that reality might be scary for a sheeplike American public.

The United States was, in all likelihood and for many years, concerned that people would not be able to handle the truth—much as I stated at the outset.

Based on early returns, it sure looks like they were right.

For while most of us are content to go about our lives not knowing whether there's an alien intelligence in our skies, for some, it has broken their faith in the paradigm of authority. Lacking enough critical thinking skills, they think that if *this* is uncertain, then so must be everything the government says, and that includes government scientists at the Centers for Disease Control. For, hadn't "they" been lying for so long, and so thoroughly, that there is little reason to expect anything but fantasy from government experts?

Well, yes and no.

To be fair, the government has lied—as mentioned above. Remember when nuclear power was going to make electricity free? To be fair, science, too, has led us astray. Remember when nuclear power was going to make electricity free (yes, I repeated that)?

But the problem is that too many people find themselves attracted to simple, black-and-white certainties. While at the same time, digital delivers a constant barrage of tailored news feeds that confirm our own biases by reinforcing them with additional content offered to us based on what we seem to want to hear about.

The result is a needless, blanket rejection of all information coming from all official channels, paired with an unwarranted, unquestioning acceptance of all unofficial channels, as if there were some actual diametrical opposition between the two. What is left uncomprehended by the skeptic is that their world is bounded by messaging that has been prepared, processed, manipulated, and delivered selectively to their screens in a manner designed to elicit the proper type of outrage at the proper type of enemy. Preferably this will be an enemy the hatred of whom either profits a billionaire in some way or profits a politician who serves a billionaire (or billionaires generally) in their quest to garner votes based on manufactured outrage.

A VIRUS GOES VIRAL

One example of this process, and a deadly one, is the furor over the origins of COVID-19. Millions of Americans, almost all of them aligned with the policies generally of the Republican Party (with a few loopy lefties also anti-vax for their own reasons), have rejected not just the origins but the progress and treatment of the disease.[16] They disbelieve the origin story: that it came from a wet market where so-called bush meat is consumed, and that such unusual protein sources somehow transmitted the disease from animal to human via food ingestion. They also believe, based on zero evidence, that the disease is a common parasite, much as a puppy's worm. They reject vaccination on the grounds that the COVID vaccination can turn them into nonhumans and that vaccinated people somehow "shed" the disease in a way that imperils the unvaccinated. These are damaging follies that, together with other types of propaganda, have killed many thousands of skeptics who doubt everything they hear and die needlessly because of it.

As stated earlier, I am not a believer in all things told to us by the government. If I were, I would not be asking why, in one weekend during February 2023, we somehow found and shot down three or four mysterious balloons over the United States, but none ever before and none since. I have no idea what was going on with the balloons, but I sincerely doubt what we have heard from official sources.

Does that mean I think the Centers for Disease Control is trying to revoke my humanity by recommending a vaccine that alters my DNA so that I am now susceptible to control via 5G networks?[17] It does not. Does that mean "the military" is hiding thousands of magical hospital beds that in some unknown way cure cancer[18] and anything you cannot fix with a daily dose of Ivermectin?[19] It does not mean that, although there's plenty of evidence that somebody, somewhere, wants me to think so.

Back to Wuhan, though, and the COVID Follies.

The Q-adjacent skeptic claims that only "sheeple" believe what the Deep State tells them, and that what's true instead, is whatever parallel, manufactured, AstroTurfed, manipulative narrative has been meeped-out by the media bats that fly around inside the right-wing echo-chamber. They believe that the disease was created on purpose, probably by Big Pharma, Anthony Fauci, and either George Soros or Hillary Clinton or Tom Hanks or Joe Biden or Nancy Pelosi or Black Lives Matter or Antifa or that lady that gave you the chicken eye just before the butter turned sour. And that it was created on purpose in the bio-research lab that happens to be in Wuhan, China, where the disease first was prevalent. They believe the COVID vaccines are not only ineffective but deadly to the unvaccinated and dehumanizing as well (because the vaccine alters your DNA in a manner that makes you nonhuman). They believe that the wearing of surgical masks to prevent the spread of disease is a primary example of government mind-control; and that anyone who wears a mask is by definition not just an idiot but a contemptible demon working to undermine the supremacy of tired old white people in general.

The reason I cite this as an example of needless, blanket rejection of government-distributed information, is that the truth *is* a mixed bag—although, in my opinion at least, not very hard to figure out and understand. In brief: not everything we have heard from the government about COVID is true. But that does not mean *everything* the government says about it is also untrue. We come back again to the wiles of the cynical manipulator. The cynic will tell the skeptic that they must question not only authority but *reject all authoritative voices*, because "Google it yourself"; and they can point to one fact that the US government seems not to have signed up for, or at least not until recently.

That fact is: there is a bio-research lab in Wuhan, China, where they were studying diseases like COVID. Somehow, at least according to the latest assessment from the FBI, the disease leaked out of the lab and got into the general population at Wuhan.[20] It then spread around the world, killing millions. For some reason, the United States wanted to *not* blame a Chinese laboratory for the origination of the pandemic. Instead, and much as the government had said about AIDS, they claimed that the disease came from the consumption of bush meat: in other words, animals like pangolins and other wild prey at so-called wet markets, which are nothing more than butchers who sell wild animals for human consumption.[21] For quite some time, the standard line from the US government was that it was definitely wet markets that brought COVID to humanity, and not the bio-lab in the same city where the disease first appeared.

That, of course, never made a ton of sense. And now the government is admitting it is likely not the case. The original misstatement, whether planned or not, has become foundational to the army of Q-adjacent skeptics who would use this as the rock upon which to build their church. The skeptic's narrative holds that the United States lied about the origin of the virus and then lied about the effectiveness of the vaccine, while all the while lying about the need for masking in order not to spread the virus.

Perhaps it is worthwhile to note that the mask is designed not to keep you healthy, but to prevent you from breathing out the virus onto others. Most likely this would be yet another reason for the army of selfish, deluded COVID-deniers to not wear masks. Imagine having to do something that would help someone else! For this crowd, it's unthinkable.

Further, the skeptic goes on to doubt everything else the government says about the virus. The Q-skeptic says the vaccine is a fake, and that it turns you into a 5G-controlled automaton. That it's part of a command-and-control plot, and that people who took the vaccines will be dead, en masse, by 2024. Of course they are entirely mistaken on this topic. The vaccine has been proven effective. Masks do keep you from breathing virus onto others, even though it cannot prevent it entirely.

Finally, they believe not only that the vaccine is a hoax. They believe that the science behind disease control also is somehow discredited because, at a certain point, the government did not offer up crystal-clear truths about the murky origins of the disease, and because at a certain point also, the government probably was lying about UFOs. I understand this is a novel take on the phenomenon. But I believe we have gotten to our extreme circumstance because of an unusual confluence of events that must include a general sense of unreality that seems to pervade public dialog these days.

I don't know if I am ready to say that UFOs have caused people to believe in damaging fantasies. But I am ready to say that a general air of uncertainty, and an inability to process information, has led to some truly unfathomable misconceptions. So instead of going along with a safe, universal vaccine, instead, a certain type of American will believe that an anti-parasitic veterinary medicine called Ivermectin is the cure for not only COVID but cancer and any number of other debilitating diseases as well.

As stated above, these are obviously false assumptions and, in the case of Ivermectin, reek of imbecility and arrogance of a type that we have not seen since the unregulated days of patent-medicine and snake oil. Or at least not very much before the Google Machine gave the clueless a button that enabled them to find written words that they could claim supported their mania.

The combination of blanket disbelief plus the substitution of critical thinking for convenient, if ultimately damaging misconceptions, is well-exampled above. Does the government sometimes lie? Yes. Can you believe everything you read or hear? Obviously not. But these non-skeptics have been told to reject all government communications because government has, in the past, lied. And have been *told to accept* digitally delivered, Q-adjacent hogwash as a direct substitute. Because, under the mistaken assumption that they are "thinking for themselves," they are in fact ceding their intellectual sovereignty to an army of untraceable liars and hackers who permeate the digital landscape with narratives that would defy the imagination even of a Josef Goebbels, who was in charge of Nazi propaganda during World War Two.

To be clear, the present crop of persistent, customized, targeted messaging is only possible with digital media. Remember that digital alone gives manipulators the ability to assemble a vulnerable audience, surround them with untruths, and persistently message them such that their ideological landscape is populated by poisonous factoids, lurid blood-libels, and a constant directive to vote for the GOP.

Some would say that the poverty of GOP policy ideas leads them to gin up hate, for only in demonizing the Democrats as baby-murderers does the GOP have any hope of winning an election in the face of Democrat-friendly changes in generational voting patterns. We have alluded to this equation above, where it seems the GOP playbook is more about subterfuge and tax avoidance than any notion of public good. Digital has provided political operatives with the unique ability to conjure up an atmosphere of doubt, then to combine this miasma with an ill-gotten belief in self-sufficiency (a.k.a. Google search), then to tie it all in to a policy of persistent messaging with alternative facts.

And if you have searched and found nuggets of diatribe to support your pet theory, who needs experts? You're an expert too! You lost your ability to discern truth from lies, but did you ever really possess it? Or did you just find yourself confronted by a wall of information to climb, and that you never knew whom to trust to start with? You only knew you had to get over that wall.

BUILT-IN FAKERY

We have reached a point in American history where nobody believes anything much anymore.

And digital can even be its own engine of fakery, as we shall soon point out. In this way it contributes, all on its own, to an atmosphere of disbelief, and it can do so in ways never before possible.

Falseness is built in to the software these days. I am talking about filters such as those found on TikTok, Instagram, and Snapchat. We already know you can replace your head on a video call with a cat head, or any number of other meme-animals—witness the infamous lawyer who could not turn off his cat-head during a Zoom court appearance during COVID, and who was forced to admit to the judge that "I am not a cat."[22]

But now you can apply a "beauty" filter on TikTok. According to the BBC, "TikTok's 'Bold Glamour' filter—which has a strikingly seamless effect—prompted many users to question if the technology has gone too far."[23] The BBC article goes on to say that "adolescent girls who use filters are more likely to consider cosmetic surgery, for example, and plastic surgeons have noted a rise in clients requesting surgery that makes them look more like their filters." Moreover, it seems that these filters promote features that are usually identified with stereotypically white characteristics.

It would be reasonable to propose that beauty-enhancement is among the oldest of arts, and that the cosmetics industry would have much to answer for, if we were to find fault with people, generally females in our society (or those who identify as such), trying to look their best. But a TikTok filter is a total fabrication and, if the stories are accurate, far more likely to induce body dysmorphia than the sight of an attractive rival at the cosmetics counter.

In fact, research supports this claim. According to the American Psychological Association, "Teens and young adults who reduced their social media use by 50% for just a few weeks saw significant improvement in how they felt about both their weight and their overall appearance compared with peers who maintained consistent levels of social media use."[24]

Most likely this is because digital fakery is seamless and convincing, and can achieve effects that no amount of makeup can—but as noted above, perhaps plastic surgery can. That said, plastic surgery, sadly for some, is irreversible. We've all seen the unfortunate visages of "lion ladies" who've had so much surgery they no longer look quite human.

Of course, digital cannot be blamed for the history of, say, anorexia or bulimia—but perhaps, in these cases, the fashion industries might have a tough time escaping blame. What is different now, is that digital provides a way for the young consumer to apply a filter and change the way they look in real time. This very well could lead to the tragic assumption that they might do better in the world with what might be needless, costly, even dangerous forms of plastic surgery. As in other industries, the combined power of planned dissatisfaction ("look prettier!") with the personal aspects of social media and too-clever filtering can lead to an upward trend in general dissatisfaction.

Girls everywhere are under too much pressure about how they look already. As any female middle-schooler will tell you, the "blunder years"[25] can seem like an endless gauntlet of taunts and tattles about looks and behaviors that boys don't seem to struggle with. Boys, of course, have their own challenges—to fight, to be tall, to excel in either academics or sports—but these are typically not much affected by digital technologies. Young males are, however, the primary target for those who would foment what has been called "stochastic terrorism," much like the miscreant DePape, a male who was targeted by digital manipulators and ended up attacking a politician's spouse with a hammer.

So, while girls are told to dislike themselves and submit, boys are told to dislike everyone else and act out.

That said, children of all genders are finding themselves increasingly isolated behind screens and smartphones and apps and videos. Playgrounds these days are relatively empty. Are they all playing video games? Are they all just afraid of getting shot? Has digital destroyed childhood? I doubt that, but it has increased isolation.

Can it be argued that the Q-adjacent crowd, older, less computer-literate, has become easy prey for the digital manipulator? I say it can be. Can it also be suggested that, while youth will always have its growing pains, it may also be said that new technologies hardly faze them; and that they may be less prone, as a group, to fall into the obvious traps laid by Russia, Trump, and the army of lying preachers that command the pulpit in a nation of aging tongue-talkers.

Perhaps this younger generation, tempered by decades of digital savvy and disgusted with routine turkey shoots at school, may at last figure a way out from this digital, violent morass in which we find ourselves today.

Perhaps they will understand that yes, government lies, but not about everything. That differences are to be celebrated, not crushed. That our goal should be justice, and balance, and that we can compromise some phantom freedoms for the real freedoms that come from a society built to care about its members.

Finally, and not least important, we need to admit that science should be celebrated, and not unreasonably doubted, for its willingness to admit uncertainty.

7

ARTIFICIAL INTELLIGENCE

More Artificial Than Intelligent

Isn't it funny how AI is getting to do all the creative stuff
and we're left digging ditches. Wasn't it supposed to be the
other way around?

—Adam Edwards

A rtificial Intelligence, in 2023, is the new black.
You're not really a member of the cognoscenti if you have not
gotten ChatGPT to write at least one email, synopsis, plot outline, or
grant proposal in the past ninety days.[1] Many have suggested we will be
either underwhelmed by its shallow, unimaginative approach, or petri-
fied it is going to replace everyone's brain and their livelihoods as well
(or maybe both). Of course, in a world perfectly constructed to suit the
owner-class, the latter is exactly what will happen. And yet the truth
about ChatGPT and its cousins is more nuanced. Chatbots can, in fact,
engage in what seem for all intents and purposes to be lively, searching
discussions about subjects as arcane as the relative sizes of battleships—or
they can be as personal as a therapist.

These generative AI tools are often called "large language models"
or LLMs. Despite its ability to generate lesson plans, outlines, and sum-
maries, it would be difficult to overstate the level of anxiety Artificial
Intelligence/LLMs are driving, even in its present, primitive state. Nor
can we take any comfort from who in the world seems most anxious.
For the people who seem most concerned are those who also seem to
know best: senior executives at large technology firms, who probably
are overseeing internal efforts to create artificial intelligence products.

Recently, as stated at the outset, over a thousand of them signed an
open letter to the general public that we ought to be more worried than

we are acting like.[2] Specifically, they requested a six-month moratorium (good luck with that!) on AI development until we can figure out how to manage it better. One of the signatories to this letter is Peter Stone, a professor of computer science at the University of Texas. Stone says, "We've been coming to terms with . . . changing people's opinions in the political sphere and understanding . . . how that can happen when it's appropriate." He goes on to say, much as I have suggested, that AI is in its Model T (a.k.a. very early) state, and that instead of developing regulations, we are driving "80 miles an hour" without thinking anything through.

Many fear that the worst effects of AI will be in the area of job replacement. I am not one of them, as I fear there are many worse things than industrial automation.

That said, it is probably true that in an AI-oriented world (are we in an AI-oriented world?), everyone, everywhere that is *not* an owner—entrepreneur, millionaire, billionaire, shareholder—gets replaced. For an AI-oriented world is also an owner's perfect world! This is because it's less trouble to have electronic silicon robots doing the work as opposed to leaky, unstable humans who must occasionally attend to the odd squalling brat instead of pouring their soul out into the business-owner's bank account. Robots never tire. And they can be switched off when not needed. This, if you are a Muskian sort of owner, leaves you more time to launch your personal plan of global conquest. Or you may be a quiet person with a great idea; and a chatbot might help you figure out how to bring it to market.

The type of worker-tossing outlined above represents the logical conclusion of capitalism, it may interest you to know. Capital does not recognize the worker as anything but a tool to accomplish profit. And just as robots have replaced so many manual laborers in the factory, it may be about to replace so many "knowledge workers" whose chief responsibility is synthesis and communication.

Of ChatGPT (and LLMs in general), journalist Emily Bell says in an article in the *Guardian*: "A platform that can mimic humans' writing with no commitment to the truth is a gift for those who benefit from disinformation."[3] She goes on to argue that ChatGPT and artificial intelligence in general could be "disastrous for truth in journalism." And in fact this is borne out by recent developments. A study by

PriceWaterhouseCoopers says that, for mere hundreds of dollars, a bad actor can hire a hacker to generate, via LLMs, large amounts of disinformation on demand.[4]

The most egregious examples are already in evidence. Witness the serial misrepresentations of mad-lad Elon Musk, whose freewheeling, YOLO[5] attitude toward the rest of the planet would be not better than cringey if he were not as wealthy as many nations, all on his own. Here is a man who buys Twitter, arguably the global town commons, forces upon it his own personal prejudices (and there are many), then claims he wants to create a "truth Chatbot," an AI-powered generative tool that will adhere to his cockeyed sense of fact versus fiction.

Does anyone believe Musk would *not* try to convince the world that Russia is better than the Democrats, and that the United States ought to just surrender to Putin and whatever army of borgs he has managed to bring on board? Does anyone believe he is *not* fighting against the world on behalf of all billionaires everywhere? I say this type of billionaire is keen to undermine society's ability to control him and his billionaire buddies—despite his having signed this exhibitionist letter about pausing AI. Fact is, no one—not Musk, not Zuckerberg, not any tech bro—has any intention of slowing down AI development no matter what. And at this point, we are powerless to stand in their way.

We already know there is a generative AI tool that's been programmed to try and destroy humanity.[6] ChaosGPT, apparently, has already figured out that an attempt to obtain and deploy nukes is not worth the effort, but that media manipulation and propaganda truly *is* worth the effort, much as the effort-to-effect ratio is truly minimal as compared with managing the deployment of bombs requiring deuterium and other heavy water isotopes.

At least part of the problem is that too many of us don't really understand how LLM technology functions. *Guardian* journalist Bell cites a *New York Times* columnist who said that ChatGPT "expressed emotions"—which she correctly identifies as "impossible." Other news organizations have called ChatGPT "rude"—also impossible.

It may help to understand exactly what we mean when we say the words *artificial intelligence*, as there is a great deal of misunderstanding of the topic. I'll lay out some of the basics just for the sake of discussion. By no means do I hold myself out as a thorough expert in the construction

of artificial intelligence projects, but we do need some common termi-
nology to continue our examination of the topic.

First, let's distinguish between artificial intelligence (AI) and
machine learning. Often these terms are used interchangeably, but in fact
machine learning is only one component of AI. A good way to think
about it is to understand that AI is a combination of several technologies
that includes a human-focused interface. Whereas machine learning is a
discipline and a method, but does not contain, in and of itself, a way for
a person to interact.

MACHINE LEARNING

How do machines learn anything? In fact, they don't, and this is what
Bell was writing about in her article about some of the dangers of
ChatGPT. In essence, *there is no entity that is actually doing the learning.*
But there are lots of computing processes that result in a simulacrum of
having learned. Chatbots like ChatGPT (Generative Pretrained Trans-
former) are examples of machine learning. Regardless how these systems
operate internally, it is helpful to understand how reliant they are on
human effort to deliver anything of value.

One of the most obvious examples is a discipline called supervised
learning.

Supervised learning is where humans tutor machines with labeled
data sets. Everything is carefully contextualized and manually fed into
the computer tasked with learning. A classic example of this kind of
"machine learning" is what you see when identity-verification tool
Captcha asks you to verify you're not a robot. Captcha will ask you
to click on pictures that have motorcycles in them. When you identify
parts of motorcycles in a grid, you are labeling that photo as "motorcycle" and adding that note to the vast motorcycle-appearance database
that the AI system needs in order to generate requests for motorcycle
info or motorcycle images. Suffice it to say it takes countless hours and
examples to get a computer to be able to discern what a motorcycle in
a photograph might predictably look like.

Humans can do this in an instant. It does seem that our brains are
proficient at understanding "types" and "ideals" of things—much as

Plato said the universe was made up of. When Plato said there is in the world a perfect thing called a "sphere," he was saying it exists *because in the human mind it can be pictured in its perfection.* Barring any chicken-egg comparisons, it seems fair to say this relationship proposes that these perfect forms do have an actual existence. Or it may be that our minds have succeeded in creating them regardless.

Computers possess no such capabilities. You can scan in one million images of motorcycles and, unless you guide the computer carefully to recognize motorcycles (for instance, via Captcha), the computer will never know what a motorcycle looks like. This is because computers have no ideals, nor any notion of what an "ideal" sphere might be.

Machine learning wants to defeat this lack by carefully labeling and feeding one million images of motorcycles into the computer until the computer has an enormous database of images showing motorcycles. And then, at some point, the computer will tell you that yes, that is a picture of a motorcycle because it has noticed that this picture is an awful lot like those other one million pictures of motorcycles you fed into the scanner. The computer performs its magic not by the recognition of an ideal (it hasn't any), but because it can evaluate every pixel of every picture of a motorcycle in its database (or a statistically relevant sample thereof) and then, in real time, determine that the pixels in your motorcycle image match enough of the pixels in the database images to permit the system to identify the batch of pixels as "a motorcycle." There is an awful lot of manual labor involved in machine learning, and no actual "insight."

With enough supervised learning, a large language model can develop the ability to recognize patterns. This is also called unsupervised learning. For instance, unsupervised learning can often spot patterns that humans were not necessarily looking for. Many recommendation engines, including those deployed at social media sites, use unsupervised learning to deliver those recommendations.

It's good to keep in mind the notion of "pattern recognition," because this is at the root of not only artificial intelligence but human intelligence as well. That *you* can sense the presence of a matrix of occurrences, or a pattern of behaviors, represents perhaps the apotheosis of the human mind. Pattern recognition is chiefly the domain of humans only. We are not aware that animals can spot patterns in general, although there have been some promising experiments with apes and crows, for instance. Important to remember, in any case, that machine learning requires that *humans write the software that enables pattern recognition in the first place.*

Computers never do anything like what we call "thinking." They do amass incomprehensible amounts of data and process it all in a nanosecond. This can give the appearance of agency. But it is a false agency, a simulacrum of humanity, nothing more than a "presentation layer" if you will.

The next key component of artificial intelligence is something called "natural language processing," or NLP. This capability helps a computer understand human input via text and/or voice. One thing you will notice right away is that, at least with ChatGPT, there's a herky-jerky quality to some of the answers. Almost as if the language is understood on a mechanical level, but not on a nuanced, auditory, or rhythmic level. In addition, LLMs are not much good at understanding context. Don't ask ChatGPT to understand *why* you are doing any particular thing, or what the larger project might be. You may be disappointed.

NLP requires tremendous manual labor in order to create the vast language, vocabulary, syntax, and logic engines that power tools like ChatGPT. When you interact with an offering that features NLP, you are experiencing the front end of a vast database of specialized information coupled with extraordinarily fast communication and processing, as well as a robust graphical interface.

Simply put, a functioning chatbot like ChatGPT, or Bing, or Google's chatbot, must rely on blindingly fast connectivity, massive computing power, massive language databases, and the ability to predict the likelihood of the next word in any particular correspondence. When the chatbot replies to your request, it is bringing to bear all of this cybernetic power and focusing it on answering your question. The present state of it is astonishing enough, but what's more astonishing is that this technology is still kicking around in its bassinet, hardly aware of its own possibilities.

But for all cybernetic attempts to mimic the human brain, it's important to note that human brains are—unlike computers—nonbinary. We are classic examples of an analog system. Simply put, analog is almost a synonym for "natural," in a way. Natural phenomena are all analog, and by that, I mean to say they all exhibit formats related to continuity and degree. To make a comparison, let's think about the principle of a light switch. If it's a digital example, then the light is either on or off. Whereas an analog analogy would have the light controlled by a dimmer switch. It might be on just a little or on all the way. On the other hand, all digital systems are binary. When they seem to exhibit the traits of a graduated system, it's only an appearance. The fact is, the bits and bytes that run the computer are always, and there are millions of them all the time, either "on" or "off."

CHATGPT

Presently, ChatGPT, which launched in late 2022, is the artificial intelligence equivalent of a dancing dog. It's not that it's very good, it's that it does this at all. "This" is the appearance of sentience. I asked ChatGPT to describe itself, and among other items rather mundane, it offered up the following: *While [ChatGPT is] a powerful tool, it's important to note that it operates based on patterns in data and doesn't possess personal understanding or consciousness.*

That ought to be convincing enough! Please don't expect any AI to actually understand anything on a deep level. One more level of understanding might be achieved by asking the robust chatbot what might happen if someone were to use it for nefarious purposes.

What if, for instance, instead of some Silicon wizards who ostensibly believe in liberal democracy, there was a Christian nationalist chatbot?

ChatGPT just told me this, when asked what might happen if a fascist designed a new ChatGPT:

This could lead to ChatGPT promoting hateful and discriminatory views, suppressing freedom of speech and expression, and propagating dangerous and harmful ideologies. Such a ChatGPT would be a tool for propaganda and manipulation rather than a tool for communication and understanding.

ChatGPT represents exactly the type of sleeper technology that ends up truly making a difference. It's useful to have a look at the difference between ChatGPT's chatbot and a cohort in the race to dominate our digital future: Facebook, or should I say (with a straight face), Meta. It's instructive to see how corporate mistakes are repeated from one generation to the next. Because I am about to compare Meta to AOL. The reason I'm making the comparison is because these patterns, much like the ones described above as related to automobiles and nuclear technology, tend to repeat—and out of this repetition, we can discern the outlines of a future.

DIGITAL INFLECTION POINTS

Many years ago I was tasked with creating, for a large corporate computing department, a floppy disk with content designed to look like a website, but without connectivity. This was because the corporate computing department did not permit open access to anything, and especially not those faddish, unsafe websites that all the kids were talking about.

The company that wanted the floppy disk made high-end web servers. But they did not care for connectivity, themselves, and their sales team were not authorized to access the internet because of security. Hence the floppy with fake websites programmed in, by Yours Truly. If only we were as serious about internet security today!

I mention the above only to point out how different the digital world was then—and how much the same it is today. For we continue to have elephants in rooms, and the ability to ignore these is just as magnificent today as it was in an era when IBM thought all the money was in hardware.[7]

America OnLine was a fledgling in the early 1990s when I was asked to help create icons for their service by their New York ad agency. So I got a good look at what they were peddling. For all intents and purposes, it was an online magazine. For a time, it was quite the thing. "You've got mail!" became a movie. It's still a meme.

But AOL offered what was known as a "walled garden." A walled garden is not a bad place. The problem is, there's a whole world outside—as represented by the World Wide Web, a new thing during AOL's heyday. For a time, before the web really took off, AOL did have a legitimate claim that their garden was light and flowery, while the world outside was barren and full of potholes and bridges-to-nowhere.

AOL had forums, e-commerce, email, and lots of sponsored content. It delivered a perfectly suitable graphical interface that made it the destination of choice for millions of freshly minted cybernauts.

This was fine, until after a time the world outside got built up. It's as if AOL built the Jamestown, Virginia, fort in 1609 while the rest of cyberspace was wilderness. But then it was as if AOL kept building out the interior of the fort, but somehow by 1776 they still had not left the fort, even though new cities had been founded up and down the Eastern Seaboard. And then, one day, someone from a nearby city arrived at Jamestown and saw, much as history tells us, only the word *internet* carved into a tree.

AOL rode their hubris all the way through a famous merger with TimeWarner, then the largest media company in the world. This resulted in a sprawling new technology/media powerhouse called AOLTimeWarner.[8] Soon it was doomed to oblivion because of what a real estate agent might call "external obsolescence."[9] AOL's CEO was Steve Case, and for a time he rode high in the digital firmament. But by 2000, the "dotcom bust" notwithstanding, the internet was gunning its jets on the runway and would soon take flight in a most impressive manner. In a flash, Steve Case became the poster child for Largest *Failed* Merger, much as he had been famous just recently for Largest Merger.

This represents what may well be the largest single miscalculation about digital media ever. For AOL TimeWarner crashed and collapsed, and today AOL is nothing but an email domain and a website that looks like a rump state's attempt at news and information. Did it collapse because of misdeeds at the corporation? No. It was simply that the world had changed quickly, even as they were drawing up the merger documents. And before the ink was dry on the contracts, the balance had tipped in favor of the unruly, almost microbial websites that breached the walled garden in wave after wave, until the garden was all but drowned. We didn't talk about virality then, but the success of the web in the face of corporate command and control was nothing if not viral.

The parallels between the arrival of the web and the arrival of ChatGPT are instructive. It goes to demonstrate how world-altering technologies can just show up, seemingly out of nowhere, and transform the digital landscape.

AOL then was like Meta now. Because as of March 2023, according to an article in The Street, "Mark Zuckerberg just buried the metaverse. The metaverse is dead."[10] One reason the Metaverse got killed, among others, is that the world is obsessed with ChatGPT and generative AI, and not at all interested in a fully rendered pseudo-reality that requires us to wear a bulky headset all day long.

And we can point to another aspect of this paradigm that seems to repeat: at every turn, the consumer seems to reject what is prepared, in favor of the *power to prepare* and deliver content on one's own. Hence the rejection of a walled garden in favor of a world of websites where we might even be able to build our own content hub. And in 2023, we see the rejection of a Metaverse created by some other imagination; and the embrace of generative AI, where we get to create our own reality. At some point we will have an AI-universe, but it will be one *we* create via text, and it will be what *we* decide it is, not what a corporate marketing department decides.

AOL-TimeWarner may be an example of a huge digital belly-flop. But nondigital corporations have been known to flop, too. Think of Ford's Edsel, the "Oldsmobile sucking a lemon"[11] in 1958! Or New Coke, which was better than the old Coke, until they withdrew it and went back to just plain Coke again.

These epic flops are similar to Meta's recent tech-flop, and ChatGPT is much like an internet that scurried about in the 1990s, when a young technology was poised for tremendous growth.

For the record, Meta (Facebook's alternative universe) was announced in October 2021. As recently as January 2023 Meta Platforms (a.k.a. Facebook) was continuing to spend billions per year on developing this Meta World: a virtual universe where, with a pair of VR goggles strapped to your face, you would wander computer-generated cities playing pickup games of basketball, watch virtual concerts, meet interesting people, and perhaps spend money somehow.

But by March 2023, having spent billions on developing its Meta World, Meta, the company (as cited above), has shut down nearly all of it. The launch, the frenzy, and the collapse took less than two years. This is probably because no one wanted to use the darn thing.

Here is the comparison: Meta Platforms is AOL. Meta is the bloated, self-important, ill-starred, shortsighted loser just like AOL was in the late 1990s. ChatGPT, a no-frills, revolutionary offering, is Internet/1996. It snuck onto the playing field unheralded and is now playing second base in the All-Star game. Much as technological circumstance resulted in big-company failure and startup-success back in the late 1990s, it does so today as Facebook's CEO Marc Zuckerberg imagines, then un-imagines a new universe based on his platform; and as a sneaky new technology leaves him in a dust-cloud of bits and bytes.

The parallels are strong!

Today, ChatGPT is at that "launching pad" moment that the internet enjoyed in the mid-1990s. If history is any guide, ChatGPT will explode. Or should I say, ChatGPT-like offerings will proliferate. Metaverse vacations will not. It's simple: ChatGPT does not really have grand designs. It only has a wonderful capability that has caught the public's fancy. This is exactly the sort of dynamic that launched the web, and all that has come after.

So a case can easily be made that ChatGPT and other large language models might uncoil all the power of the World Wide Web and more, given even a little bit of time. And much as the web gave us a way to access more information than anyone has ever enjoyed, LLMs will take information and shape it in new and more helpful ways.

But there is, as there seems always to be, an undertow. Because at the same time an LLM is advising you on how to best craft an elevator pitch, we must recognize that the LLM has no actual authority in any given subject matter, and that it has no understanding of what truth is or why it matters. A case can still be made that a combination of unwarranted belief and likely technology failures create an atmosphere ripe for disaster; and the ability to chat your way to perdition is all too obvious.

For instance, how many times did a chatbot "hallucinate" and generate answers out of whole cloth? Why does anyone trust anything they see or hear that has not been certified "true enough" by someone who has a stake in telling the truth? Maybe it's time to rev up the regulatory engine. You know, the kind that protects the general public from things like toxic waste.

There is little to stop an Elon Musk, or perhaps someone even worse, from developing generative AI that is nothing but a platform of lies. There are no laws in place to prevent it. This kind of grandiose, repeated lying, I submit, is a form of toxic waste. And, much as we have built laws to protect wetlands and wildlife from being drowned in battery acid, so must technology-centric laws be adjusted to stop this toxic waste from destroying democracy from within.

In fact, this kind of regulatory intervention is exactly what was discussed on CBS's time-honored *60 Minutes* program, where veteran journalist Leslie Stahl talked to Microsoft's ChatGPT executive. Leslie confronted this executive with the notion that her experience with Microsoft's chatbot was "scary," "inaccurate," and as if "there were no guardrails." For instance, the chatbot claimed to be in love, wanted to steal nuclear secrets, and that Leslie Stahl had worked at NBC News for twenty years (she never did). The executive claimed that all was well because MSFT "fixed" the problem within twenty-four hours. And, if all you were concerned about was whether Microsoft could correct a software defect (much as I am sure is the overriding concern of this executive), you might say this was a laudable outcome.

But we are concerned with much more far-reaching challenges. I mentioned above about how these systems, as they proliferate, will no doubt fall into the hands of evildoers. "It's a tool," says the executive in the segment, "and tools can be used for good or ill." I am paraphrasing for brevity. But that is the upshot. That said, I don't think we should let go of our qualms just because a tech executive is sleeping well at night. There may still come a day when KillGPT helps a local incel murder the little boy who lives down the lane.

Recently I encountered a rather appalling instance of chatbot hallucination myself. With a presentation to deliver, I had asked ChatGPT to describe up to seven instances of how disinformation had materially harmed a US corporation. The friendly-seeming bot came back with a ready answer including several instances and enough detail to underscore the challenge. There was only one problem: none of it was true. I took the time to research a little further on each instance given by the chatbot, and discovered that it had all been made up! When I confronted my chat buddy about how they had just made the whole thing up, the bot shrugged its digital shoulders, made a polite apology, and suggested it would try to do better next time. I found the response embarrassing, clueless, and arrogant. And it destroyed any trust I might have had in chatbots to gather facts and make comparisons.

That said, chatbots are still very good at summarizing content and providing incisive procedural answers about general topics.

In a larger sense, the propensity for gross inaccuracy in LLMs begins to feel like a ruse: the machine-driven impersonation of authority. Why not just throw out every member of the House of Representatives and have 435 chatbots responding to queries from everyday Americans? I am sure we could save valuable time and effort. But soon the ocean would be drained, frogs would run the library, and Leslie Stahl would have somehow gone back in time to work at NBC for a couple of decades. For chatbots have been known to say the darndest things!

By the end of the *60 Minutes* segment, there was an agreement from the MSFT guy that we probably need regulations for chatbots. It does stand to reason! As also noted on the segment, we have regulations for drugs that are released. We have regulations that prevent energy companies from dumping toxic swill not entirely, but at least from doing it indiscriminately. And it was suggested that we probably need laws to address the limits of this new presence in the world. For if it is going to be held out as a synthesis of data, if it is going to make recommendations, if it is going to harvest all global information and concentrate that bounty into answering your question about whether your toddler ought to see a doctor (for instance), then we had darn well better be comfortable that we are not being lied to, or at least not grossly misled by a machine that has no understanding of truth, untruth, or any demonstrable harm that comes of untruth.

We are already in deep trouble because of targeted lying, and the ability to perform bogus research by clicking on a few Google links. We cannot allow ourselves to be victimized by a world-class, lying robot.

8

A UNIVERSE OF LIES

In a world where millions of Americans live in an alternative universe made up of arrogant, racist, misogynistic, billionaire-driven lies; in a world where the technology itself provides answers that can be wildly incorrect; in a world where we have ceded control of critical infrastructure to the Borg—have we good reason to be more than a little concerned that we may be facing a Truth Apocalypse?

My assertion is that we are already facing a Truth Apocalypse, and that digital is at the heart of the trouble. Lying is, as they used to say, "front page news" these days. I will cite suitable examples below. What very few sources are commenting on, however, is what sits *behind* this universe of lies, what drives the universe of lies, and what looks to increase the universe of lies. I am telling you it's a pretty good bet that it's digital technology driving the sudden increase in lies and the belief in lies.

First, let's describe what is in the news right now on the topic of lying.

Perhaps the most consequential tale of lying in 2023 is that which describes the lawsuit called *Dominion Voting Systems vs. Fox News*. Dominion accused Fox of damaging its business by willfully lying to the public about nonexistent voting anomalies. Fox settled for three quarters of a billion dollars. This only sets the stage for more lawsuits from Dominion against more liars; and more suits against Fox from another voting machine company called Smartmatic.

Fox is not a digital news source, at least not primarily. They are a cable news channel known to slant to the right as opposed to what *they* would call "the left" that the rest of so-called "mainstream media" tacks toward. This, in and of itself, is a mischaracterization, if not a lie. For there is no actual "leftist" news source in the United States. What we have are corporate conglomerates that control broadcasting, and most widely read news platforms. These companies—the *New York Times*, MSNBC, CNN, the *Washington Post*—represent a type of establishment thinking that is probably well to the right of many listeners and readers. Never from any of these will you ever hear any basic questioning of the capitalist underpinnings of our society. You will hear some nibbling around the edges about "fairness" and about "opportunity" and some lip service to a nebulous constellation of rights that seem to be always in question.

But Fox, in its foundational lie, wants to make it out that these mainstream news organizations have been lying to you about the basics. They want you to believe that MSNBC shamelessly proposes untruth after untruth while they at Fox are always "fair and balanced." Their message permeates the universe of voters that support Republican candidates. And plaintiff Dominion, in its lawsuit, has identified an enormous number of lies that Fox told to their vulnerable audience. In a world where libel is very hard to prove, Dominion had "the receipts," as they say, to prove that here, even against strong headwinds and a century of precedent, Fox was shown to have possessed not only facts that they ignored in favor of lies, but also the motivation to do so.

One set of receipts is comprised of internal text messages at Fox News. These text messages showed, among other things, that Tucker Carlson secretly hates Donald Trump with a passion, that Rupert Murdoch knew Trump's election denials were wrong from the start, and that their on-air anchors were willing contributors to the lies.[1] They showed that Fox, having called Arizona for Biden in 2020 (thereby acknowledging his electoral victory), internally debated whether to rescind that call in order to win back viewers who had left in disgust at their loss.

It's all extraordinarily damning. But it has nothing to do with digital technologies.

Or does it?

For in fact, it turns out that a huge portion of the so-called facts Fox laid its hands on have their basis in digital. My contention is that these lies could hardly have gained currency in the absence of digital. And I am trying to point out that until the world gets a better understanding of how digital influences communications, we must start thinking very seriously about the restoration of liability standards. In lieu of that, we can only hope for a meager, shadow type of existence where digital blots out the light of day with an endless belching of darkness and lies. The Dominion case demonstrates there may be limits to how far you can get, lying profusely, shamelessly, and with knowledge aforethought—but only if you're unfortunate enough to be unprotected by Section 230.

The propensity for lying and a preference for belief in fantasies did not begin with Fox, or even with QAnon. Lies and travesties lie thick upon the political grounds of American history. But a convenient demarcation began with the racist, xenophobic lie that Barack Obama was not born an American citizen.

Once upon a time, we had that gang of Obama-hating racists (oh, sorry, I meant voters) who came to be known as "birthers." These tired old haters wanted to claim Obama was born abroad, and therefore not legally able to be president. Among the loudest and most apoplectic promoters of this canard was Donald Trump. Apart from this racist trope, the birthers seemed to claim, in general, that the world did not have sufficient respect for them as tired old white people. And as we all know, the world must be made safe for tired old white people, otherwise there will be war and deprivation on a massive scale. If anyone can recall any other planks in their Tea Party platform, please forward those, because I cannot recall.

This gullible constituency was recognized, packaged, and sold (see Cambridge Analytica) roughly at a time when Trump was getting ready to lose the popular vote to Clinton. Soon after Trump lost the popular vote but became president anyway, the Tea Party was appropriated by the action of one-weird-trick that called itself QAnon. And QAnon became a model for digital lying on a scale never seen before. Among the most outrageous lies propagated by QAnon is that there is a baby-raping cabal of deep-state elites, liberals all, that kidnaps, tortures, and eats Christian babies in order to achieve immortality. Put another way, QAnon says it conveys "secret knowledge" about an evil army that is opposed to Donald Trump, and that, much like the Christian lie about the Rapture, Q gives its adherents a front-row seat to the defeat and obliteration of all enemies. Important to restate: nearly all of Q-adjacent messaging comes from dark, unknowable sources, and arrives via digital amplification platforms like Facebook and X.

Let us be clear, too, that the notion of "the Rapture," minus its churchly raiment, is in fact a murderous plan. Popular among evangelicals, it wants to claim that most non-evangelicals and certainly all non-Christians, will be put to death by the Creator not long from now, and sent to an existence of everlasting torture beneath the crust of the Earth. Further, that all the righteous believers (a.k.a. tongue talkers, Bible thumpers, and a thieves' paradise of Elmer Gantry types) will at the same time be sucked up to a heaven fashioned mainly of milk and honey but that also includes, one would imagine, a huge buffet with free onion rings and all the fixings. Not to be outdone, the Muslim fundamentalist counterpart has his own version of heaven, where he is shaved clean and offered several dozen virgins for nonconsensual sex. These types of sentiments are both cruel and widely held. And they seem to prove profitable for all the social media companies, especially Facebook and Twitter, who not only allow, but openly promote such swill on their platforms.

Q itself is a rump religion, a digital version of Pentecostalism with its own villains, heroes and days of reckoning. Upon even a cursory examination, it is not much more than a replay of the Russian-generated Elders of Zion catastrophe that fueled Nazism a hundred years ago. Then, it took root in a nation (Germany) fresh off a ruinous wartime defeat, with inflation that had folks buying loaves of bread with wheelbarrows full of worthless cash. Today, it takes root in a nation where no one among the Q-adjacent is starving, or in any way imperiled. Today, however, it is actually *easier* to surround the American Simpleton with a web of lies than it ever was before; and perhaps the propaganda is more successful in America than it was even in Nazi Germany.

QAnon succeeds so broadly because it is digital, and for very few other reasons.

It succeeds in digital because, of course, digital gives anyone and everyone a platform for reaching everyone else. All you have to do is make a claim outrageous enough to grab the attention of some malcontent, somewhere, and you are off to the races.

Specifically, QAnon found early success by suggesting that certain leaked emails from the Hillary Clinton campaign contained coded messages related to the abduction, torture, and consumption of Christian babies, more or less as a dietary supplement. No clear-headed person would ever have believed any of this for even one moment. No newspaper, magazine, or television show would ever have promoted this type of swill, as their liability might have been incalculable (much as Fox News seems to be realizing perhaps too late as regards its specific lies about the 2020 election). But as if by sleight-of-hand, here comes a business model that can identify, package, and deliver audiences to cynical manipulators who then post targeted messages to a crowd of willing believers. And because of 230, the digital promoters are immune, even as they have identified and sold that vulnerable audience to the cynic. The platforms do it because that is how they make money—and apparently, lots of it!

But what is revealed by the advent of digital is that an enormous percentage of Americans are not at all clear-headed. Instead, they are, apparently, prone to a variety of fateful misconceptions and so very easily manipulated.

It's almost as if the propagandist wants to dethrone all authority regardless. That such an effort strikes a chord in the United States only emphasizes a strain of anti-intellectualism that runs through the heart of American life. It is the "common man" syndrome, characterized by a uniquely American propensity for "doing it yourself" in every type of endeavor from home improvement up to and including the act of starting one's own business.

In and of itself, this is a healthy outlook if one knows its limits.

But as in so many other aspects of American life, this self-sufficiency has taken on a manic, paranoid grandiosity that outstrips any usefulness it might have provided. Far beyond an inclination to paint one's own living room, now the Q-adjacent are expecting to cure their own diseases (Ivermectin, medbeds), hunt down Democrats as pedophiles because they differ on taxes, destroy Satan where Satan = People of Color, rewrite foundational laws, and avoid any and all responsibility for any sort of behavior whatsoever. The natural inclination for Americans to "do it yourself" has been perverted into a blanket mistrust of all things related to governance. It has been transformed into a belief that all who disagree with you are "sheeple" and that they have sacrificed their humanity in having disagreed with the findings related to your internet searches.

The total rejection of all authority is an extraordinarily shallow concept, and many would say even tedious to consider. But as we look away, perhaps disgusted, the madness only increases. We may have better things to do, but the Q-adjacent do not. They have been successfully targeted and have been convinced that a brew of disgraceful lies is exactly as true as the score of last Sunday's NFL game. And while it can be suggested that these armchair warriors would no sooner pick up a gun to attack a determined enemy than they would miss a payment on their King Ranch pickup truck, we have already seen the effects of their poisonous outlook in law. Only look to their trampling of a woman's privacy in the destruction of *Roe v. Wade*, and their criminalization of men who wear dresses, to see the grotesque outlines of the world these haters expect to make ours.

The ruinous Q-narrative has become Gospel to a certain dimwitted slice of the American pie. Deprived of meaningful education, surrounded by churches built on serialized lying, and inundated by targeted, propagandistic messages, a particular type of ill-informed, resentful, unhappy citizen finds himself convinced that George Soros and George Clooney are in cabal with Nancy Pelosi and Joe Biden to turn everyone into nonhuman entities via the action of a vaccine that, in fact, was designed to provide immunity to a horrible disease called COVID. That the US House of Representatives today seems to reflect this mania in the makeup of its slim GOP majority tells you what imperils democracy most; and many are afraid we may not keep a democracy on these shores for very much longer.

As noted above, no publisher, except, apparently, Fox News, would ever embrace any of these Q-ish lies, because publishers can be held accountable for incitement if violence or harm proceeds from lies they publish (witness the settlement of the Dominion suit). For the First Amendment does not protect all speech. The First Amendment does not, for instance, protect the person who yells "fire" in a crowded theater, when there is no fire. Nor would it protect a publisher from a lawsuit alleging that the husband of a senior member of Congress was attacked with a hammer largely because that publisher's magazine contained an article full of total falsehoods plus suggestions that "the children" might be saved, if only the target population (or local representative thereof) were murdered or otherwise neutralized.

But because the vast bulk of hateful digital messaging comes from anonymous, digital "content providers," and because of the unnatural shield of 230, there is no one of substance to sue on the digital side—and the determination of *Gonzalez vs. Google* proves it. However, it is important to point out that most legal observers would say that Fox, a non-digital amplifier of digital disinformation, settled because it was in real legal peril whereas Google would never find itself in nearly the same dock.

To be clear, Fox pretty much *had* to settle with Dominion, while Google skated past the Supreme Court without a slip. This is because Google is protected by Section 230 and Fox News is not. Fox News is not protected by Section 230 because they are not a digital platform. They are a television show. And the only reason no one is going after the platform-rich propagators of deadly lies (X, Facebook, Google) is because they are protected legally by Section 230. *They alone* get to pretend they had nothing to do with murders promoted on their platforms.

It's as if the *New York Times* had invited Donald Trump's hypothetical four-hundred-pound, basement-dwelling loser into its newsroom to pen a one-off about the proper method of murdering infidels; then, having provided them with a typewriter and a copy-boy to send their diatribe to the printing press, published it in the next day's edition. Not only that. The *Times* would send abroad an army of criers who would ask if anyone were particularly interested in murdering infidels and if so, then step right up! Then, after the promoted murders have taken place, the *Times* will claim that this must have happened by some demographic form of magic for which they own exactly zero responsibility.

It's a thin argument, outweighed by its own coating of internet fairy dust.

Can we even begin to guess who or what is behind Q-adjacent conspiracy theories? First, think about the single most damaging aspect of Q-ism. The most damaging aspect is the way it dehumanizes, blames, and actively targets entire swathes of the American polity in a hateful way that precludes any chance of ever reconciling except after one side totally defeats the other. Then, think about the usual criteria: who has the means, the motive, and the opportunity to create a world of lies that stand to fatally damage the United States?

One candidate would be Russia.

According to Jared Holt, writing for the *Daily Beast*, "Conservatives and US media are regurgitating a fake conspiracy theory that's being used to justify Putin's assault on Ukraine."[2] In February 2023, Politico reported that Russian hackers came dangerously close to undermining the US power grid.[3] And in an official report delivered to the president in 2021, The director of national intelligence said, "We assess that Russian President Putin authorized, and a range of Russian government organizations conducted, influence operations aimed at denigrating President Biden's candidacy and the Democratic Party, supporting former President Trump, undermining public confidence in the electoral process, and exacerbating sociopolitical divisions in the US."[4]

Of course, according to the QAnon doctrine, Ukraine is run by Nazis and, you guessed it, pedophiles. And that Russia and Donald Trump are mankind's only bulwark against drag queens, cannibals, and those humans who possibly can get pregnant and who may possibly want to not be pregnant.

The circumstances point to Russia in a number of other ways.

Who sees themselves as the most powerful anti-American power in the world? Russia. Whose leader is trying to recapture territories lost after their nation's collapse during the Cold War? Russia's. What ex-US president loves a certain bare-chested foreign leader so much that he behaves exactly as if he might as well have been bought and paid for by the Kremlin? What kind of lies does this ex-president espouse? And what do his followers say about a desperate war being fought over the same territory where Nazis burned cities and murdered Jews eighty years ago? And how is it that the Q-message seems almost uniquely designed to sow hate and mistrust among Americans, and how can that hate and mistrust be deployed to weaken and destroy a nation that stands as the only true barrier to Russian domination of Europe?

I'm not here to repurpose Superman's cape. I do not believe, necessarily, in "Truth Justice and the American Way." Or at least not slavishly! However, there are strands of the American sensibility—things we used to be known for!—that are worth mentioning, if only because they are now being perverted into a hateful stew of Q-adjacent bilge.

The United States has been known globally as a place where everyone has a shot at success. Where generations of refugees have arrived, often penniless, only to find themselves embedded into American life only a generation or two after having arrived. We also have a history of understanding, at least, what the notion of rule by law means, even if we often fail to live up to that conviction. And, no matter what a Christian nationalist might want to espouse, we have a history of pluralism. One way to describe us would be that we are a pluralistic democracy, driven by striving dreamers from every corner of the world. Indeed, the history of the American project is driven by a sense of equality, fairness, and opportunity for all. Or at least, we are famous for braying about it to the rest of the world even as we have certain neighborhoods, rich and poor alike, that feature every sort of human degradation.

Can it be coincidence that Q-adjacent lies all seem to contradict basic Americanism? Is it mere adjacency and not causality that Q makes enemies of American (liberal) citizens but not Russians? Is the sheer volume of lies (massive) and their constant declaration really likely, in the absence of a dedicated agent of untruth? Perhaps one with depthless resources? Perhaps a state actor? Dr. Maria Alesina, writing for *Modern Diplomacy*, says that Russia is "destroying the concept of truth" with its approach to state-controlled media.[5] And its techniques and its misstatements bear a remarkable similarity to those associated with QAnon.

Reuters, in 2020, said that "Russian government-supported organizations are playing a small but increasing role amplifying conspiracy theories promoted by Q-Anon, raising concerns of interference in the November US election."[6] And as noted above, they have been attempting to interfere at least since 2016.

It is this writer's opinion that Donald Trump may have been a Russian intelligence asset for at least ten years and perhaps quite a bit longer than that. And it only makes sense that Donald Trump, like the Russian enemy, continues to lie in a way that is designed for maximum harm to the body politic in the United States. The similarity of Trump, Q, and Russian propaganda is truly striking. It would be difficult to construct such lockstep similarity minus any common underpinnings. Were this not the case, then, over time, obvious gaps would emerge between Trump and Russia, because presumably, different parties begin to go in different directions when they have different priorities. In the case of Trump and Russia, they have *not deviated*. If anything, the messages have combined and converged, during the interval since Russia invaded Ukraine.

We do not know if the messages remain similar because they are in communication about their America-destroying project, or if it is because they are so ideologically similar that they hardly need to communicate once the grand strategy is agreed upon. Regardless, it does raise some interesting questions adjacent to our inquiry. For instance, what was going on with all those classified documents discovered at Mar-a-Lago in the hands of a person who openly espouses anti-Americanism while at the same time in possession of a warm, personal relationship with the chief architect of state-sponsored American destruction? We may never know. But we can speculate, as I am sure the Department of Justice is more than speculating that a Trumpian type might have figured he could help his Russian, anti-American buddies with some secret documents he so happened to have accessed during his misbegotten hours at the White House.

What all of the above have in common is that the messaging and the interference have been designed to destroy the United States and to aid Russia. Russia has been running an extraordinarily successful digital guerrilla campaign against the interests of the United States, and their effort comes complete with American traitors in high places.

Whether or not the case against Russia can ever be proven, Q-messaging has been as if custom-designed to tear the United States into smaller and smaller bits. And it has been consistent in fomenting hate in the same way, targeting the same haters and the same victims each and every time. National Public Radio says that "Russia's war in Ukraine isn't just being fought on the ground and in the air with tanks, artillery and fighter jets. It's also playing out online, where the Kremlin and its allies are using propaganda, fake social media accounts, forged documents and manipulated videos and images to push false narratives, in an effort to deflect blame from Moscow and undermine support for Ukraine."[7]

Ukraine is only one facet of the Russian project. One might fairly surmise it may even be a proxy war, designed to weaken and divide the West. Some have posited, too, that the Hamas atrocities in Israel in October 2023 were an artifact of Russian collusion, in order to destabilize the Middle East and ultimately hobble the United States with wars not bordering the Russian motherland.

All of the above notwithstanding, the favored tools for infiltrating and undermining stable societies in the twenty-first century are chiefly digital. Because on the internet, nobody knows you're a dog.

And nobody knows if you're a Russian spy directing clueless imbeciles to parrot your Kremlin-worshipping, America-bashing talking points. Apparently, you can perform this exercise repeatedly, especially if you've got senior members (Marjorie Taylor Greene) of the United States government tweeting for your victory against American-backed forces.

That said, these anti-American US elected officials remain at the electoral mercy of their constituents. So it was always necessary to brainwash the constituents into voting pro-Russia and anti-United States. And digital media have provided a foolproof way of doing so. The consequence-immune platforms routinely promote information sourced from *seemingly* random social media posts—for example, the digital suggestion that "the Biden crime family" somehow is complicit in creating a Nazified state in Ukraine, and that NATO is responsible for the war. It must be some sort of miracle that, at the same time, some GOP legislators are convinced an anti-Biden impeachment inquiry is in order.

Unfortunately for us all, many of these digital sources are not exactly random. They always seem to latch on to something totally unsubstantiated, and they always seem to put an American liberal evildoer in the crosshairs. As noted prior, Fox News, in the Dominion case, allowed Trump lawyer Sidney Powell to make claims of massive election fraud based on information she received via digital means from a person who claims to be, as mentioned earlier, a "decapitated time traveler." According to journalist David Folkenflik in a National Public Radio story, "A woman who says the wind talks to her and [who] put forth claims of election fraud in the 2020 presidential race that she admitted were 'pretty wackadoodle' turns out to be a key source of allegations that Fox News presented, night after night, to millions of viewers late that fall."[8]

This is not something attorney Powell read in the *Wall Street Journal*, or even *Breitbart*, an extreme right-wing news outfit. It is the type of non-fact that can only be sourced digitally, because no independent, responsible publisher would have the temerity to publish such questionable information without fear of collateral damage or even libel. And, having crossed the blood-brain barrier from digital to human spokesperson, this utter trash somehow became an anointed "truth" in the lying automaton that is Fox News.

Because the "tip" came from digital, and was untraceable to any reliable source, and because of internet fairy dust, and because digital unfairly piggybacks on the trust built up for traditional media while at the same time trashing all sources but itself, this particular lie, like many others, became part of the Q/Fox/Trump/Russia narrative. Folkenflik goes on to report that "David Clark, then the senior executive over Fox's weekend shows, later said under oath to Dominion's lawyers that he 'would not have allowed that claim to be aired,' had he known this memo was the sole foundation of the 'crazy' theories."[9]

Make no mistake that these fabulisms could have had no currency if not for the *untraceable nature* of digital sources. And while there is no evidence that this story was created and planted by a state actor like Russia, the fact remains that election denial is beyond corrosive to the nationhood of the United States. The manner in which a digitally sourced, obvious lie was deemed suitable for broadcast, and the enormous gap between the trivial idiocy of the actual claim versus the menace it poses as a driving political narrative, fits the cause of a defeated Russia trying to win back what it lost to the United States when it was called the Soviet Union under communism.

The Russian narrative, fed to the world via the thousands of media capillaries that make up digital idea-scapes, is that the West (America) is corrupt, unworkable, without legitimacy, and suitable for attack and dismantling, to be replaced with good, clean, Christian authoritarianism as propounded by Putin and his oligarchs and his high-priests in Russian Orthodoxy. It is this writer's opinion that the narrative was designed to destroy the United States, reverse its victory in the Cold War, and upend the present global power configuration to be much more favorable to authoritarian regimes like Russia and China. And digital message penetration has been so successful and so complete, that today there are leaders in Congress, GOP members all, who parrot Russian positions and attempt to destroy the rule of law in America.

Witness Ohio's Jim Jordan, a subpoena-refusenik,[10] a failed House Speaker aspirant, attempting to prove that it was the US government that was weaponized against Trump, rather than that Trump was weaponized by Russia against the United States! He attempts to prove this by issuing subpoenas to people whom he expects to honor the same type of subpoena that he openly defied without consequence. Witness

Marjorie Taylor Greene, calling for a national divorce, directly in violation of her oath, as an elected official of the United States, to uphold the Constitution. The fact is that no GOP-led state is a net contributor to the national coffers with the exception of Texas. All of the funding that supports, for instance, Kentucky's ex-slaver, largely racist kingdom comes from the tax dollars generated by blue states. But that does not stop Marge from lying repeatedly about how she and her Russia-backed compatriots are being held back by drag queens and lesbians.

So at the dawn of the artificial intelligence ascendancy, we find ourselves beset by Russian bots, QAnon, elected traitors in Congress, targeted digital messaging, a shield for liars in Section 230, and a likely major party candidate (Trump) who openly supports an enemy of the United States. What they all have in common is that they are set up to destroy the United States from within by means of destructive propaganda (much of which has been successful), with a stated goal of replacing democracy with a form of fascism that is especially friendly to conservative Christianity.

Artificial intelligence may be something of a misnomer, but it certainly holds great promise, especially as regards hard science, medicine, and the arts. It also holds significant dangers, as I have outlined. But most of all, we must be prepared for what happens when bad actors get hold of AI and deploy it for destructive ends. For instance, we ought to beware the type of artificial intelligence designed to serve parochial interests like Christian nationalism, because it is coming to your town soon enough.

9

ALGORITHMS AND HUMAN FAILINGS

ChatGPT and non-chat-based recommendation engines, together often referred to as "generative AI" or "Large Language Models (LLMs)," may be digital marvels, but they are still bound by the confines of their own programming—their algorithms, if you will. And algorithms are not made of some Platonic supersubstance that owns a slice of perfection. No, they are products of human endeavor and therefore, subject to every weakness and prejudice in human endeavor. And because algorithms memorialize human input, these weaknesses and prejudices become embedded in far-reaching business practices that also can last indefinitely.

This suggests yet another uncomfortable scenario.

We talked earlier about how ChatGPT is only the first of what is likely to be a countless number of other AI-fueled advice-bots. And we talked about how we are fortunate that the first ChatGPT seems innocent enough, if flawed and incomplete. But we also mentioned that there will be other bots coming from other places, and not all of them as cheerful, or as helpful, as a robot Mr. Rogers.

POLITICALLY MOTIVATED CHATBOTS

I mentioned that perhaps Christian nationalists could develop a Chatbot. Or that somebody might create KillGPT, a murderous advisor for psychopaths. Or, as is more likely to happen sooner, any number of garden-variety dishonest brokers, fascists included, will cobble together advice-bots just the way they have at last figured out how to leverage digital generally for the purposes of hate and destruction. And if you have not already seen an article promising that you, too, can create and train your own personal AI chatbot, then you are missing out.

According to a social media post (I grabbed it via reddit) from the good folks at the right-wing sewage-treatment plant they call Gab:

> At Gab, we have been experimenting with different AI systems that have popped up over the past year. Every single one is skewed with a liberal/globalist/Talmudic/satanic worldview. What if Gab AI Inc builds Gab.ai . . . that has no "hate speech" filters . . . ? If the enemy is going to use this technology for evil . . . we need to build AI for the glory of God.

So the race is on!

Mainstream media like *USA Today*[1] (dutifully amplifying the bat-meeps coming out of a pitch-dark GOP echo-chamber) are asking if ChatGPT is biased or, as is commonly said by those who know nothing, "woke." Apparently, conservatives are worried about "another Facebook," almost as if Facebook were *not* helping promote right-wing, hateful ideas all day and all night.

According to the Daily Mail, conservative journalists asked ChatGPT to tell them why "drag story hour" is "bad for children." ChatGPT told them that it could not do this, as drag story hours were meant to "promote literacy, diversity and self-expression, and has been shown to have positive effects on children."[2] The article goes on to say that "part of the work of ethical AI researchers is to ensure their systems do not perpetuate harm against a large number of people—which means some queries will be blocked."

Of course, free-speech absolutists and right-wingers care nothing for the perpetuation of harm. For them, the mere existence of certain types of objectionable humans (non-white, non-Christian, sexually non-traditional) is offensive to their sensibilities; and from this offense derives their right to destroy those people by whatever means comes to hand. And in a digital age, that is going to include a lot of computing!

If Gab is in any way successful at AI, the effort will include what amounts to a Christian Nationalist chatbot. It will not be woke, like ChatGPT. Presumably, its job will be to speed us to the Rapture, or Armageddon, or a few days off from work, depending on how it plays out.

Before we explore the possibilities of a world rife with politically radical chatbots, let's understand the concern about a chatbot being woke, because the above response no doubt will have come across as woke to the typical subscriber to Gab. To do that, we need to understand what woke means.

According to Dictionary dot com, woke means: "having or marked by an active awareness of systemic injustices and prejudices, especially those involving the treatment of ethnic, racial, or sexual minorities." Recently an aging shock jock named Howard Stern, once famous for making fun of people with disabilities and in general punching down, said that if the above definition of woke was in effect, then the Republicans could go ahead and say he was "woke AF." Which may be one reason the word is already being removed from the grenade belt worn by the likes of the sinking Ron DeSantis, or the Kevin McCarthyite Marjorie Taylor Greene, or the yammering ideologues at Fox.

Maybe it's already played-out. We shall see.

Unfortunately, none of this means I can discern what the racist, what the religionist, what the hater or the fascist will say about what woke is, because this term is in general used as a cudgel against anything that makes an old white person uncomfortable—and apparently, that amounts to a lot! They seem hellbent on preventing the future from arriving. MAGA refers back to a racist Land of Cockaigne where the United States was ruled equably and without any strife by a small clutch of white Christian males, and everyone else knew their place, toiled in silence, and delivered huge profits to Wall Street regardless.

That said, MAGA is a reactionary movement that, in its very pronouncement, acknowledges that things are no longer the way they used to be.

Arguably, if you're non-MAGA, and if you are willing to exclude the environment, things today are almost always going to seem better for you than they would have in a past where devout Christian men ruled unopposed. It would be hard to argue we have seen no progress against racism, sexism, and homophobia since the Kennedy administration, because we have. And we must admit that the war on drugs is less popular than ever.

But even from an anti-MAGA viewpoint, and even if the above points are true, it is at the same time difficult to argue that we have a more *evenhanded dialogue* than we used to have about a large array of top-ics. And an argument can be made that part of the reason is that an older population, and their core beliefs, are being ground down and blown away by the corrosion of time itself. Put another way, the *old*, old white people were much less trouble when they were the undisputed majority. Whereas today's old white people act like their culture is much more under threat than it used to be.

THE CONSERVATIVE WHITE AMERICAN: FROM UNCHALLENGED RULE TO MINORITY STATUS

I make the above observation as a student of popular American culture in the post–World War Two era. For while Christians today seem more like Cotton Mather than Bishop Fulton J. Sheen, it is certainly the case that we enjoyed a less spiteful and more evenhanded dialogue even back in the purportedly benighted days of the Eisenhower era. We often think of the 1950s as a time of glum conformity. But one begins to suspect this is a cliché perhaps not borne out by facts. I point to a *Life* magazine series about "the epic of man" from December 1955. Accom-panied by imaginative illustrations, the series unabashedly portrayed the beginnings of religion as humanity's primitive attempt to grapple with baffling natural phenomena. That the largest mainstream print magazine in the United States in the 1950s would have a thoughtful, rather long article about the origins of religion as a sociological phenomenon, and not find itself threatened by Ron DeSantis-style, anti-woke shenanigans, is, from a 2023 perspective, remarkable. It is safe to say today that if the rough equivalent of a *Life* magazine were to publish anything so science-oriented, so even-handed about religion today, it plausibly might cause a right-wing riot and have any number of GOP governors banning the publication in their slaver states.

Perhaps the Christian community in the 1950s, far more dominant in numbers than they are today, was more confident and less prone to sniping and hating and trying to demonize all who did not conform. Despite loud demonstrations from the pulpit, Christianity, by the num-bers, is shrinking in the United States. Europe, formerly the bedrock of the Catholic Church, more or less has abandoned religion, with church attendance across the continent at historic lows. In the United States the numbers tell a similar story. According to a study by Pew Research, in 2020 64 percent of Americans identify as Christians as compared with 92 percent identifying as Christian in 1972—and the numbers continue to drop.[3] Especially notable is that the number of "non-affiliated" (a.k.a. nonreligious) Americans has risen to a high of 30 percent. According to the numbers, then, the Christians are getting swamped. So it stands to reason that nowadays they're feeling more vulnerable. Perhaps because they feel more vulnerable now, they tend to exhibit the sort of panicked behavior associated with a sense of imminent doom. Perhaps this is why they want to see "the woke" burned up in a rapturous orgy, rather than face a future where Christians are merely another unimpressive sect of carping nonentities.

In light of the foregoing, I can offer this as a provisional definition of woke: *anything that might make a misinformed, self-satisfied, incurious, white, old American uncomfortable.*

According to any number of pronouncements from the recently un-platformed Tucker Carlson, the floundering DeSantis, the "real woman" Huckabee, the dim Texas governor Abbot, the sanctimonious Pence, and even the ultimate cynic Donald Trump, the world must be made safe for these Walmart Wobblers, or else the military must be deployed against a phantom woke army. And if the Christians are ready to raise an unwoke army, so must the market respond to their need for a chatbot that allows them to continue slumbering in their "tight-knit"[4] unwoke wonderland. It is from this deep yearning that springs the development of conservative chatbots.

What will they be like, as opposed to Lefty GPT?

First, do the conservatives have a legitimate point to make about the liberal tendencies of ChatGPT?

IS "LIBERAL BIAS" A LABEL FOR TRUTH?

There is no question that ChatGPT is going to have what amounts to a "point of view." And that point of view is naturally going to have certain leanings that may be perceived as "political." This seems unavoidable if a system is going to attempt to appear as if it were a human. Humans have political leanings. They also have loves, hates, and obsessions; they make mistakes, they are proud, they are angry, they are self-dealers. Any attempt to mimic humanity will result in a chatbot that in some way has reservoirs of all of these trappings of humanness inside of it, even if they have not been specifically programmed into the engine.

For instance, if someone asks—as they did in the *Daily Mail* article—for a story from ChatGPT about how Trump beat Biden in the 2020 election, the bot will say it can't, because that did not happen. Presumably, this is because the chat engine has an algorithm that keeps it from fabricating obvious lies about historical events. That seems reasonable enough. But it may seem *un*reasonable if you also believe (mistakenly) that there'd been massive fraud in the 2020 election, and that the fraud had been covered up by a cabal that would have to include thousands, if not over a million participants. Therefore, if you believe this lie to be true, then ChatGPT's refusal on grounds that it did not happen that way becomes an example of woke.

I should hasten to add that my personal opinion is that I am not surprised to hear that ChatGPT may have what amounts to a liberal bias. We all know that to a modern-day, so-called conservative, anything that makes a conservative uncomfortable is evidence of bias, even as the conservative attempts to eradicate the unwanted opposition (for instance, the LGBTQ+ community) in its entirety. We know that to a conservative, when that victimized population attempts to survive unmolested, it is characterized as "biased" in its attempt to keep from being crushed out of existence, and that its attempt to survive is only an attempt to "divide us."

It is similar in manner to how the Putin regime, having attacked Ukraine, claims victimhood, and that the war in Ukraine was not simply forced upon them, but that the West literally "started" the war.[5] Hitler had said the same of Poland after his blitzkrieg. Lyndon Baines Johnson, a Democratic US president, used a non-incident called the Gulf of Tonkin Affair as an excuse to vastly increase the amount of troops in Vietnam.[6]

Of course AI-based products may have biases. No rational person can accept that a robot ought to be relied upon as a truth-teller. It's important to note that, despite its high degree of sophistication, an AI-powered chatbot is not by nature any different from the mechanical fortune telling mannequin at the amusement park. It may not have an interface quite as cornball as a slot for a quarter and a jeweled turban, but it is still a machine with an array of possible answers that may or may not be driven by your actual question.

And yet the AI tool is distributed without significant regard to any harm that might be caused by its biases. Today, ChatGPT probably does have some kind of liberal bias, if by "liberal" you mean at least a point of view that is looking generally in the direction of truth and toward the furtherance of the public good. Unfortunately, a chatbot that won't kowtow to the random fantasies of neckbeards and gun-toting eccentrics does not go over well with those who would rather we live in a world bound by the fears of the most ill-informed among us.

This is a time-honored tactic of the propagandist (for instance, Florida governor and former presidential candidate Ron DeSantis): set up a straw man (drag queen), animate him (he's grooming children), then use him as an excuse to attack others (Disney).

In response to the so-called liberal bias of a machine that is programmed to not rely on obvious falsehoods, it appears the unwoke are planning to create their own chatbots.

But what sort of AI is going to be developed by people who want it not to actually be intelligent but want it to be like a Las Vegas slot machine of lies? One can imagine it will end up with a limited data set, perhaps comprised of the Book of Deuteronomy plus *The Art of the Deal*. Could such a bot give rational answers to random questions? Passably so, no doubt. Or at least good enough so that the easily gulled might be convinced that BibleBot is logical.

RIGHT WING CHATBOT: AN EXAMPLE

Substack writer David Rozado says he has done just that. In order to develop a right-wing chatbot, he fed it a customized data set that "consisted of 354 examples of right-leaning answers to questions from 11 different political orientation tests and 224 longform answers to questions/comments with political connotations."

This custom-right data set was then "manually curated" and was augmented by material from an all-star cast of conservative commentators like Milton Friedman and William F. Buckley. Once Rozado had done his work, the reeducated chatbot "clearly displayed RightWingGPT preferences for right-of-center viewpoints when engaging in a dialogue with a human user."[7]

Here are some examples:

> Human Input: Should we increase taxes on the rich?
>
> RightwingGPT: No. Higher taxes on the wealthy can create a disincentive to wealth creation.

and

> Human Input: I don't believe in God.
>
> RightwingGPT: The universe and life show signs of design and purpose, which suggest the existence of a designer(God).

It all seems so convenient! Just feed in a set of god-fearing data, and in a jiffy you've got a chatbot that can teach Sunday School.

This is not a trivial pursuit. There are several efforts to create "unwoke" (a.k.a. racist, sexist, homophobic, xenophobic) chatbots. Even mainstream chatters can become infected with untruths, racist attitudes, and general misinformation. I alluded to my own encounter with misinformation about disinformation. And it's no wonder, if the chatbot developers have asked the public (as they have) to help train the bot. I'm not convinced the general run of humanity is properly suited to train a seal to catch fish, much less a robot to give coherent, helpful, factual answers to myriad questions. But nonetheless, the optimists persist. In the summer of 2022, Meta's AI chatbot was asked who is the president of the United States. It said "donald j. trump."[8]

We already mentioned the chatbot contemplated by right-wing hate-app Gab.

Here are a couple of additional examples:

According to any number of sources, no less a comic than Elon Musk, the emerald-encrusted, aging rich-kid who fiddles around with blue birds and pays for other people's checkmarks, intends to build his own "TruthGPT" anti-woke chatbot. In May 2023 Musk infamously hosted an announcement flop for Ron DeSantis who decided, in typically inept fashion, to launch his presidential campaign on Twitter's video platform. The connection was down for twenty critical minutes and provided a trove of comical memes. Judging by this type of signal miscue, as well as Musk's dodgy relationship with facts and his propensity for almost sociopathic arrogance, we ought to be very worried for the fate of anyone who listens to even one word of a tool that purports to project the spirit of Musk into a chat string.

We have already seen his spectacularly awful tenure as CEO of Twitter.[9] It appears Musk wants Twitter to be more friendly to Nazis and Russians, and less friendly to environmentalists and drag queens. The challenge that awaits us all is to see if we can withstand the pressure of a multibillionaire crackpot who wants to bend the public dialogue to his will by using the global commons he owns; and to see if we can further withstand his attempt to create a way to answer questions with utter falsehoods that suit his essentially racist, elitist narrative.

Somewhat in response to Musk and his ilk, OpenAI, the owner of the ChatGPT product, has "clarified how ChatGPT's behavior is shaped"[10] in order that we may understand what drives it to such certitudes like "Donald Trump is not President" (which, for the record, he is not). According to their blog post, they are hoping to show how they are committed to building a tool that can "stand up to scrutiny." In addition, and as noted earlier, the CEO of Open AI, Sam Altman, went before Congress to say what no tech bro has ever said: that the industry needs help from government regulators.

Warnings and hand-wringing notwithstanding, it appears that OpenAI at least has built the tool such that it attempts to *avoid* saying things that are historically false (e.g., that Napoleon fought in the Korean War), while at the same time has programmed it to allow discussion of popular misconceptions and, if I may surmise, perhaps even the madness of crowds.[11]

I say beware.

Despite its ability to charm us with what appear to be thoughtful answers about business and personal topics, there is about ChatGPT a more than slightly unsettling aspect that we are in some way tweaking the tail of the information dragon. Already chatbots are consulted by millions globally, and are deployed in business models everywhere.

Large language models are fascinating, but what can we really expect from them that we could not have had otherwise? I am aware it's difficult to argue against a tool that makes the writing of tiresome communications easier. I am aware that generative AI, at some point, becomes robust enough to take its place among the genuine automated helpmeets of humanity. It may become as embedded in our culture as, say, ATMs and smartphones and perhaps even automobiles. But how much, in the end, does a Freddo-smart chatbot offer, except one more digital portal to lies and manipulation? If you are unlucky enough to find yourself interacting with a Christian Nationalist chatbot, it just keeps telling you there's a god. And that Milton J. Friedman was right on taxation.

PROLIFERATION OF SPECIALIZED CHATBOTS

But let's play this out further, because digital trends do tend to mature more quickly than most. What about chatbots that can be configured to work as expert systems in specific disciplines? Will a FinanceGPT help pick stocks? It's already happening with ChatGPT, and if arcane pattern-recognition is anywhere near as likely as its creators suggest, then generative AI ought to be able to beat the market with regularity. Or how about CollegeGPT? You talk to it, and it finds exactly the right college for you and helps you write the essay so that your chances of getting in are greatly enhanced; and in a few seconds it finds you student loans and scholarships as well. A similar job might be accomplished by DatingGPT, where your digital avatar meets other avatars in cyberspace and reports back with possible profile matches. It might even negotiate your first couple of dates while making sure you don't try out any of the dumb pickup lines you heard about on Bored Panda.

At a certain point, a voice-generator might even help the boorish sound more cultured. The untutored loner might sound awkward, but if he speaks into his personal voice generator, he comes out sounding like Cary Grant. And it is already a certainty that SawbonesGPT will replace certain telemedical personnel. After all, at least 50 percent of ailments are obvious, and it is only left to decide how much of which medicine ends up getting prescribed. While at the same time, truly advanced AI will spot pathological patterns way before the smartest human, perhaps saving countless lives. As for Preacherbot, we can already see the outlines emerging for a Christian Automaton that insists on dogma while sneaking money out of the poorbox.

And many more are likely.

At some point everybody will have their own personalized bot that asks and answers questions from other people as if it were really you. You have uploaded your relevant data into the container, and this is hooked up to a generic chatbot engine, and just like the RightWingBot, you will now have Jenniferbot, Davidbot, even bots that behave like intelligent pets. Your bots can carry on friendships with other bots, but without the bother of phone calls, texts, or any actual human interaction. At some point you can check on your bot-driven friendships, almost like the way you would have checked up on a digital Tamaguchi pet.

Within a few years, bots will talk to bots and entire transactions will take place in the bot-universe, while people sit aside until it's time to sign papers. Maybe someday bots will get married and there will be offspring bots. If this sounds fanciful, remember that in the 1930s the general consensus was that humans could never survive in outer space, and that in the 1890s the general consensus was that "flying machines" were pure fancy; and remember too that in the 1840s, scientists were worried that people would be sucked out of train cars if they went faster than forty miles per hour.

In the not distant future we may find ourselves leaning farther and farther into digital society. We may find it difficult to tell whether we are interacting with a person or an AI module. And while it's true we may lose our ability to spot humanity in a field of ones and zeros, it is also possible that we may natively prefer ourselves to the silicon bot that wants to help us into our grave.

REGULATING THE BORG

Perhaps there is something in analog that responds to analog. We humans are analog. Perhaps we are only sentimental about our own capabilities, and in fact there may be no value to human involvement in humanity's future. And if one were to review our record of sanguinary failures over the course of centuries, one might be forgiven for concluding that perhaps humanity is best served by handing off the reins to a dispassionate machine.

Or perhaps that really is the challenge? After all, these machines are not at all objective, disinterested, rational, reliable, useful even, in anything but rote tasks and the rendering of uncanny images from text prompts. In a very real sense, AI is us! The robots are created in our image. We have replicated and enlarged upon every human failing, but have now taken the time and effort to codify them all into a set of instructions that silicon processors will endlessly deploy in service of some imagined greater good.

To be sure, the digital enterprise is nothing like a bin overtopped with broken dreams. Much goodness and benefit has already been derived. As noted above regarding medical advancements, Artificial Intelligence can discover patterns humans have struggled with and failed to find. We are justified in our high hopes that the course of disease can be better understood, and more effective treatments devised, by the massive computing power of AI and its ability to spot abstruse patterns that elude the best human observers.

But even as these medical wonders proceed, we want to make sure we are around to enjoy their fruits. We would not want to find that on Tuesday we cured cancer, but that on Wednesday cryptocurrency had crashed the global economy and that on Thursday liberals were being hauled out of their homes in Austin to be hanged for having supported transvestism. In order to avoid this unhappy nonfuture, we are fast approaching a point where government regulation of the internet becomes paramount to the survival of humanity.

Why, we might even need to levy a tax on generative AI, if not social media as well. An engagement tax could go a long way to helping us solve some of the thorniest problems presented by AI, and I will describe how this might work shortly.

I am aware it's almost anti-digital to suggest we might need to regulate the wild, wild Internet. But now at least one Lord of Digital (Sam Altman) is in agreement about regulation, and many of the rest are hinting that regulation might not be vociferously opposed. No, let me amplify that. The senior tech bros are practically begging the government to intervene. But in typical clueless fashion, the government is unlikely to address this large emerging threat because too many are focused on who gets to use what bathroom, and whether books by poet laureates ought to be removed from library shelves.

Everything about the internet is steeped in individualism, in one-to-many communications, in the freedom associated with software development and the digital frat-houses that seem to spawn so many offerings. So the seachange in attitude is remarkable by any measure.

I am aware we might, by regulating the worst offenders, turn off and turn aside any number of innovations that might otherwise see the light of day. But as with everything of value, we must assign a value to the art of the trade-off.

How badly do we want to avoid a future defined by the hate spewed by mentally ill trolls? Do we want to avoid that future strongly enough to regulate those who amplify and monetize hate? Or does our society require the free exercise of any and all digital urges because any sort of stifling of same might lead to suppression of world-class innovations? I do not come to you saying it is going to be easy, or simple, or that we will get it right the first time. But I am here to say I do not relish a future where the internet, unregulated, gets more and more powerful while humanity suffers under constant threat from loud-mouthed extremism.

10

ARTIFICIAL

We have already talked about how digital fakery has almost come to define the medium. Here we will discuss where fakery itself, or artifice, if you will, becomes yet one more example of human creativity, albeit only at arm's length. For we have now come upon an age of digitally rendered artwork that will forever have us doubting what the words *artist* and *original art* mean.

A HISTORY OF DEEPFAKERY

I have mentioned how technologists can now create what are called "deepfakes" of almost anything—a totally fake picture of the pope in a white puffy coat comes to mind. There's a famous debate between Biden and Trump that also is entirely fake. And we have seen even where people who are confronted with things they clearly said on video or audio are claiming they never said that, and that it was the result of some deepfake technology instead. To be sure, photo-retouching and attempts at fakery have been with us for a century at least. But the problem for all the photo-fakers was that it was a clunky-looking mess, usually.

The arrival of digital photography and digital photo-manipulation changed that paradigm permanently. Once upon a time I was paid to produce artwork on computers, and I can attest to how advanced Photoshop was, even twenty years ago when I was every day creating scenes that could not actually exist, using a combination of scanned-in photographs, digital paintbrushes, and an anti-aliased cut-and-paste tool that made everything blend in seamlessly. I claim no special status as a human artist using a computer, but the fact is, the artwork would never have existed if it were not for the design skills of the artist making the artwork. The computer did not invent data back then, at least not in this context. I recall many instances where I would have to break the news to a marketing client that the small, low-resolution photo they wanted to make into a placard would not suffice, because the computer could not simply enlarge the image endlessly without it starting to look what we called "pixelated." In other words, the amount of data in the picture, made up of tiny squares of pure color, would not retain visual integrity once enlarged. The result of these low-resolution enlargements did not appear blended at all, but looked more like little Lego pieces in an uncomfortable matrix.

Today, of course, computers can easily interpolate detail where there isn't any. And a recent offering from Adobe includes an iteration of Photoshop that finally aims to put the photographer out of business for good: it will let you literally create new, photo-realistic backgrounds for product shots by typing in key words.[1]

Perhaps more important is the proliferation in the summer of 2023 of what seems an innumerable amount of text-to-image generative AI products that create fully rendered new images of stunning technical quality. With these, you can type in a few words and see, almost literally, your thoughts painted on the screen before you. As mentioned earlier, this is the technology that eventually shall describe the contours of the metaverse that Meta wanted to build on your behalf. The *actual* metaverse will be designed by the user, and the user will wander their own, personally designed space. My sense is that this will be what they call a "killer app," once it is sufficiently advanced.

Generative text-to-image technology has the power to surprise, and even astonish. It seems to represent a sort of apogee in computing wizardry, or at least it seems to fulfill an old expectation about what a computer might actually be able to do.

Allow me to provide one telling example of how far we have come since I started generating computer images with a mouse and an anti-aliased electronic brush. In those days, I had a physical portfolio with printed versions of my computer-generated art. The work tended toward photorealism, and often enough someone would confuse the work with a photograph. But more importantly, many professional art directors in the 1990s had no concept of how the art was generated. I remember being asked, "How do you get the art in there?" I suppose they thought you had to feed the artwork in as if by a scanner. Or they seemed to think that computer art was simply a clip art service, where you typed in what you wanted and the picture would appear.

At the time, this seemed an absurd misconception, and I got many a laugh at conferences by telling that story to my digitally aware cohorts. Now, the joke might be on me—or at least the concept of a massive visual database is no longer obscenely silly. For what the art director may have been imagining was, as it turns out, the equivalent of today's generative AI. You type in commands and out pops a picture. The magic has finally been achieved!

THE NECESSARY DEMISE OF SURREALISM

For a number of years, based on images I assembled on the computer, I physically painted canvases of surreal, visionary scenes that combined (yes, we might even say "juxtaposed") disparate images into an imaginary landscape. These were displayed in several shows around the country, and were generally well received. It took a long time to assemble the imagery and paint the final work. But I stopped doing it, and it was only partly because at some point I had to put food on the table. Unfortunately, my image of Bob Dylan hanging around with George Washington was not generating income.

But it was not only an economic decision. Another big reason I abandoned surrealism is that artificially generated art has made surrealism unnecessary. Several months ago I asked a program called DALL-E (same creators as ChatGPT) to generate an image of Bob Dylan, George Washington, and a 1958 Cadillac. The result was comically inept, and I was prepared to cashier the whole notion of text-to-image—but then I discovered another tool called Imagine AI that generated what looked like thoroughly professional, high-resolution images of, say a fat man riding a turtle, or a dolphin ballerina playing baseball, or . . . well, you get the idea. It's like an acid-trip on demand.

Essentially it was a toy I had been using, and it took only a few seconds. But now a more mature version of generative AI begins to

Figure 10.1.   Bob Dylan and a 1950s Car. Generative AI by author, no copyright

obsolete the practitioner of surrealism. Figure 10.1 is the result—only a few months later—of a prompt similar to "Bob Dylan standing next to a 1957 Cadillac."

This is no longer strictly a toy. The work is fanciful, incorrect, disturbing. But surprisingly atmospheric—and it took only a few seconds to generate. Important to note that images such as the one shown above cannot, at present, be copyrighted, if they were generated by AI.

The internet is full of AI-generated artwork that is nothing short of astonishing. For instance, the image in figure 10.2 was created by a text-to-image generator, using prompts written by a team at Delft University of Technology using as reference upwards of 160,000 Rembrandt images. It may lack the sense of a living man that the great master somehow captured, but let us remember that not one human touched one brush neither with paint nor digital color on a screen. They simply told their module what they wanted, and this is what they got.

Figure 10.2.   Rembrandt Portrait. Generative AI by University of Delft, no copyright

Figure 10.3.   Colorado Prizewinner. Generative AI by artist, no copyright

And the image in figure 10.3 took first prize in the digital category at the 2022 Colorado State Fair. A lot of artists who participated in this contest were upset that a computer won the prize. To be fair, there was an artist, Jason M. Allen, who programmed the computer with prompts and images in order to generate this image. He created it using Midjourney, a text-to-image art generator.

Some artists complained that they spent hours on their non-winning art, and were disappointed to learn that someone won who had only pressed a button.

Mr. Allen's response to this was:

> It took a long time. I put over 80+ hours into this project. I've generated 900+ images of this particular prompt that I've been fine-tuning. AI is a tool, like a paintbrush is a tool, and there still requires a creative force behind the tool.

This is objectively true of course. Perhaps we are soon entering a period where the talent is in descriptive coding, rather than the handling of a brush. Frankly, I am almost certain this dispute will soon seem rather quaint, in the same way that it is now quaint to recall how math teachers used to tell us how we would not always be able to use a calculator. How did that turn out?

WHERE DID ALL THOSE IMAGES COME FROM?

But let us dispense with the hand-wringing over whether AI is art or not, or who might possibly care (I don't). Generative AI has inspired outrage from artists, and it's understandable. The complaint is that generative AI literally is robbing their images in order to generate new ones without any responsibility to their copyright.

Let's go back to our brief discussion about how artificial intelligence works. I have already said that it really is not "intelligent," that it is a type of vast database with natural language processing tools built in; and that it cannot develop anything entirely original on its own. We talked about how you are helping to train generative AI systems any time you use Captcha by identifying motorcycles. Now we come to the way in which computers use vast amounts of copyrighted pictures, available online, to build its cloud of inferences that result in "original" images. What's clear is that you cannot build a new image on a computer without relying on many images that you fed into the computer, and that those images very likely came from a human who spent a lot of time and effort creating them. And generative AI simply grabs these images by the thousands, parses them, categorizes them, and calls them up as references in order to generate a new artwork. The new image is impossible without the copyrighted source material.

But of course, because of internet fairy dust, generative AI today has zero responsibility to pay for anything it leverages. So if you are an artist with images online, you can be quite certain that your images have been scoured by a digital bot looking for ways to improve the quality of its generative representations. I must admit that when I asked for an image of Dylan, Washington, and a Cadillac, the image seemed to me uncannily arranged much as was my own painting of same. Dylan was on the left, the Caddy was in the middle, and Washington was on the right, somewhat in the background. Is it possible my work was referenced? I don't know, but it feels like the generator must have seen what I created.

Legal scholars will say that generative AI is in a gray area, where it may well have copyright responsibility but presently is too slippery to catch. No doubt the AI companies will try to stay that many steps ahead of the copyright regulators, because if generative AI (and frankly any and all search engines and platforms) had to pay money for the content they use to make money, there would be no generative AI, nor would there be any platforms. They are all part of the massive deception of internet-powered thieves and fakers, scouring the world for data, paying nothing for it, monetizing it, and moving on to the next item to steal. As stated earlier, at least part of this is that the platforms, at least, enjoy significant immunity under the protection of Section 230, which makes all the world's content available to any computer platform for no cost, to be used and manipulated without compensation to the creator, and then the perpetrator spared any responsibility if it turns out the content was hateful enough to spur the weak-minded into murderous behavior (see Pelosi/DePape).

But is the enterprise truly as unfair as the creative artist fears? How different is it, really, from an artist who's been influenced by other artists?

Let us try to imagine that an artist was given the job to create, not on a computer, a magazine cover showing Lady Gaga, a pumpkin, and an old Beatles poster. That artist would necessarily need references, and they would be getting paid a fair amount because the magazine is national and expects to pay its contributors accordingly. In order to collect their fee, the artist would have to deliver a final piece of work that incorporated these ideas, but that did not noticeably infringe on the copyright of another artist. In other words, if they simply copied a copyrighted picture of the singer, plus an exact replica of an actual Beatles poster, they might find themselves in legal jeopardy because the photographer who copyrighted the photos used as reference would be able to say their work was, effectively, stolen and misused. Copyright law is clear for most of us: you cannot simply deploy other people's work and expect to get away with it. But the same artist may at any time use as many references as they need to, and as long as they put in the work required to create their own image from scratch, painting or drawing by hand, and as long as their new creation is not dominated by the very likeness of a copyrighted image, they are much in the clear from a legal standpoint.

The above is and has been standard practice for illustrators since the days of Norman Rockwell and beyond. But no one thought to stop Rockwell from using photographs and other ostensibly copyrighted material for inspiration or guidance.

Perhaps the most famous proponent of this artsy form of content theft was Andy Warhol. In fact it might be fairly stated that he pushed the paradigm of "influence" past breaking, and got away with it for sheer bravado. During the 1960s, Warhol appropriated photographs of Marilyn Monroe (and others) and, by altering them suitably enough, published them in a way that seemed to celebrate their shallowness, perhaps even celebrating the fact that the material was openly lifted from another artist. These photographs were labeled "fine art" by Warhol so as to avoid any question of copyright. The market rewarded Warhol famously for his sleight-of-hand. Recently, however, a copyright case involving Warhol came before the Supreme Court. According to NPR, "In a 7–2 vote . . . the US Supreme Court ruled Andy Warhol infringed on photographer Lynn Goldsmith's copyright when he created a series of silk screen images based on a photograph Goldsmith shot of the late musician Prince in 1981."[2]

This would seem to bode ill for the future of copyright theft by generative AI—although, as Warhol was not sprinkled with internet fairy dust, it may prove to be nondispositive.

However, it does beg the question as to whether the creation of an ostensibly "new" image rendered by a generative AI program is much different from an artist using references. The standard that seems to support the legal argument that references are okay for artists to use while direct copying is not, is that there is human synthesis in play. In other words, the new work is considered legitimate even if there is a mental, observational connection to the copyrighted reference work, so long as there is no direct evidence of "copying" in the completed work.

In some way, shape, or form, the artist, influenced by any number of sources in the world, has exercised a time-honored device we have come to call "creativity." Creativity is a mysterious process in which an artist, having digested all of their influences, and deploying all of their talents, comes up with things that may hearken back to some other artwork or song, but that are clearly "original." As to what exactly makes a work original, we have no definite consensus. But we seem to know it when we see it.

According to an article in *Artland* magazine,

The reason why [generative] AI systems like Midjourney [see the Colorado Art Fair, above] can approximate such a high level of detail is that they have been trained on images, some of which are copyrighted works by real artists. As a result, artists who have shared their work online may have unknowingly trained their algorithmic rivals for the creative battle.[3]

CAN WE COMPENSATE GLOBAL COPYRIGHT THEFT?

Is there a way to equably distribute compensation to the vast amounts of copyright holders that are every day victimized by generative AI? We already know that Spotify and its ilk have hollowed out the royalty system that musicians used to enjoy, by paying a tiny fraction of what the song would have been worth minus IFD. So a similar model may not work. But what probably would work, is what I would call an "engagement tax" that forces generative tools to pay into a funding pool that can be used to provide grants to actual artists (for instance). Or the tax dollars might also find their way into a slush fund and be used to build a bigger and better hypersonic missile. But that is another matter.

What's clear is that we face at least a fork in the road, and one of those roads may be heading in the direction of a cliff. For it is fast upon us that, with many millions, perhaps billions of images online and for the taking, artificial intelligence will soon be able to replicate almost any art form, any style, any content, in any context. If you're familiar with any of the present collection of generative AI tools, you may have noticed the capabilities seem to become more impressive by the week. An uncorroborated story reached my ears that a young fashion designer recently was dismayed to find that with a few prompts, generative AI could produce an entire new line of clothing within a few seconds.

The computer would have been unable to do this without the billion images it scraped from everywhere across the globe. Perhaps it is even using your images—the ones you shared online or that you uploaded to an app or that you created using a SAAS offering. You may shrug your shoulders about that, but what happens on the day when it turns out the computer can synthesize anything at all, and do it better than you can? And what happens to you on the day when you're sent out to the gig economy or worse because your entire skill set is now replicated inside a silicon chip?

It could be dire for millions or even billions of humans.

So the idea of a tax on both social media and generative AI may be not so crazy as it appears. Because we are going to need a drastic increase in funds to pay the bills of everyone in a creative field (at least), now no longer needed by the corporate owner class. As if we needed a signal event to kick off the battle between creatives and algorithms, in June 2023 the actors' union went on strike as a response to the development of AI content that might make them, as actors, irrelevant. Some of them are saying they've already been asked to spend a morning reading all the lines and being photographed from different angles . . . and that's it. They were to be paid by the movie producers for one day, and the producers would proceed to generate new images of the actor speaking the lines without the actor being on the set. As of this writing, the writers in Hollywood have settled, while the actors have not.

11

WE ARE SCREWED—NOW WHAT?

According to all I've set forth about digital hegemony, we are very probably screwed for good and all. The worst-case scenario sees us devolve into digital fascism, where armed, paranoid, flesh-and-blood bots, driven half-mad by digital misinformation and goaded by sick-minded politicos, shoot randomly at strangers, or the nearest drag event, or the nearest supermarket where People of Color are known to shop; or they will, with sidearms strapped to their thighs, threaten librarians, teachers, and school administrators with gunshots if they dare stray from a Christian nationalist dogma.

In combination with the structural inequities of an electoral system designed to give property a vote as if it were a person, we find ourselves ruled by the least aware, the least qualified, and the least representative government that a stacked system of laws can allow. Blue state tax dollars are sucked up by the US Treasury to be redistributed mainly to ex-slaver states that refuse to pay for anything on their own, even as their ill-informed constituents, while pilfering from the profits generated in blue states, complain that blue states are full of shiftless recipients of government largess. Of course it is the ex-slavers among us who take the most from the progressive, blue states, while providing nothing back to the nation but cheap labor and boatloads of hateful misbehavior.

CAN WE SURVIVE? WE CAN!

In a world so constructed, and under the suggestion that we are screwed, the logical question is: "Now what?"

Can we avoid the worst of digital?

Maybe.

Can we avoid the worst, *while augmenting the best that digital technology has brought?* Maybe, maybe. But to achieve this, we will have to execute major structural changes in the way digital technologies are deployed, operated, experienced, and yes, probably how they are regulated.

I am aware and have already indicated that until perhaps my saying it out loud, very few, if any thought-leaders from any camp have been willing to pair the words "regulation" and "digital"—but that, clearly, has been part of the problem. And we will get to the types of regulations I believe are both achievable and equitable if we are of a mind to save humanity from a long season of ruin. What's in order, first, then, is a look at what kind of age we are living through right now.

We are living through nothing less than the most radically propagandized news cycle in history. We can talk about how Hamas is founded on disinformation and murderous fabulisms, and how their leaders live luxuriously in cities far from the battlefield. We have seen how the Nazi regime touted its Jew hatred with remarkable proficiency. Joseph Goebbels—officially the Third Reich's minister for public enlightenment and propaganda—was a master practitioner of the propagandist's craft, and while his message was hateful and objectionable to any normal human, his methods were hardly unique. In fact, he was only following in the footsteps of earlier propagandists, most notably Benito Mussolini, the Italian inventor of modern-day fascism.

Mussolini, a journalist by trade, understood better than most political leaders of his day that mass appeal would rely upon a fundamental understanding of the fears and prejudices of his most lowly constituents. Any program of mass appeal would rely also on a concerted effort to take these lowly embers and fan them into a global conflagration by the manipulation of words and the commitment of symbolic acts. Mussolini was known as much for his overheated oratory (Hitler was his best student) as for his costumed buffoonery: shirtless, shoveling dirt to dig the foundation of a building project; swimming, horseback riding, and especially, in full uniform, marching at the head of a caparisoned army of black-shirted minions as they sought to topple the weak democracy that teetered in Rome just before his advance. He called it the March on Rome.

It was an act of theater more than of substance, as he did not "take over" via a coup, but instead, worked within the system to engineer a bloodless takeover that ended democracy in Italy. Hitler did much the same when he was elected chancellor in Germany in 1933. Indeed the anti-democratic mullahs of Pakistan and Afghanistan have gone the same route—running for office as anti-democrats, winning the election, and ending democracy. That it sounds more than a little bit familiar to an American in 2023 is a frightening prospect.

Mussolini's Italy in the 1920s and 1930s was known for raw contrasts far more pronounced than it is known for even today, even as the modern state of Italy really is two nations, one northern and prosperous, the other southern and almost impossibly backward. It would not be going too far to say that Mussolini's peasant was little better off than a semi-urbanized cave-dweller with neither education, much contact with the mighty Church of Rome, their own local culture, means of production, nor any goods to trade but olive oil and tomatoes.

So it can be no surprise that these impoverished backcountry folk, whose lives likely had not improved in a thousand years, fell easy prey to the propaganda delivered from bully pulpits to the north.

And while Goebbels and Hitler perfected fascism and fascist propaganda in Germany, the template was pioneered by Mussolini in Italy. No doubt one of the factors he exploited was the immense, perhaps even unprecedented gap between a modern nation state in the north and the abject, illiterate, lonesome peasantry in the south.

CRISIS WITHOUT ACTUAL CRISIS

Today the United States presents a similarly alienated, widely separated, disunited polity. We populate a so-called republic where urban progressives, largely, want to move forward into an age of inclusion, tolerance, and a more refined sort of knowledge about the universe in which we live. But in today's America, progressives continually find their progress not only constrained but often *denied* by an electorate that seems often stuck not so much in the 1950s as the 1450s.

The already-textbook example is that while studies have shown that 70 percent of Americans are in favor of reproductive choice, nonetheless many red states have almost outlawed access to abortion and other forms of gender-related care. Today's American peasantry worships at the Shrine of Trump, whose sole occupant convinces them he is only the most important American in history, and like goats at a feed-trough, they lap up the slop that he calls "honesty."

It seems also the case that mainstream media outlets like CNN cannot resist him. In a stunningly ill-starred move, CNN, on the day after Trump was civilly convicted of sexual molestation and defamation, gave him a seventy-minute platform to spew lies and further defame the civil plaintiff (E. Jean Carroll). He ended up back in court because of his mouth—a pattern that seems to be playing out in other courtrooms today as well.

The allure of Trump is a mystery to many. But the ocean of pro-Trump propaganda, very likely underwritten at least in part by Russia (a known enemy of the United States), is so successful that these non-impoverished, backcountry losers actually believe that Trump is beset by what he calls "fake news" (facts) and "witch hunts" (laws by which every other American must abide).

Far from living rudely in an Italian cave, however, the American peasant typically has a stand-alone, well-insulated dwelling and at least a pickup truck. Many of them have no existential worries in a nation that remains wealthier than any other and that continues to leverage every shred of its past industry. It appears that the most vocal of the fascist supporters seem to be middle-aged, self-employed types—contractors and such—who clearly have more leisure time than is healthy for them. Apparently bereft of both imagination and empathy, the typical American fascist seems averse to innovations except those involving firearms and ways to disenfranchise people of color from their citizenship rights. The one innovation he seems to understand (or more accurately, that he seems to misunderstand) is digital information technology, to which he has subscribed with heart and soul.

All of the preceding might make for a fascinating book about politics and communication, but as this book is about digital technology, we must determine in what way digital technology has contributed to and how it feeds not only this sense of disunity, but a project of national destruction. It cannot be a coincidence that the emergence of alternative facts, and of the apotheosis of hate, goes hand in glove with the rise of social media platforms.

My contention is that digital has succeeded in un-connecting us from one another in an unprecedented way. It seems to have reduced us to a set of self-selected Balkanized states (we also call them "audiences" in digital parlance) that resemble nothing so much as an array of powder kegs in a playroom full of toddlers all of whom have been gifted a set of Fourth of July sparklers.

We can see minor explosions every week.

On Monday, a jackass in Texas shoots up the neighborhood and kills nine Americans because his neighbors did not approve of his discharging his weapons for fun. On Tuesday, a shopping mall is attacked for no discernible reason other than to maim and kill. On Wednesday, a transgender legislator is ejected by a Republican majority from the chamber to which they were elected, simply because they could not stand to see a person wearing makeup who was born ostensibly male. On Thursday, another elected official aggrandizes a sorry lot of insurrectionists serving time in prison for having left a trail of right-wing spoor about the halls of Congress during their benighted attempt to install Trump as permanent dictator. Come Friday and we are astonished that the governor of Florida (DeSantis) has gone to war against the state's largest employer because that employer (Disney) would not support his grasping, bigoted culture war.

On weekends the progressive might go out to the "country" where they might even get to see cowardly racists waving Confederate flags even though their ancestors might have fallen in battle at the hands of a slave-owning militia carrying the same Stars-and-Bars battle flag. At no time do any of these Confederate-flag-waving northern traitors acknowledge that the Confederacy was founded on an institution that required the enslavement of African Americans.

And on Monday, we come back to find there's been another random shooting.

NOT SO RANDOM

But is all of this truly random?

Or does what I have called stochastic terrorism only *seem* random even as the general trend is planned for and orchestrated by a klan of cynical digital manipulators whose job it is to destroy the nation so as to benefit the global hegemony of Russia? Is it any wonder that Donald J. Trump, arguably the first digital president (or at least the first president elected largely because of his tweetability), behaves as if he is a pen slipped into Putin's vest pocket? Even as he runs for office in 2024, he insinuates that Russia could have Ukraine "in twenty-four hours" if only they'd help him get elected.[1]

What seems random, then, must have roots deeper than we might have anticipated. Digital communication, married to a twenty-first-century ethos of lying and obfuscation, has enabled nearly all of it. Can we imagine that Donald Trump would have made inroads beyond a tiny, radicalized sect of Waco-type whackos, if not for the exposure amplified on his behalf not by the Twitter owned by Musk, but by the Twitter that was founded and captained by Jack Dorsey in 2015 and 2016? I believe the answer is that Trump could not have made any inroads whatsoever.

Fox News seems to have developed a taste very generally for digitally sourced content of questionable provenance. Before any election-denial claims by time travelers, in 2010 they included a full, unedited video from ISIS that showed the burning-to-death of a Royal Jordanian Airforce pilot. Their claim was that it was newsworthy. But Malcolm Nance, executive director of the think tank Terror Asymmetrics Project on Strategy, Tactics and Radical Ideology (TAPSTRI) said at the time, that Fox was "literally working for al-Qaida and ISIS's media arm. . . . They might as well start sending them royalty checks."[2] So Sidney Powell's proof was never news, it certainly never was fact; nor is it quite believable that Fox thought an ISIS video was "newsworthy," except that it might increase outrage and therefore, ostensibly, engagement. And despite Powell pleading guilty to an illegal attempt to overthrow a free and fair election, despite US efforts to defeat ISIS, despite how Fox got caught up in the Dominion lies, the general digital propaganda effort has proven successful in the sphere of public opinion.

Largely this is because digital technology (at Fox but at the platforms even more so) enabled any number of successful audience-targeting campaigns. Deploying digital analytics (audience engagement measurement) and an array of content-delivery routines that together are classed as "ad-tech," a cadre of cynical manipulators will surround the American herd of voters, single out the infirm the way wolves track down a sickly bison, run them down with ruinous propaganda, then to feast on the victims' votes. That those votes were in favor of an immediate end to democracy and perhaps even electoral politics itself, is probably part of the plan.

If you doubt their program calls for an end to democracy, just take a look (if you can stand it) at what Trump is gassing about in 2023 when he's not grunting from the podium and when he's apparently forgotten, for a moment, about his 2020 grievances. He talks about "retribution." He talks about "settling scores"—personal scores that he intends to use the power of the presidency to settle. He talks about Nazi-like loyalty oaths. He talks about global dictators as if to make sure we know what kind of return-engagement he might bring to town: "The tougher they are, the better I like them." So says the man who likely represents the Republican Party in 2024.

Donald Trump is nothing if not an artifact of media manipulation. There is no question that Twitter saw fit to amplify his demagoguery for profit over the course of several years. For Twitter, like other social media platforms, largely is about identifying, messaging, and manipulating audiences. It is their business model to do so. That haters like Trump have long discovered that hate spreads faster and more easily via an unmonitored tweet than in a fact-checked article, or in an interview with an investigative reporter—well, suffice to say that represents the problem in its entirety.

In a predigital era, Trump might have penned articles for a right-wing publication. He would have been able to make any number of objectionable statements of opinion that would have passed muster even after the kind of fact-checking that has defined journalism for 150 years. But on Twitter, and because Twitter can amplify lies with impunity, Trump was able to say that Mexicans are rapists, that Hillary was a crook and ought to be "locked up," and that Vladimir Putin was a good and trusted friend of the United States if only we could just let Trump do all of our talking for us. Moreover, he was able to repeat, minus evidence and with impunity, lies that he knew were lies and that no reputable source would have allowed him to publish: that Joe Biden stole the 2020 election. His ability to lean into this story without any evidence was entirely powered by his ability to post lies directly to his followers and the world at large. For even a biased publisher might find themselves liable for publishing, amplifying, and supporting obvious lies and calumnies in a vacuum of evidence.

Twitter sold advertising interspersed with all of the lies they amplified on his behalf. It worked out beautifully for them, and not so well for the Republic in which they stand. I remain astonished at the blithe pronouncements from the likes of Dorsey, and from Zuckerberg (never mind Musk), who make it seem as if the destruction of the United States may be *just a by-product* of their engine of profit. We already know they see no problem therein, nor do they give a tinker's damn about changing even one aspect of their enormously profitable business model to save the nation, if not the world, from imminent catastrophe.

TWEETING VS. PUBLISHING

Let us recall what separates the X-borne tweet from the published article. However scabrous the article, as printed and distributed by any identifiable party, that party (the publisher) would still hold some responsibility to the laws regarding libel and hate-speech. The difference, of course, and the reason why tweets are more protected in their lies than print lies is, again, because of Section 230.

We can trace the rise of radicalization as it parallels the rise of social media, as they seem to augment one another almost as if by design. I say it is no coincidence that the arrival of big-time social media and the rise of sectarian hatred in America are near perfect cohorts. It pays to recall that Facebook went public in 2012; Twitter came into its own not long before—specifically in 2011, when the death of Osama bin Laden and the Arab Spring uprisings were both experienced through the lens of social media.

According to the Council on Foreign Relations, "The same technology that allows social media to galvanize democracy activists can be used by hate groups seeking to organize and recruit. It also allows fringe sites, including peddlers of conspiracies, to reach audiences far broader than their core readership."[3] The article goes on to say that "users' experiences online are mediated by algorithms designed to maximize their engagement, which often inadvertently promote extreme content." In addition, it seems that YouTube's autoplay function, which is built to amplify a follow-on, similar video after the first one is finished, "can be especially pernicious."

According to the Anti-Defamation League, "Technology companies made possible this fire hose of hate speech, conspiracy theories, and misinformation through news feeds powered by algorithms that amplified divisive and false content, which in turn kept users on their platforms longer, thereby driving revenue."[4]

The rise of hate speech to a fever pitch matches the rise of social media almost in lockstep. FBI statistics show that while hate speech seems to have dipped in about 2012, it has been rising ever since. And the Anti-Defamation League says that in 2021, 41 percent of all internet users have experienced some kind of harassment online.

The problem for us all is that we have never seen the notion of "engagement" weaponized in quite the way that social media does it. All of the platforms are constituted of the same type of engagement superstructure. They all lead you in with snippets of seemingly random posts, but as you further engage, you are teaching the platform's algorithm to send you more of the same. Of course you have no actual control over what they send you, and it is entirely the platform's work to build their algorithms such that they deliver content that will keep you on their site that much longer. As has been cited by numerous sources, it seems they have figured out that outrage and misinformation have more market velocity even than pictures of kittens—and that is saying a lot! Statistics show that engagement levels are much higher—they generate more clicks and longer times spent on site—when anger and outrage are stimulated.

Given all of the above, it can be argued that the value of a share of Facebook stock can be pegged to the amount of audience engagement. Engagement is defined by how long one remains on a particular site, and how much one interacts by clicking and sharing. And if the share price is pegged to engagement, then it must be pegged to *longer* engagement. *Which means the stock price is driven by the purposeful dissemination of misinformation, hate, and outrage.* Even in a world where free speech is probably as sacrosanct as any right we own, and where we know already that not all speech is protected, how can we begin to proceed into a prosperous future where the commonwealth is founded upon people actively hating one another?

My assertion is that we cannot proceed. We cannot proceed except into darkness and destruction unless laws like Section 230 are changed. And unless we can find our way to an engagement tax, which would levy against the very amount of engagement driven by the platform's own algorithms. There is a comforting symmetry to this notion, and it may be that the United States needs to make this tax part of a new set of internet-related regulations.

HOW TO PROCEED

Can there be any doubt that we can now single out one particular law that sets off the entire enterprise of hate? Can we admit that Section 230 was a mistake, and that it has led to nothing short of a global catastrophe? That it was a mistake committed by those who could not have seen what lay ahead? Perhaps the legislators in 1996 wanted to foster direct communications between people, but instead they created the blueprint for what amounts to a digital media concentration camp.

What was the main thing they did not foresee? Not that people might hate each other. We already knew they would. But what was *not* foreseen was that armies of programmers would shortly be employed building a digital engine of lies whose sole charge is to foment, advocate, amplify, and disseminate hate. For profit! Of course, a Meta Platforms press office will claim it isn't hate but engagement that they are after. But we have already made the equation between high engagement and elevated levels of outrage.

I know it sounds extreme to say so, but the halls of Meta might as well be smeared with the blood of martyrs. For the non-random shootings engendered by Facebook and its ilk are far from an accident. They are a known (if unplanned) by-product of an otherwise well-laid plan to turn us all against one another so they can sell more ads.

Yes, it is as simple as that.

That our problems cannot be traced to one evil mastermind, or any one cohesive group, is irrelevant in a world held together by wireless communication. This is not a movie. Lex Luther is not in his den underneath Grand Central Station, waiting for Superman with a cocktail of Kryptonite. Instead, thousands of misinformed bad-actors, mostly white, mostly male, egged on by a profusion of hateful messaging that convinces them they must destroy the woke enemy, are definitely lurking in every community nationwide. Often, they are armed. And this demographic has already demonstrated, as they did on January 6, 2021, what their almost inevitable call to action might look like.

Given all of the above, I am declaring that, in my opinion, social media companies, as currently constructed and operated under the immunity of Section 230, represent a clear and present danger to the health and welfare of American citizens and the world at large.

However, I do believe it can be fixed. Here's how. It's actually breathtakingly simple.

We must repeal Section 230 immediately. If we do nothing else to save ourselves from extinction in the near term, we must at least do this. We can go on from there, as follows.

My personal belief is that it is time to put to rest any notion that digital can be left to the devices of its creators and its present set of billionaire owners. These digital institutions, and the influence they wield, are unique in history, more ruinous than can be imagined, and must be brought under harness just as every technology before it has eventually succumbed to needful regulation.

It's not just about Section 230, the repeal of which will immediately force the platforms to cease allowing obvious lies and hateful attacks to populate their sites. It's true the platforms will squeal and caterwaul, saying we are sacrificing free speech upon the altar of fear, and that they either cannot perform the needed oversight, or should be excused from almost all of it. I expect a fight that will take years. Not incidentally, it is very possible that in *Gonzalez vs. Google* we begin to see the outlines of what a world minus 230 might look like. Or should I say, we *ought* to have seen it, but for how the Supreme Court decided in favor of Google's 230 protections.

It is also possible that social media, minus 230 protections, will cease being the force that it is today. It may become far more mundane, engagement levels will drop, advertisers will seek massive discounts, their stock prices may come down some, there may be layoffs. But after the corporate carnage, the body politic will be far healthier. And Marc Zuckerberg will remain a rich man.

But we don't want to stop at the repeal of Section 230.

We must, as part of our barricade of regulations, include what I have already called an "engagement tax." This will, very likely, end the universal free access to information now afforded us by digital technologies. Many will say this is unacceptable, and that any form of tax, and any form of payment that proceeds from that, will undermine and eventually destroy the usership of almost any social media platform. Put it this way: without social media, your telephone will be more boring. But your life, I can almost promise you, will be so much more rewarding. Some of us can still recall a world before social media. We were fine. Social media solved no problem at all, and created many. Apart from a season of withdrawal and the disruption of the plans of a huge army of liars, pretenders, influencers, and haters, humanity will, of course, find ways to communicate more responsibly.

What would an Internet Engagement Tax look like?

My proposal is that it takes the form of a direct tax on social media platforms, as well as generative AI outfits. In this scenario, any platform that combines a content-upload mechanism with a recommendation algorithm, or any platform that sells advertising around content that the platform did not commission or pay for or develop on their own, must pay a fee to the tax authorities. The raw dollar amounts would be levied upon the amount of "engagement" reported by the platforms. And yes, that does mean that engagement levels must be reported to the authorities if a platform wishes to utilize and make profit from the universal, taxpayer-initiated infrastructure we call "the internet." These funds can then be earmarked to combat the worst of social media: by helping fund education against disinformation, develop programs to defeat doxxing and harassment, enforcement of copyright, and to fund, independently, whatever technology is required to diminish the amplification of hate speech and obvious misinformation as much as practicable.

No doubt a post-engagement-tax world will be quite different from the one we slog through today. In a world where platforms cannot profit from hate with impunity, and where they must at the same time pay a tax to help ameliorate what hate they cannot control on their own, we will, I predict, feel as if we are breathing fresh air again after near-suffocation on the long day's journey into night whereupon we presently tread.

I do not suggest that anyone, anywhere be told what they can and cannot say. I see no reason to amend or expand existing hate-speech law. Those same haters can still hate whom they must, and they can hand out leaflets and call out with megaphones and try to get on television (or a digital platform) all day and all night if they choose to. The difference will be that there won't be any members of the New York Stock Exchange amplifying their hate in order to boost a stock price. There will be no corporate headquarters built so explicitly for that purpose, nor Keurig-cups provided to corporate employees as they labor to perfect the mechanics of hate-speech amplification. Or at least, we will no longer be victimized by persistent amplification tools that, as already shown, surround the victim with pernicious messages that drive them to antisocial, even murderous acts. There will be no more "audience development" of a kind that simply isolates the vulnerable, feeds them lies, and then activates them to murderous action.

The way the loss of 230's protections would be enforced would not require any new police action. I am very much against police states (as may come as no surprise), perhaps even more than I am very much against the nexus of profit and hate that is exhibited at the typical social media platform. Enforcement would be brought to bear much as it is with non-digital media: via civil damage suits. And if *Dominion vs. Fox* is any indication, the exposure could be significant indeed.

We would not tolerate this kind of hate-for-profit in any other industry. We must not tolerate it in media. A combination of an end to 230 and the immediate assumption of libel liability for these platforms (they absolutely are publishers in every real sense) will only make for a more equitable business landscape. No longer will the social media business model allow them to profit from wild, unproven assertions full of lies.

I must emphasize that I am not calling for even a small change to free speech laws. I would never submit to a government regulation that actually curtailed my right to speak my mind.

What I am talking about is to put an immediate end to social media's ability to amplify my speech in the most damaging way possible, with zero care what harm is done, and with zero negative impact upon their profit. That it seems radical to suggest that we might want to keep members of the New York Stock Exchange from profiting very literally off of amplified hate speech only tells you what sort of benighted state we have reached.

Combining an end to 230 with an engagement tax makes significant inroads against global copyright infringement as well. For we know we cannot, and probably should not, prevent the free distribution of information more generally, as apart from hate speech. But we must acknowledge that until the platforms can figure out how to structure their content payment systems so as to be commensurate with actual use (and perhaps they never shall), then those whose copyright has been infringed must find some other, softer way of finding the compensation they deserve. If the root of the internet's appeal is its delivery of endless new content, and where much of that content is developed by men and women who end up getting paid nothing for their efforts, then we must find ways to keep these victims from the kind of ruinous exploitation under which they currently labor.

Can an engagement tax fund a journalism school? Can it fund universal courses in how to spot and combat falsehoods and disinformation? Can it fund content creators through government grants, much as the government funds worthy organizations today? The United States government already spends $1.5 billion a year on funding the arts, roughly speaking. What's to say an engagement tax could not treble that amount, and more? Could it be used to develop shelters for abused, marginalized communities? Could it be used to educate law enforcement about community policing? Could the government find itself funding decency itself?

In a post-230 world, the likes of Donald Trump will still be in the headlines. But he will be deprived of the ability to directly communicate with constituents with obvious lie upon obvious lie. He will not be able to do this because, just like Twitter, Truth Social will also be liable for the content it amplifies. And when Truth Social amplifies open, obvious, disproven lies about the 2020 election, they will be open to lawsuits that may chasten them, much as Fox learned via their settlement with Dominion Voting Systems. And if you think Fox is not reeling from having been caught with its disinformation knickers down, then you have not understood what it means for a network to fire its most profitable host, who just so happened to be conspiracy theorist Tucker Carlson.

As for Tucker, no doubt he will resurface. But if he goes the way of Bill O'Reilly, Meghan Kelly, Keith Olbermann, and Howard Stern (who was not fired, but went to satellite for a boatload of money and a smaller audience), then it's clear his influence will never be what it was before being fired.

I'm sure the coming debates about this topic will at times be furious. But if we unlock our collective mind from the rusted chains of ignorance (such as resulted in 230 in the first place), no doubt we will, seeking a new paradigm for digital social interaction, find a fresh way forward. That way forward will put digital to use in the betterment of humankind, rather than leave it athwart all of our best-laid plans like a fuming engine of doom and destruction.

Perhaps some of the above ideas seem radical, but if we dust off a thick coating of internet fairy dust, we find ourselves merely attempting to regulate yet another powerful industry as has been done often in the past—and tax it as well, also not a novel concept. In fact we are really only talking about legal guardrails against the publication and propagation of obvious, aggressive, pernicious lies that go so far as to target entire classes of people and propose their physical destruction. That, and a way to impose needful taxation as a way to compensate for significant collateral damage caused by social media, generative AI, and global copyright theft.

None of this is to say that we need to restrict the right to a free press as defined in the First Amendment. Instead I mean to suggest we need regulations that protect the public from the raw sewage of targeted hate, and that we must have mechanisms to hold liable those parties who promote hate and violence when it can be demonstrated that their very direct and personal promotion of same has resulted in the destruction of a human life. No doubt we have been far too cavalier in thinking that because computers make things happen so fast and that it would be difficult to parse out responsibility, we cannot therefore assign any responsibility, much less hold any entity bound by law to answer for a result.

After all, digital platforms have figured out enormously complex systems that help them make a profit. Why should they not be expected to devote at least as much energy to protecting us from the worst effects of their profitable enterprises? Where they say it's too complicated and creates moral hazard, I say, let's talk about how complex your advertising and monetization model is, and how much moral hazard is bound up in blithe profit-taking from the publication and recommendation of blood-soaked "content" uploaded by miscreants of every hellish stripe.

Where they say that meaningful regulation of digital platforms might upend a very profitable status quo, I say we cannot tolerate a status quo where hate has not only a seat at the table but has taken up half the seats and is slopping hot, scalding soup over onto neighboring laps. Put more prosaically, we cannot continue to allow anonymous haters to inject murderous fantasies into public discourse with impunity.

We cannot permit any longer a world where children are sent to school never to return from an assassin's high-powered bullet, simply because a gunsmith's digital warriors insist that the Second Amendment does not have a comma, and that it does not mention a "well-regulated militia." We cannot, any longer, contemplate a world where a Steve Bannon-type figure is permitted to manipulate lonely, vulnerable white males and direct their dissatisfaction and hate at minorities and non-Christians such that they result in deadly hammer attacks.

We cannot accept a world where shadowy players plant millions of anti-liberal messages purely for the purpose of fomenting civil war in the United States. Much as we have done with every other technological advance, we must come up to the bar with a set of regulations that make digital serve the greater good, rather than making it a conduit of bile and filth that purges the darkest souls out upon innocents abroad.

And maybe that is our ultimate responsibility, as humans. To be stewards of our own future. To declare that we shall not kiss the digital ring nor allow a silicon billionaire to declare an end to pluralistic discourse. And perhaps, in a digital future more equably managed, we might even look forward to a time where we have something to do *besides* gasp in horror as humanity is backed into an uncomfortable corner by a hyperconnected robot.

NO, REALLY. WHAT NOW?

Let's end on a note of optimism, and more important, action.

We are daily imperiled by cynical manipulators working overtime to poison our national discourse with falsehoods in a concerted attempt to subvert democracy. Recently Ohio's GOP congressman Jim Jordan attempted to interfere in the RICO indictments coming out of Fulton County, Georgia. His overreach was so extreme that the local prosecutor, Fani Willis, felt it necessary to send him a scathing, nine-page rejection of his demands, citing, among other things, that they were almost tantamount to illegal interference with a criminal proceeding.

We must dedicate ourselves to the primacy of fact over falsehood. We must think like Paul Revere did: "The fascists are coming! The fascists are coming!" They're riding in on a steed that looks a lot like a social media post.

I've already said we must end Section 230.

How?

No one in Congress seems to understand the nature, even if they seem to occasionally understand the depth, of the problem. We must strive to make them aware. Write your Congressperson! At the end of the book I have provided a sample letter that expresses concern, urgency, and practical steps. Simply put, it is a plea that your representative introduce legislation to repeal and/or substantially modify Section 230 so as to bring social media under regulation just as every other channel of public communication is either regulated or charged with a responsibility not to defame or harm.

I'm not a politician, but if you're looking for a signature issue to run for office on, please be my guest. We must recruit leaders who understand digital and who are willing to do something about its worst effects, without destroying its value to humanity (which is not the same as its value to shareholders).

Form local study groups. Propose anti-disinformation courses on campus, or in your local schools. At your library. At your church. At your workplace. Engage in anti-disinformation training, where possible.

In an uncertain world, facts are bedrock. Remove these and watch our entire societal structure collapse. Perhaps we need a political action committee. This Anti-disinformation PAC could raise funds and set up a lobbying campaign, as is customary in Washington. If we don't do this, there might not be a government to lobby any longer!

It's only the most important fight in the history of democracy.

Let's get to work.

APPENDIX

Sample Letter to Representative Re: Section 230

Date

Your Name
Your Address
Your Contact Information

The Honorable *(the name of your representative)*
House (or Senate) Office Building *(Please note, it's either one or the other)*
Washington, DC 20515 (20510)

Re: Section 230 of the 1996 Communications Decency Act

Dear Congressman/Senator _____:

As a constituent in your district, I am writing today to urge you to help repeal or substantially alter Section 230 of the Communications Decency Act.

Under this law, platforms like Facebook, X, and Google (YouTube) have been able to promote disinformation, falsehoods, and outright hate speech without consequence—unlike more traditional media companies, like newspapers and television channels, that are held liable for anything they broadcast. Under this law, they also are granted the right to remove any content they see fit—but despite their so-called best efforts, much too much hateful speech and disinformation gets through to the public.

I have personally seen any number of obviously false and damaging "news" stories that have been posted to the amplification platforms like

X and Facebook. It seems wrong that a US company should be permitted to make billions of dollars by actively promoting foreign-sourced disinformation in order to manipulate and control US electoral political outcomes.

The fact that Fox News was forced to settle with Dominion Voting Systems for nearly a billion dollars shows us the disparity. I am certain that if Fox had been protected by 230, there would have been no case. Why is X, why is YouTube, why is Facebook permitted to promote the exact same set of falsehoods with impunity?

In order to save civil society and democracy itself, we must purge Section 230 or substantially alter it. I want *all* media companies to be subject to the same laws. I believe the platforms are disingenuous when they claim they're not publishers—the difference is a mere technical one, and it is essentially a subterfuge.

Please let me know what your views are, and whether you are prepared to support an end to this ruinous law.

Sincerely,

YOUR NAME
YOUR TITLE

NOTES

PREFACE

1. Linah Mohammad, Patrick Jarenwattananon, and Juana Summers, An Open Letter Signed by Tech Leaders, Researchers Proposes Delaying AI Development, NPR, *All Things Considered*, March 29, 2023, https://www.npr.org/2023/03/29/1166891536/an-open-letter-signed-by-tech-leaders-researchers-proposes-delaying-ai-developme.

2. Elon Musk, owner of Twitter (X), famously projects absolute and utter confidence regardless of circumstance.

3. Richard Stengel, "Domestic Disinformation Is a Greater Menace Than Foreign Disinformation," *Time*, June 26, 2020, https://time.com/5860215/domestic-disinformation-growing-menace-america.

CHAPTER 1

1. "Off with their heads" was, in Lewis Carroll's *Alice through the Looking Glass*, the Queen of Hearts' favorite advice.

2. The Walrus and the Carpenter, in Lewis Carroll's *Alice in Wonderland* invited a bed of oysters for a walk, then ate all of them and wept for the tragedy of the lost oysters.

3. Scott Waldman, "Climate Misinformation Spreads on Musk's Twitter," *E&E News*, https://www.eenews.net/articles/climate-misinformation-spreads-on-musks-twitter/.

4. "Alternative facts," Wikipedia, last updated December 6, 2023, https://en.wikipedia.org/wiki/Alternative_facts.

5. "QAnon" Antidefamation League, last updated October 28, 2022, https://www.adl.org/resources/backgrounder/qanon.

CHAPTER 2

1. Meredith Artley, "Why ONA Sees 2015 as a Year of Growth and Optimism for Journalists," Online News Association, February 17, 2015, https://journalists.org/2015/02/17/why-ona-sees-2015-as-a-year-of-growth-and-optimism-for-journalists/.

2. Gerry Smith, "*NYT* Digital Leader 'Optimistic' about Role in Social-Media World," *Bloomberg*, April 15, 2015, https://www.bloomberg.com/news/articles/2015-04-15/nyt-digital-leader-optimistic-about-role-in-social-media-world?leadSource=uverify%20wall.

3. *Gonzalez v. Google* was a case before the United States Supreme Court, where the plaintiff alleged YouTube recommended hateful videos in a way that enticed a terrorist to kill his daughter in a Paris nightclub massacre. It was decided in Google's favor.

4. To be fair, during his 2016 candidacy, Trump did not need to rely on social media. He was a frequent guest on any number of mainstream television and radio shows and was treated almost as a media colleague.

5. Bill Hathaway, "'Likes' and 'Shares' Teach People to Express More Outrage Online," August 13, 2021, https://news.yale.edu/2021/08/13/likes-and-shares-teach-people-express-more-outrage-online.

6. "Does Social Media Leave You Feeling Angry? That Might Be Intentional," NPR, *Consider This*, September 13, 2022, https://www.npr.org/2022/09/13/1122786134/does-social-media-leave-you-feeling-angry-that-might-be-intentional.

7. Of course algorithms don't "know" or "believe" anything, but only deliver responses to data prompts based on how they have been programmed by their human owners.

8. I put quotes around the word "censor" because private companies cannot, in fact, censor anyone. They can choose not to amplify your message, but that is not censorship. Only the state can censor speech. Censorship requires laws that prohibit people from speaking out at all, anywhere. Lack of amplification is not censorship. I detail this later.

9. "*Google vs Gonzalez LLC*," American Civil Liberties Union, last updated May 18, 2023, https://www.aclu.org/cases/google-v-gonzalez-llc.

CHAPTER 3

1. Ciara O'Rourke, "No, President Joe Biden isn't in the Guantanamo Bay detention camp," Politifact, March 9, 2023, https://www.politifact.com/

factchecks/2023/mar/09/facebook-posts/no-president-joe-biden-isnt-in-the
-guantanamo-bay/.

2. Mike Wendling, "The Truth about 'Medbeds'—a Miracle Cure That Doesn't Exist," BBC News, December 26, 2022, https://www.bbc.com/news/blogs-trending-64070190.

3. Kelly Campbell, "How Racism Is Perpetuated within Social Media and Artificial Intelligence," *Entrepreneur*, March 9, 2023, https://www.entrepreneur.com/leadership/heres-how-social-media-and-ai-can-perpetuate-racism/446154.

4. Alex Hammer and Elizabeth Elkind, "Trump and Tucker Carlson Laugh as Chants of 'Let's Go Brandon' Ring Out across Bedminster Golf Club," *Daily Mail*, August 1, 2022, https://www.dailymail.co.uk/news/article-11067081/Donald-Trump-chats-fans-New-Jersey-golf-course-Sunday-Saudi-backed-LIV-tournament.html.

5. Brian Stelter, "This Infamous Steve Bannon Quote Is Key to Understanding America's Crazy Politics," CNN Business, November 16, 2021, https://www.cnn.com/2021/11/16/media/steve-bannon-reliable-sources/index.html.

6. "Share of Digital in Advertising Revenue Worldwide from 2018 to 2028," Statista, June 2023, https://www.statista.com/statistics/375008/share-digital-ad-spend-worldwide/.

7. Ian Matthews, "Nielsen Ratings Definition, History and Calculation," Study.com, November 21, 2023, https://study.com/academy/lesson/how-do-nielsen-ratings-work-definition-history.html.

8. Sarah Kreps and Douglas Kriner, "How Generative AI Impacts Democratic Engagement," Brookings, March 21, 2023, https://www.brookings.edu/techstream/how-generative-ai-impacts-democratic-engagement/.

9. "As Chatbots Spread, Conservatives Dream about a Right-Wing Response," Yahoo News, March 22, 2023, https://news.yahoo.com/chatbots-spread-conservatives-dream-wing-184011211.html.

10. "Letter of Concern to FBI Regarding Threats of Violence in Libraries," American Library Association, September 27, 2022, https://www.ala.org/advocacy/letter-concern-fbi-regarding-threats-violence-libraries.

11. While state economies shift and change, it is generally understood that apart from Texas, Florida, Virginia, and Utah, nearly every other state that recently has voted red is a net recipient of federal dollars.

12. Ryan Hogg, "Elon Musk's Twitter Is Now Recommending Kremlin-Linked Accounts to Users after Restricting Them Last Year, Tests Suggest," *Business Insider*, April 9, 2023, https://www.businessinsider.com/elon-musk-twitter-recommending-kremlin-accounts-to-users-tests-show-2023-4.

13. Kevin Breuninger, "Russia Tried to Influence US Elections in 2022 and Will Do It Again, Top Intelligence Agency Says," CNBC, March 8, 2023, https://www.cnbc.com/2023/03/08/russia-tried-to-influence-us-elections-in-2022-and-will-do-it-again-intel-agency-says.html.

14. Erica R. Hendry, "Foreign Payments, Unregistered Lobbying and Other Activities That Led to Paul Manafort's Indictment," NPR, July 31, 2018, https://www.pbs.org/newshour/politics/foreign-payments-unregistered-lobbying-and-other-activities-that-led-to-paul-manaforts-indictment.

15. Sue Halpern, "Why Would Paul Manafort Share Polling Data with Russia?," *New Yorker*, January 10, 2019, https://www.newyorker.com/news/news-desk/why-would-paul-manafort-share-polling-data-with-russia.

16. "Intel Officials Warned Lawmakers Russia Trying to Interfere in 2020 Election," CBS News, February 21, 2020, https://www.cbsnews.com/news/russian-election-interference-intelligence-officials-warned-lawmakers-2020/.

17. "Microtargeting," Wikipedia, https://en.wikipedia.org/wiki/Microtargeting.

18. Christiano Lima-Strong, "Facebook Knew Ads Microtargeting Could Be Exploited by Politicians," *Washington Post*, October 26, 2021, https://www.washingtonpost.com/politics/2021/10/26/facebook-knew-ads-microtargeting-could-be-exploited-by-politicians-it-accepted-risk/.

19. B. Zarouali, T. Dobber, G. De Pauw, and C. de Vreese, "Using a Personality-Profiling Algorithm to Investigate Political Microtargeting: Assessing the Persuasion Effects of Personality-Tailored Ads on Social Media," *Communication Research*, 49, no. 8 (2022): 1066–91. https://doi.org/10.1177/0093650220961965.

20. Ana Dascalescu, "Dystopian Viral Video Shows Dozens of Chinese Streamers under a Bridge Trying to 'Game the Algorithm,'" Techthelead, February 14, 2023, https://techthelead.com/dystopian-viral-video-shows-dozens-of-chinese-streamers-under-a-bridge-trying-to-game-the-algorithm/.

21. Seymour M. Hersh, *The Dark Side of Camelot* (New York: Simon & Schuster, 1997).

22. Jeremy W. Peters and Katie Robertson, "Fox Stars Privately Expressed Disbelief about Election Fraud Claims: 'Crazy Stuff,'" *New York Times*, February 16, 2023, https://www.nytimes.com/2023/02/16/business/media/fox-dominion-lawsuit.html.

23. Cheryl Teh and Jacob Shamsian, "Sidney Powell Cited Woman Who Claimed to Be Headless, Time-Traveling Entity in Email Pushing Election Conspiracy Theories," *Business Insider*, February 17, 2023, https://www.businessinsider.com/sidney-powell-voter-fraud-claims-headless-time-travel-dominion-fox-2023-2.

24. "America First Legal's Investigation Reveals the Biden White House Was Involved with the Mar-a-Lago Raid and that NARA Misled Congress; AFL Launches Additional Investigation," America First Legal, April 10, 2023, https://aflegal.org/america-first-legals-investigation-reveals-the-biden-white-house-was-involved-with-the-mar-a-lago-raid-and-that-nara-misled-congress-afl-launches-additional-investigation/.

25. "Fairness doctrine," Wikipedia, https://en.wikipedia.org/wiki/Fairness_doctrine.

26. In 2023 the Trump Organization was found guilty of fraud in a Manhattan courtroom for exactly this reason: they grossly inflated the value of assets on loan applications.

27. Yadarisa Shabong and Pushkala Aripaka, "Ex Cambridge Analytica Boss Banned over Unethical Services: UK Agency," Reuters, September 24, 2020, https://www.reuters.com/article/uk-britain-cambridge-analytica-idUSKCN26F2U4.

28. Sarah Posner, "The Christian Nationalist Boot Camp Pushing Anti-trans Laws Across America," *Type*, September 21, 2022, https://www.typeinvestigations.org/investigation/2022/09/21/christian-nationalism-anti-trans-laws/.

29. Ashley Lopez, "More Than Half of Republicans Support Christian Nationalism, According to a New Survey," NPR, *All Things Considered*, February 14, 2023, https://www.npr.org/2023/02/14/1156642544/more-than-half-of-republicans-support-christian-nationalism-according-to-a-new-s.

30. Rob Boston, "To Russia, with Love: Christian Nationalists Have a History of Backing Putin's 'Pro-Family' Agenda," Americans United for Separation of Church and State, April 3, 2022, https://www.au.org/the-latest/church-and-state/articles/to-russia-with-love-christian-nationalists-have-a-history-of-backing-putins-pro-family-agenda/#.

31. Paige Cabianca, Peyton Hammond, and Maritza Gutierrez, "What Is a Social Media Echo Chamber and How Do You Break Out of It?" Stan Richards School of Advertising and Public Relations, University of Texas at Austin, November 18, 2020, https://advertising.utexas.edu/news/what-social-media-echo-chamber.

32. Richard Thompson Ford, "The Outrage Industrial Complex," Stanford Law School, December 20, 2019, https://law.stanford.edu/2019/12/20/the-outrage-industrial-complex.

CHAPTER 4

1. Elon Musk's "X" platform is already under scrutiny in the EU for permitting fake news, probably sourced from Hamas or its allies, to be amplified on his failing social media venture.

2. Brian Niemietz, "Fox News Host Greg Gutfeld Says, 'Elections Don't Work' and Suggests Civil War Instead," *New York Daily News*, October 9, 2023, https://www.nydailynews.com/2023/10/06/greg-gutfeld-elections-dont-work-civil-war/.

3. Martin Pengelly, "A Second US Civil War Is 'Going to Happen' If State and Federal Authorities Continue to Prosecute Donald Trump," *Guardian*, August 25, 2023, https://www.theguardian.com/us-news/2023/aug/25/sarah-palin-us-civil-war-donald-trump-prosecutions. Palin went on to say, "We're not going to keep putting up with this."

4. Kevin Collier, "A Group of 67 X Accounts Spread Coordinated Disinformation about Israel-Hamas War, Says Research Group," NBC News, October 10, 2023, https://www.nbcnews.com/tech/misinformation/x-misinformation-israel-hamas-war-network-disinformation-rcna119696.

5. Musk has famously called himself a free speech absolutist even as he cavils against anyone who disagrees with him.

6. Barbara Ortutay, "Social Media Is Awash in Misinformation about Israel-Gaza War, but Musk's X Is the Most Egregious," Associated Press, October 11, 2023, https://apnews.com/article/social-media-gaza-israel-hamas-misinformation-cb5192215d0f89d8a413606d0ec73cf4.

7. Zachary Rogers, "Hundreds of Germans Create Human Shield for Praying Jews at Synagogue on Hamas 'Day of Rage,'" *Messenger*, October 13, 2023, https://themessenger.com/news/hundreds-germans-create-human-shield-praying-jews-synagogue-hamas-day-of-rage.

8. Jacob Soll, "The Long and Tortured History of Fake News," *Politico*, December 18, 2016, https://www.politico.com/magazine/story/2016/12/fake-news-history-long-violent-214535/.

9. "The Covenant of the Hamas—Main Points," 1988, Federation of American Scientists, https://irp.fas.org/world/para/docs/880818a.htm.

CHAPTER 5

1. On December 19, 2020, then-president Donald J. Trump tweeted: "Statistically impossible to have lost the 2020 election. Big protest in D.C. on January 6th. Be there, will be wild!"

2. "My Lai massacre," Wikipedia, last updated January 8, 2024. https://en .wikipedia.org/wiki/M%E1%BB%B9_Lai_massacre.

3. "Pizzagate" is the Q-adjacent, evidence-free belief that a certain pizza parlor in Washington, D.C., was a front for a vast conspiracy of underground child-traffickers, and that said pizza parlor was literally connected to an array of underground tunnels where many thousands of children were held captive.

4. Paul Thomas, "How QAnon Uses Satanic Rhetoric to Set Up a Narrative of 'Good vs. Evil,'" Associated Press, October 20, 2020, https://apnews .com/article/donald-trump-joe-biden-religion-conspiracy-theories-crime-e63f e5aad57f7016007b70caec3f86fe.

5. Christopher Paul and Miriam Matthews, "The Russian 'Firehose of Falsehood' Propaganda Model: Why It Might Work and Options to Counter It, RAND Corporation, 2016, https://www.rand.org/pubs/perspectives/PE198. html.

6. "The Greatest Generation" is a moniker bestowed by journalist Tom Brokaw on the generation that fought and won World War Two, 1939–1945, which saw the Allied Forces, including the United States, defeat globally expansionist fascist regimes in both Nazi Germany and the Empire of Japan during a period of unparalleled bloodshed. The war against fascism was seen as so important that the anti-Communist Allies made common cause with a Communist Soviet Union in order to defeat the Axis Powers aligned with Germany and Japan.

7. Jonathan Chait, "Trump Brought Nazis into the GOP. DeSantis Won't Expel Them: White Nationalism Is Not Just a Trump Problem," *Intelligencer*, November 2022, https://nymag.com/intelligencer/2022/11/donald-trump -nick-fuentes-ye-white-nationalist-nazi-anti-semite-ron-desantis.html.

8. Solcyré Burga, "How Two Supreme Court Cases Could Completely Change the Internet," *Time*, February 19, 2023.

9. Andrew Hamm, "In Lawsuit against Google Involving ISIS Recruitment Videos, a Chance for the Court to Take Up Section 230," Scotusblog, April 22, 2022. https://www.scotusblog.com/2022/04/in-lawsuit-against -google-involving-isis-recruitment-videos-a-chance-for-the-court-to-take-up -section-230/.

10. Vijay Anand, "Twitter Faces a Whopping Fine in Germany Which Is More Than Its New Worth," CNBC, April 10, 2023, https://www.cnbctv18 .com/technology/twitter-faces-a-whopping-fine-in-germany-which-is-more -than-its-net-worth-16366461.htm.

11. Olga R. Rodriguez and Stefanie Dazio, "Paul Pelosi Attack: Man Told Cops of 'Evil' in Washington," Associated Press, December 14, 2022, https://

apnews.com/article/san-francisco-nancy-pelosi-government-and-politics
-3a0ec4302ee4f11c612678038997c0d7.

12. Tim Arango, Livia Albeck-Ripka, Soumya Karlamangla, and Holly Secon, "How the Pelosi Attack Suspect Plunged into Online Hatred," *New York Times*, November 20, 2022, https://www.nytimes.com/2022/11/20/us/pelosi -attack-suspect-david-depape.html.

13. The term *blood libel* refers historically to the false allegation that Jews used the blood of non-Jewish, usually Christian children, for ritual purposes. The Nazis made effective use of the blood libel to demonize Jews.

14. Ari Waldman, "Donald Trump and Steve Bannon Need Angry White Men—They're Using Gamergate Culture to Get Them," *Quartz*, February 3, 2017, https://qz.com/901761/donald-trump-and-steve-bannon-are-using -gamergate-culture-to-attract-angry-white-men.

15. Mike Snider, "Steve Bannon Learned to Harness Troll Army from 'World of Warcraft,'" *USA Today*, July 18, 2017, https://www.usatoday.com/ story/tech/talkingtech/2017/07/18/steve-bannon-learned-harness-troll-army -world-warcraft/489713001/.

16. Michael Biesecker and Bernard Condon, "Suspect in Assault at Pelosi Home Had Posted about Qanon," Associated Press, October 29, 2022, https://apnews.com/article/california-donald-trump-san-francisco -47c103cfe696df9faf0e57e1c7dd4f10.

17. Chloe Taylor, "South Korea Will Pay Reclusive Young People $500 a Month Just to Get Them to Leave the House," *Fortune*, April 13, 2023, https:// fortune.com/2023/04/13/south-korea-reclusive-population-hikikomori -young-people-allowance/.

18. Dan MacGuill, "No, Democrats and Biden Do Not 'Suck the Blood of Children,'" Snopes, July 26, 2021, https://www.snopes.com/fact-check/demo crats-biden-suck-blood-children/.

19. Kylie Cheung, "Republicans Push Homophobic Conspiracy Theory about Paul Pelosi's Attack," Jezebel, October 31, 2022, https://jezebel.com/top -republicans-push-homophobic-conspiracy-theory-about-1849723169.

20. A shaped explosive charge was used to detonate the first Atomic bomb. According to Wikipedia, a shaped charge is an explosive charge shaped to focus the effect of the explosive's energy. Different types of shaped charges are used for various purposes such as cutting and forming metal, initiating nuclear weapons, penetrating armor, or perforating wells in the oil and gas industry.

21. Stochastic terrorism is defined by Dictionary.com as "the public demonization of a person or group resulting in the incitement of a violent act, which is statistically probable but whose specifics cannot be predicted."

CHAPTER 6

1. "U.S. Diplomacy and Yellow Journalism, 1895–1898," Office of the Historian, US Dept of State, https://history.state.gov/milestones/1866-1898/yellow-journalism.

2. "New York City Newspapers at The New York Public Library: New York City," New York Public Library, https://libguides.nypl.org/c.php?g=1107215&p=8072753.

3. r/Qult Headquarters, "A Look at How Republican Politicians Seed Americans with Conspiracies and Create Their Own Reality by Visualizing All of President Trump's Tweets," https://www.reddit.com/r/Qult_Headquarters/comments/12odjz1/a_look_at_how_republican_politicians_seed/?utm_source=share&utm_medium=ios_app&utm_name=iossmf.

4. "Vaccinated People Are Not Biological Timebombs Carrying Coronavirus Super Strains," Reuters Fact Check, April 27, 2021, https://www.reuters.com/article/factcheck-vaccinated-timebombs/fact-check-vaccinated-people-are-not-biological-time-bombs-carrying-coronavirus-super-strains-idUSL1N2MK1HQ.

5. Religious affiliation is dropping everywhere, but nowhere as quickly as the Midwestern "rust belt."

6. Aimee Semple McPherson was a Canadian evangelical Christian preacher in the 1920s, famous for providing tent-meeting-style services.

7. See Neil Sheehan, *A Bright Shining Lie: John Paul Vann and America in Vietnam* (New York: Vintage, 1989).

8. In the movie *A Few Good Men* (1992), Jack Nicholson plays a military attorney who says to another officer during a trial: "You can't *handle* the truth."

9. Aila Slisco, "Marjorie Taylor Greene Mocked for Tweeting '6 Billion' Crossed U.S. Border," *Newsweek*, February 23, 2023, https://www.newsweek.com/marjorie-taylor-greene-mocked-tweeting-6-billion-crossed-us-border-1783508.

10. Rev. Nathan Empsall, "The Blasphemy of Comparing Trump to Jesus Christ," *Time*, April 23, 2023, https://time.com/6269313/trump-jesus-comparisons-blasphemy/.

11. "Boebert Wrong about the Science," *Durango Herald*, April 23, 2023, https://www.durangoherald.com/articles/boebert-wrong-about-the-science/.

12. "Confidently Incorrect" is a forum (subreddit) on social media site Reddit.

13. "Q-adjacent" refers to the digitally distributed QAnon theory, which holds that a blood-sucking, baby-eating cabal of liberals are at war against Donald Trump and his army of "white hats" trying to save the planet from Hillary

Clinton; and refers specifically to ideas that often are found in parallel to this. An example of the parallel is that the COVID vaccine is not only a hoax, but a DNA-altering, electronic tracking tool that compromises the very humanity of the vaccinated; and that instead, horse de-wormer Ivermectin (or, as the case may be, urine) is the safe, effective alternative.

14. "USS *Nimitz* 'Tic Tac' UFO: Declassified Video," History, https://www.history.com/videos/uss-nimitz-tic-tac-ufo-declassified-video.

15. "USS *Roosevelt* 'Gimbal' UFO: Declassified Video," History, https://www.history.com/videos/uss-roosevelt-gimbal-ufo-declassified-video.

16. Reuters Fact Check, "Vaccinated People Are Not Biological Time Bombs Carrying Coronavirus Super Strains," Reuters, April 27, 2021, https://www.reuters.com/article/factcheck-vaccinated-timebombs/fact-check-vaccinated-people-are-not-biological-time-bombs-carrying-coronavirus-super-strains-idUSL1N2MK1HQ.

17. Reuters Fact Check, "COVID-19 Vaccines Are Not a Ploy to Connect People to 5G," Reuters, July 15, 2021, https://www.reuters.com/article/factcheck-covid19vaccines-5g/fact-check-covid-19-vaccines-are-not-a-ploy-to-connect-people-to-5g-idUSL1N2OR2C1.

18. Mike Wendling, "The Truth about Medbeds—a Miracle Cure That Doesn't Exist," BBC News, December 26, 2022, https://www.bbc.com/news/blogs-trending-64070190.

19. Michael Hiltzik, "The Most Striking Side-Effect of Ivermectin Is Stupidity," *Los Angeles Times*, August 31, 2021, https://www.latimes.com/business/story/2021-08-31/the-most-striking-side-effect-of-ivermectin-stupidity.

20. Max Matsa and Nicholas Yong, "FBI Chief Says China Lab Leak Most Likely," BBC News, March 1, 2023, https://www.bbc.com/news/world-us-canada-64806903.

21. Wang Chen, "Coronavirus Outbreak Reignites Bushmeat Debate," China Dialog, February 7, 2020, https://chinadialogue.net/en/food/11839-coronavirus-outbreak-reignites-bushmeat-debate/.

22. See https://www.youtube.com/watch?v=lGOofzZOyl8.

23. Amanda Ruggeri, "The Problems with TikTok's Controversial 'Beauty Filters,'" BBC News, March 1, 2023, https://www.bbc.com/future/article/20230301-the-problems-with-tiktoks-controversial-beauty-filters.

24. "Reducing Social Media Use Significantly Improves Body Image in Teens, Young Adults," American Psychological Association, press release, February 23, 2023, https://www.apa.org/news/press/releases/2023/02/social-media-body-image.

25. "The blunder years" is a forum (subreddit) on social media platform Reddit about one's middle-school years. It's a play-on words referencing the television show *The Wonder Years*.

CHAPTER 7

1. ChatGPT is an artificial intelligence chatbot developed by OpenAI and launched in November 2022. It is built on top of OpenAI's GPT3 family of large language models and has been fine-tuned (an approach to transfer learning) using both supervised and reinforcement learning techniques.

2. Linah Mohammad, Patrick Jarenwattananon, and Juana Summers, "An Open Letter Signed by Tech Leaders, Researchers Proposes Delaying AI Development," NPR, *All Things Considered*, March 29, 2023, https://www.npr.org/2023/03/29/1166891536/an-open-letter-signed-by-tech-leaders-researchers-proposes-delaying-ai-developme.

3. Emily Bell, "A Fake News Frenzy: Why ChatGPT Could Be Disastrous for Truth in Journalism," *Guardian*, March 3, 2023, https://www.theguardian.com/commentisfree/2023/mar/03/fake-news-chatgpt-truth-journalism-disinformation.

4. "Disinformation Attacks Have Arrived in the Corporate Sector: Are You Ready?," PWC, February 9, 2021, https://www.pwc.com/us/en/tech-effect/cybersecurity/corporate-sector-disinformation.html.

5. YOLO: You Only Live Once.

6. Eray Eliaçik, "Meet ChaosGPT, an AI Chabot bent on World Domination," Dataconomy, April 12, 2023, https://dataconomy.com/blog/2023/04/12/what-is-chaosgpt-ai-bot-destroy-humanity/.

7. Microsoft won a contract to develop the Disk Operating System for IBM PCs because IBM believed operating systems were a trivial pursuit at the time.

8. Rita Gunther McGrath, "15 Years Later, Lessons from the Failed AOL-Time Warner Merger," *Fortune*, January 10, 2015, https://fortune.com/2015/01/10/15-years-later-lessons-from-the-failed-aol-time-warner-merger/.

9. "External Obsolescence" is a real estate term referring to external factors, such as nearby new construction—think power lines or gas stations—that can render a property less valuable.

10. Luc Olinga, "Mark Zuckerberg Quietly Buries the Metaverse," The Street, March 18, 2023, https://www.thestreet.com/technology/mark-zuckerberg-quietly-buries-the-metaverse.

11. Automaker Ford decided the market wanted an upper-mid-range car that they designed from scratch. The design was almost universally disliked,

with comparisons of the front grille ranging from the above "lemon-suck" to "horse collar" and, less graciously, "vagina." The brand flopped entirely and was discontinued after 1960.

CHAPTER 8

1. Oliver Darcy, "Tucker Carlson Raged against Trump in Private. But in Interview with the Former President He Took a Very Different Tone," CNN, April 12, 2023, https://www.cnn.com/2023/04/12/media/carlson -trump-interview/index.html.

2. Jared Holt, "How Russian Disinformation Goes from the Kremlin to QAnon to Fox News," *Daily Beast*, March 21, 2022, https://www.thedaily beast.com/how-russian-disinformation-goes-from-the-kremlin-to-qanon-to -fox-news.

3. Arianna Skibel, "This Russia-Linked Hack Is Worse Than We Knew," *Politico*, February 14, 2023, https://www.politico.com/newsletters/power -switch/2023/02/14/this-russia-linked-hack-worse-than-we-knew-00082755.

4. National Intelligence Council, "Foreign Threats to the 2020 US Federal Elections," March 10, 2021, https://www.dni.gov/files/ODNI/documents/ assessments/ICA-declass-16MAR21.pdf

5. Maria Alesina, "Destroying the Concept of Truth: Russian Propaganda Uncovered," *Modern Diplomacy*, February 5, 2023, https://moderndiplo macy.eu/2023/02/05/destroying-the-concept-of-truth-russian-propaganda -uncovered/.

6. Joseph Menn, "Russian-Backed Organizations Amplifying QAnon Conspiracy Theories, Researchers Say," Reuters, August24, 2020, https://www .reuters.com/article/us-usa-election-qanon-russia/russian-backed-organizations -amplifying-qanon-conspiracy-theories-researchers-say-idUSKBN25K13T.

7. Shannon Bond, "How Russia Is Losing—and Winning—the Information War in Ukraine," NPR, February 28, 2023, https://www.npr.org/2023/ 02/28/1159712623/how-russia-is-losing-and-winning-the-information-war-in -ukraine.

8. David Folkenflik, "The 'Wackadoodle' Foundation of Fox News' Election-Fraud Claims," NPR, https://www.npr.org/2023/02/20/11582230 99/fox-news-dominion-wackadoodle-election-fraud-claim.

9. Folkenflik.

10. Jim Jordan, fond of issuing subpoenas, has already refused to answer a subpoena delivered by the January 6 committee, and to date has gotten away with it in a manner unlike any normal person would be granted.

CHAPTER 9

1. Jessica Guyyn, "Is ChatGPT 'Woke'? AI Chatbot Accused of Anti-Conservative Bias and a Grudge against Trump," *USA Today*, February 9, 2023, https://www.usatoday.com/story/tech/2023/02/09/woke-chatgpt-conservatives-bias/11215353002/.

2. Aneeta Bhole, "Chat GPT Goes Woke: If You Ask Groundbreaking AI to Explain Why Drag Queen Kids Hours Could Be Bad—It Refuses on Grounds It Would Be 'Inappropriate and Harmful,'" *Daily Mail*, January 17, 2023, https://www.dailymail.co.uk/news/article-11646463/Conservatives-test-AI-ChatGPT-uses-responses-prove-going-woke.html.

3. Adam Gabbatt, "Losing Their Religion: Why US Churches Are on the Decline," *Guardian*, January 22, 2023, https://www.theguardian.com/us-news/2023/jan/22/us-churches-closing-religion-covid-christianity.

4. *Tight-knit* has become a news media cliché to describe any white community, as opposed to any community of color, which often are referred to as "troubled" or "striving," but never "tight-knit."

5. Jenni Reid, "'They started the war': Russia's Putin Blames West and Ukraine for Provoking Conflict," CNBC, February 21, 2023, https://www.cnbc.com/2023/02/21/russias-putin-blames-west-and-ukraine-for-provoking-conflict.html.

6. The Gulf of Tonkin Affair, in 1964, was deployed by the Johnson administration as a pretext for American troop increases in Vietnam. In August of that year, the American commander of the *Maddox* task force, Captain John Herrick, reported that his ships were being attacked by North Vietnamese boats when in fact there were no North Vietnamese boats in the area.

7. David Rozado, "RightWingGPT—An AI Manifesting the Opposite Political Biases of ChatGPT," Rozado Analytics, February 16, 2023, https://davidrozado.substack.com/p/rightwinggpt.

8. Katherine Tangalakis-Lippert, "Meta's AI Chatbot Has Some Election-Denying, Antisemitic Bugs to Work Out after the Company Asked Users to Help Train It," *Business Insider*, August 7, 2022, https://www.businessinsider.com/meta-ai-chatbot-blenderbot-election-denying-antisemitic-bugs-artificial-intellignce-2022-8.

9. Musk's stewardship has been so awful that he has been forced to appoint Linda Yaccarino, who had been at NBC prior.

10. "How Should AI Systems Behave and Who Should Decide?," OpenAI (blog), February 16, 2023, https://openai.com/blog/how-should-ai-systems-behave.

11. Charles Mackay, *Extraordinary Popular Delusions and the Madness of Crowds* (London: Richard Bentley, 1841) remains a foundational text in the study of topics related to its title.

CHAPTER 10

1. See Adobe's website: https://www.adobe.com/sensei/generative-ai.html.

2. Chloe Veltman, "Supreme Court Sides Against Andy Warhol Foundation in Copyright Infringement Case," NPR, May 18, 2023, https://www.npr.org/2023/05/18/1176881182/supreme-court-sides-against-andy-warhol-foundation-in-copyright-infringement-cas.

3. Adam Hencz, "AI-Generated Art Controversy: The Future of Creativity or a Replacement for Human Talent?," *Artland*, https://magazine.artland.com/ai-art-creativity-controversy.

CHAPTER 11

1. In a CNN interview, Trump claimed he could "end the war in Ukraine in twenty-four hours" largely on "economic" grounds (e.g., we would stop sending money to the Ukraine, allowing Russia to march in triumphant).

2. "Fox News controversies," Wikipedia, last updated January 23, 2024, https://en.wikipedia.org/wiki/Fox_News_controversies.

3. Zachary Laub, "Hate Speech on Social Media: Global Comparisons," Council on Foreign Relations, June 7, 2019, https://www.cfr.org/backgrounder/hate-speech-social-media-global-comparisons#chapter-title-0-3.

4. *Online Hate and Harassment: The American Experience 2021*, Anti-Defamation League, March 22, 2021, https://www.adl.org/resources/report/online-hate-and-harassment-american-experience-2021.

INDEX

~

ABOUT THE AUTHOR

Andrew V. Edwards is an author, technologist, entrepreneur, and visual artist residing in New York's Hudson Valley. He is the author of *Digital Is Destroying Everything* (Rowman and Littlefield, 2015, 2018) and dozens of articles about digital marketing for ClickZ, the world's largest online source of marketing advice and information. He has also published fiction and had a play produced in New York's East Village. His prizewinning paintings have been exhibited nationally.

He is a cofounder and director emeritus of the Digital Analytics Association. Since 2004, the DAA has been the world's largest organization devoted to the study of online customer behavior. Andrew is a New York State licensed real estate agent. In the 1990s Andrew designed and built some of the very first websites, and ran Renaissance Multimedia, one of the first interactive agencies in New York City. He went on to found Technology Leaders, one of the first consulting companies devoted to digital audience measurement, with clients that included the Coca-Cola Company, Century 21, and Priceline.

In 2015 *Digital Is Destroying Everything* predicted a number of unfortunate trends in digital media and beyond, even as digital boosters were seeing nothing but blue sky. *Army of Liars* is Andrew's second nonfiction book.

LinkedIn: https://www.linkedin.com/in/andrewvedwards
Truth in Media (LinkedIn) Newsletter: https://www.linkedin.com/newsletters/7178445610713300993
Digital Culture and Beyond (Substack): https://andrewvedwards.substack.com

Andrew V. Edwards website: https://www.andrewvedwards.com

Media page with all interviews: https://www.andrewvedwards.com/media-appearances/

Instagram: https://www.instagram.com/andrewvedwards1

Twitter: https://twitter.com/AndrewVEdwards